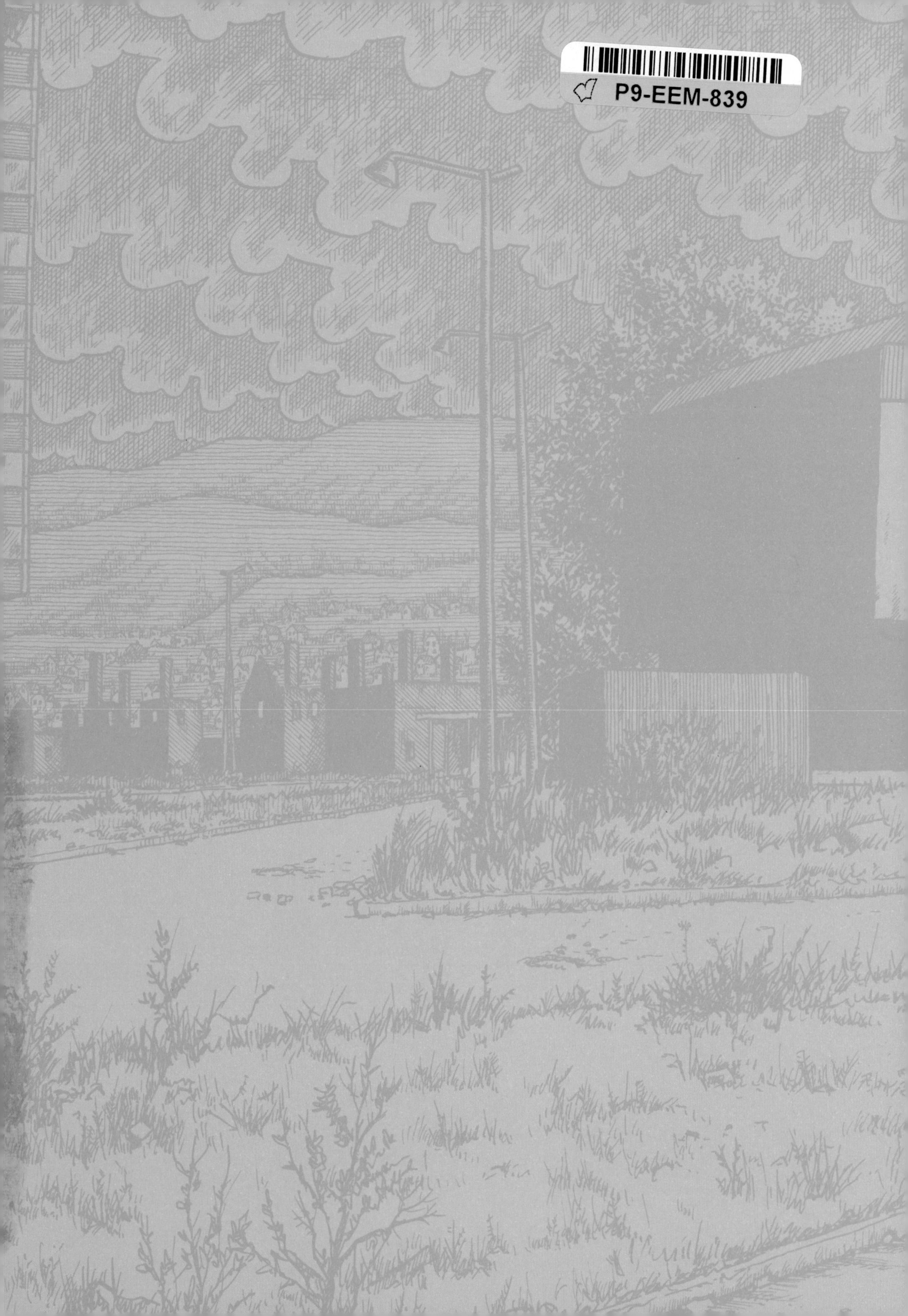

THE FIXER
A STORY FROM SARAJEVO

BY JOE SACCO

DRAWN AND QUARTERLY PUBLICATIONS

First hardcover edition: October 2003. Second edition: July 2004
ISBN 1-896597-60-2
Printed in Hong Kong
10 9 8 7 6 5 4 3 2

Publication design by Michel Vrána
Publisher: Chris Oliveros
Publicity: Peggy Burns

Drawn & Quarterly
Post Office Box 48056
Montreal, Quebec
Canada H2V 4S8
www.drawnandquarterly.com

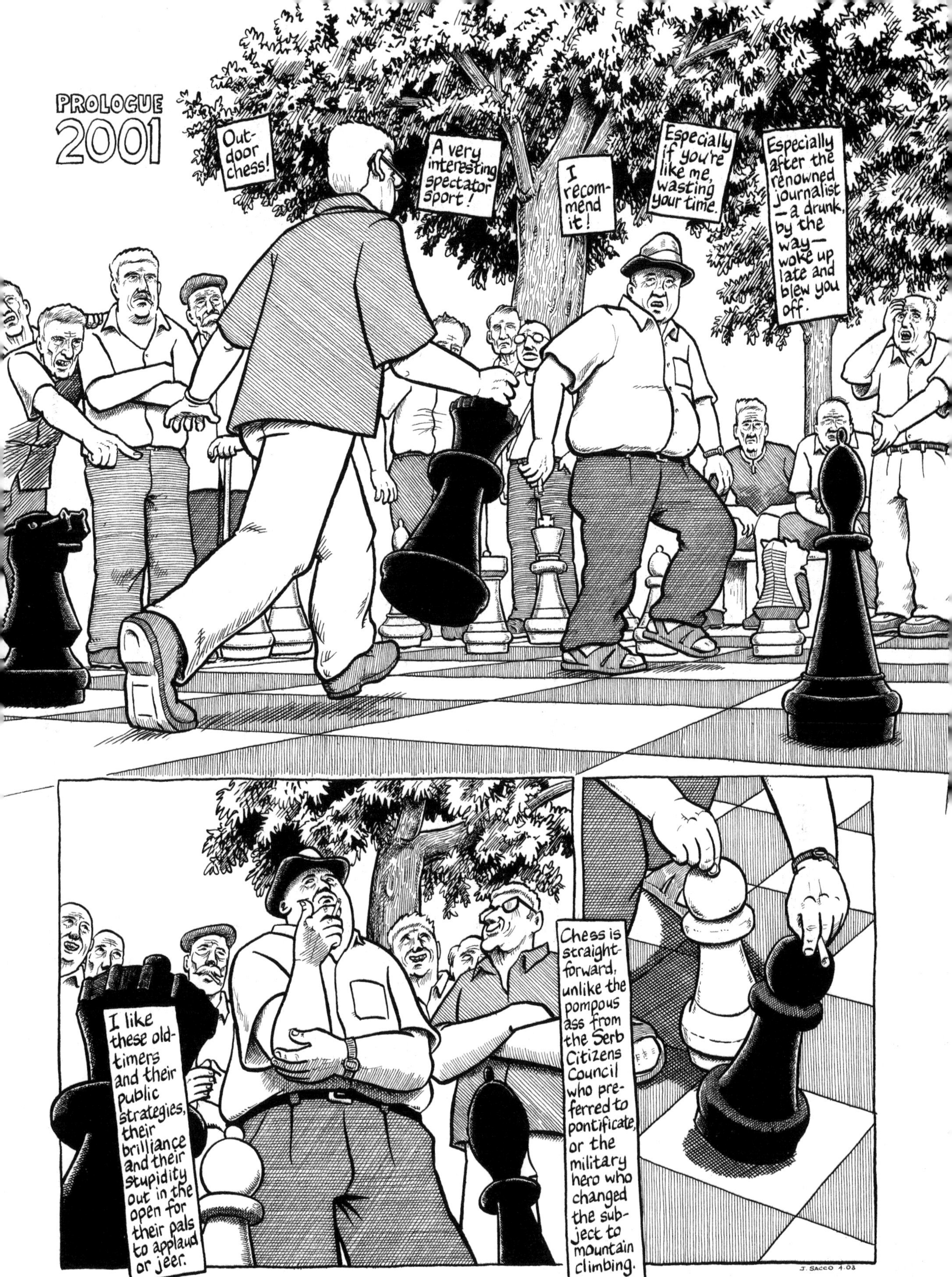
PROLOGUE
2001
Out-door chess!
A very interesting spectator sport!
I recom-mend it!
Especially if you're like me, wasting your time.
Especially after the renowned journalist —a drunk, by the way— woke up late and blew you off.
I like these old-timers and their public strategies, their brilliance and their stupidity out in the open for their pals to applaud or jeer.
Chess is straight-forward, unlike the pompous ass from the Serb Citizens Council who pre-ferred to pontificate, or the military hero who changed the sub-ject to mountain climbing.
J. SACCO 4.03

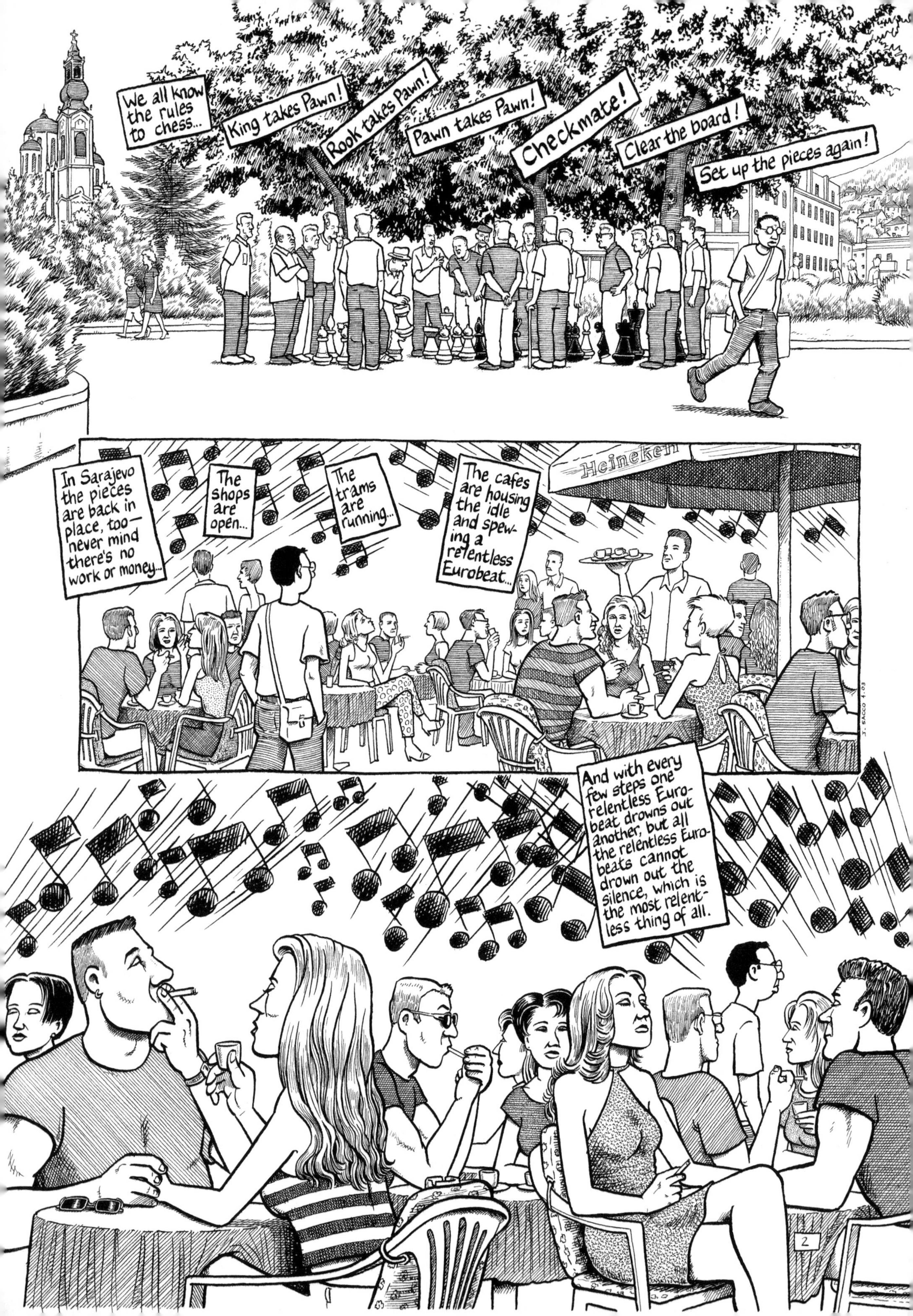
We all know the rules to chess...
King takes Pawn!
Rook takes Pawn!
Pawn takes Pawn!
Checkmate!
Clear the board!
Set up the pieces again!
In Sarajevo the pieces are back in place, too—never mind there's no work or money...
The shops are open...
The trams are running...
The cafes are housing the idle and spewing a relentless Eurobeat...
Heineken
And with every few steps one relentless Eurobeat drowns out another, but all the relentless Eurobeats cannot drown out the silence, which is the most relentless thing of all.
2

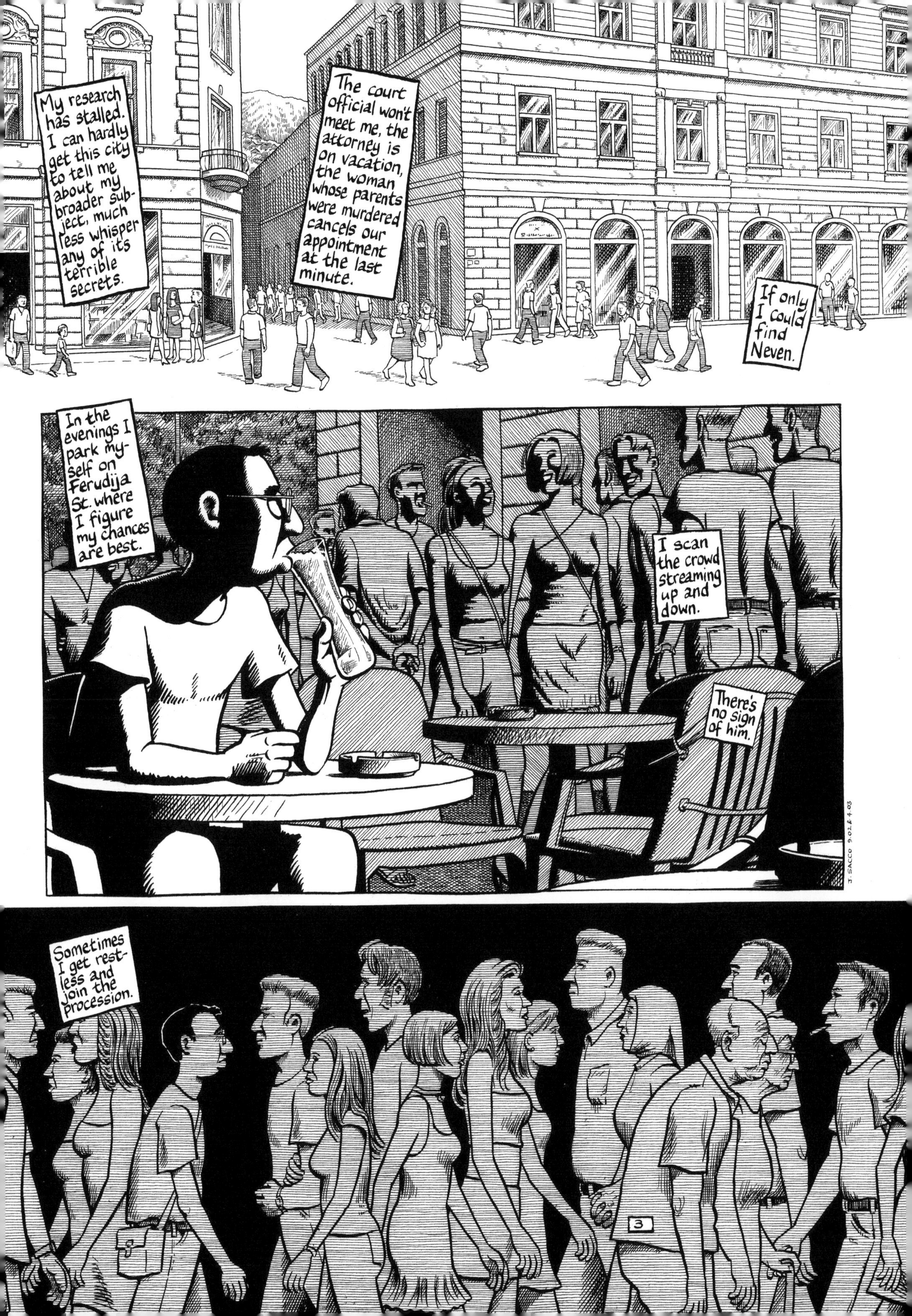
My research has stalled. I can hardly get this city to tell me about my broader subject, much less whisper any of its terrible secrets.
The court official won't meet me, the attorney is on vacation, the woman whose parents were murdered cancels our appointment at the last minute.
If only I could find Neven.
In the evenings I park myself on Ferudija St. where I figure my chances are best.
I scan the crowd streaming up and down.
There's no sign of him.
J. SACCO 9.02 & 4.03
Sometimes I get restless and join the procession.

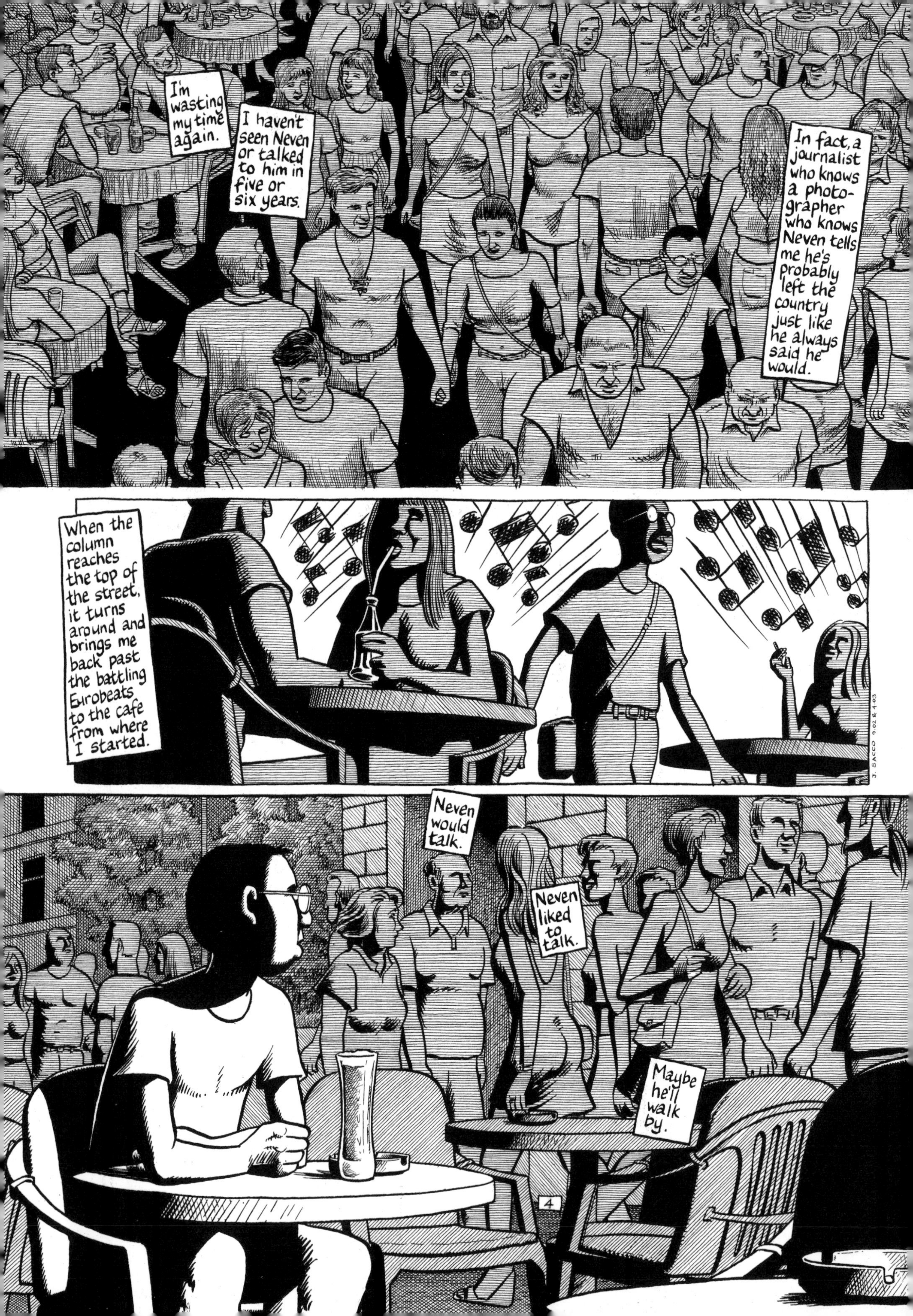

I'm wasting my time again.
I haven't seen Neven or talked to him in five or six years.
In fact, a journalist who knows a photographer who knows Neven tells me he's probably left the country just like he always said he would.
When the column reaches the top of the street, it turns around and brings me back past the battling Eurobeats to the cafe from where I started.
J. SACCO 9.02 & 4.03
Neven would talk.
Neven liked to talk.
Maybe he'll walk by.
4

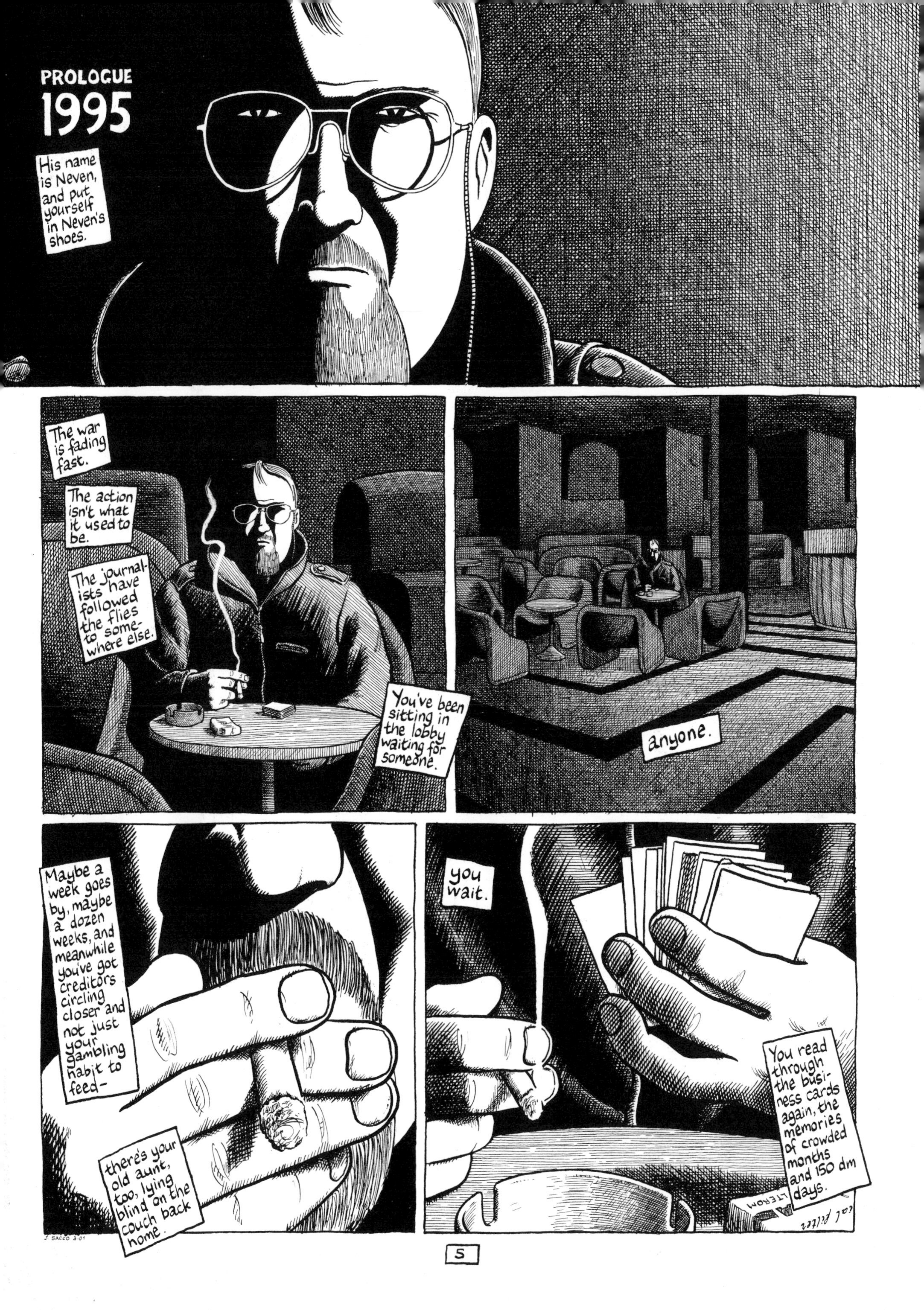
PROLOGUE
1995
His name is Neven, and put yourself in Neven's shoes.
The war is fading fast.
The action isn't what it used to be.
The journalists have followed the flies to somewhere else.
You've been sitting in the lobby waiting for someone.
anyone.
Maybe a week goes by, maybe a dozen weeks, and meanwhile you've got creditors circling closer and not just your gambling habit to feed–
there's your old aunt, too, lying blind on the couch back home.
you wait.
You read through the business cards again, the memories of crowded months and 150 dm days.
J. SACCO 3-01

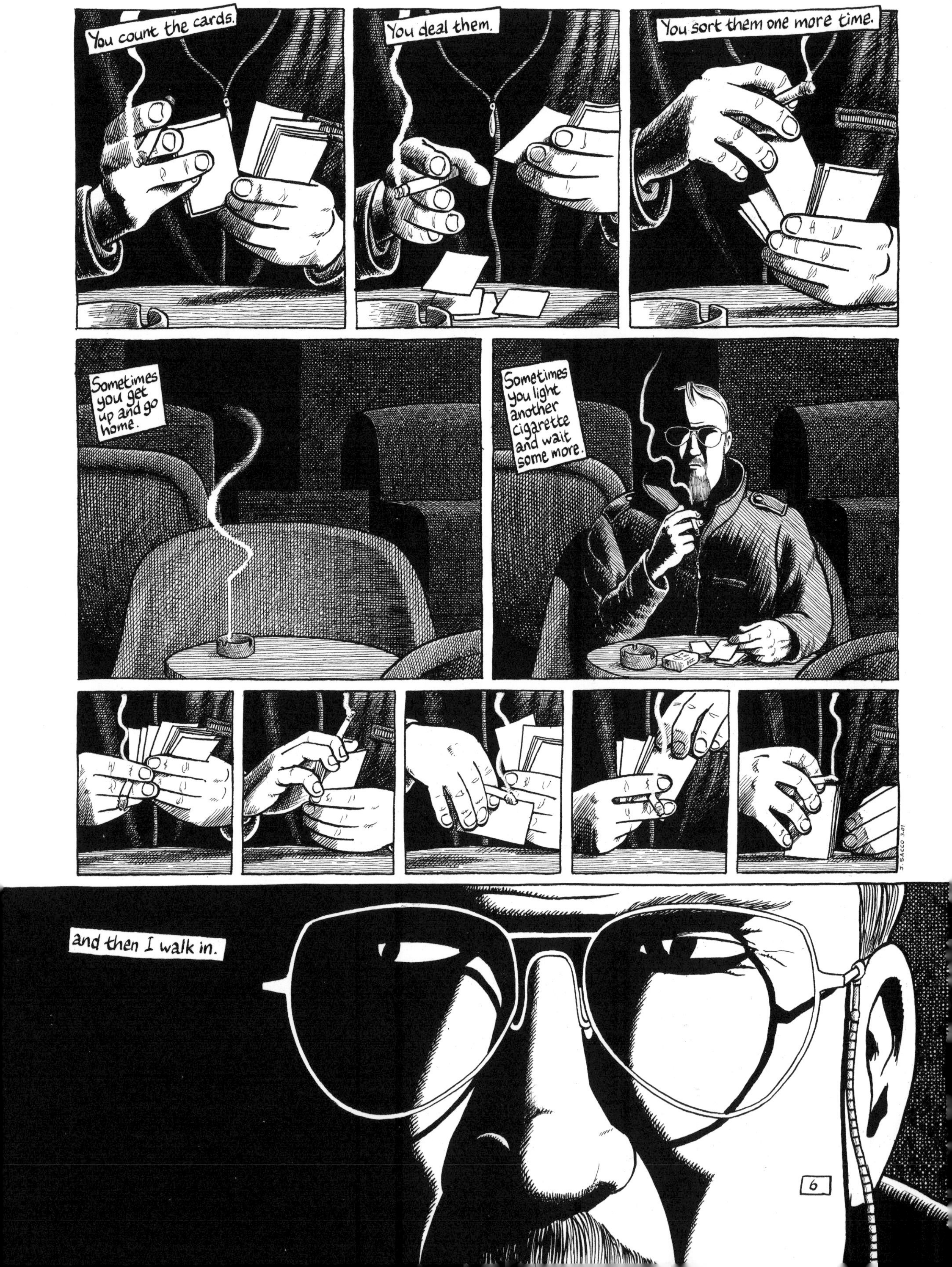
You count the cards.
You deal them.
You sort them one more time.
Sometimes you get up and go home.
Sometimes you light another cigarette and wait some more.
J. SACCO 3.01
and then I walk in.
6

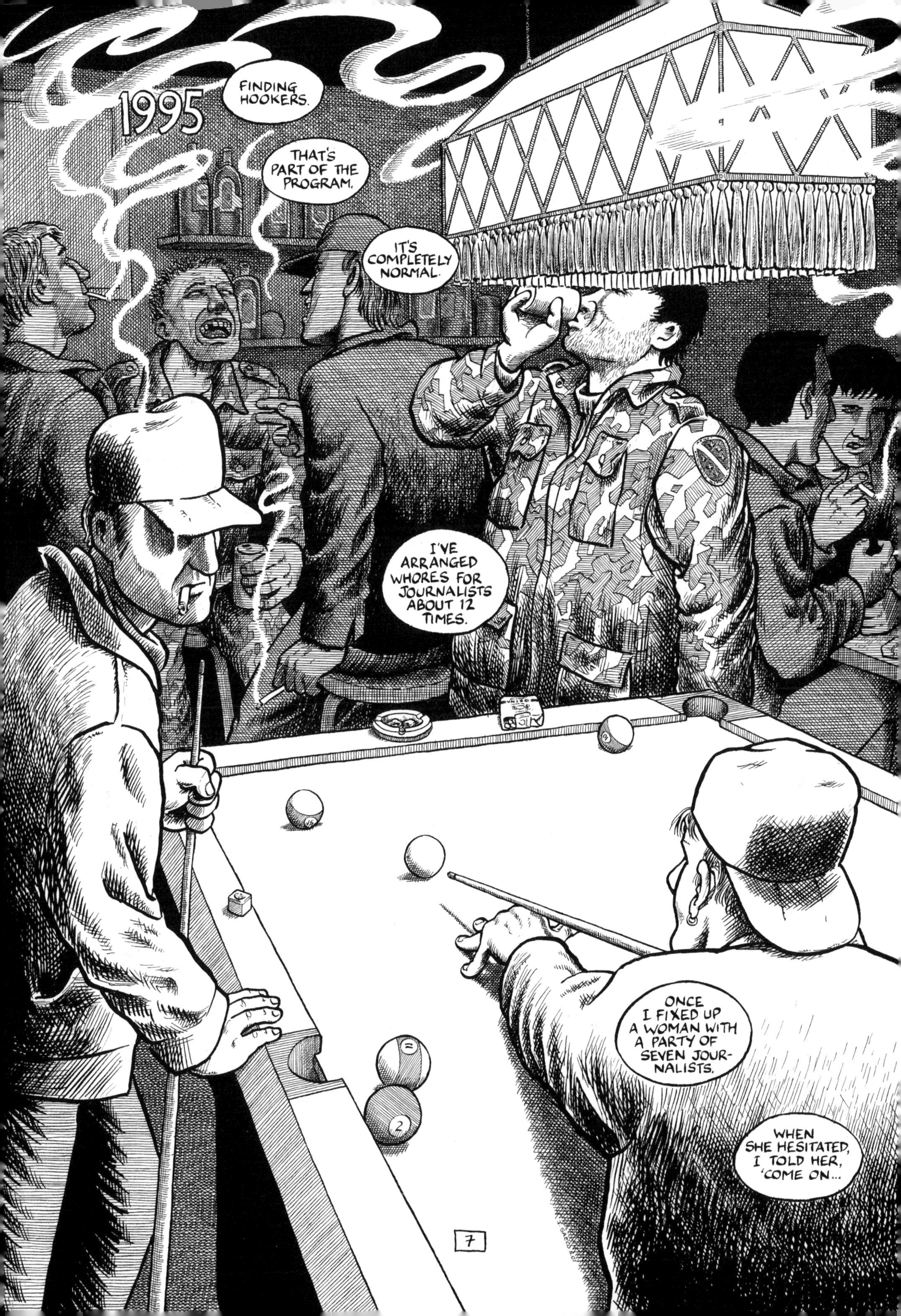
1995
FINDING HOOKERS.
THAT'S PART OF THE PROGRAM.
IT'S COMPLETELY NORMAL.
I'VE ARRANGED WHORES FOR JOURNALISTS ABOUT 12 TIMES.
ONCE I FIXED UP A WOMAN WITH A PARTY OF SEVEN JOUR-NALISTS.
WHEN SHE HESITATED, I TOLD HER, 'COME ON...

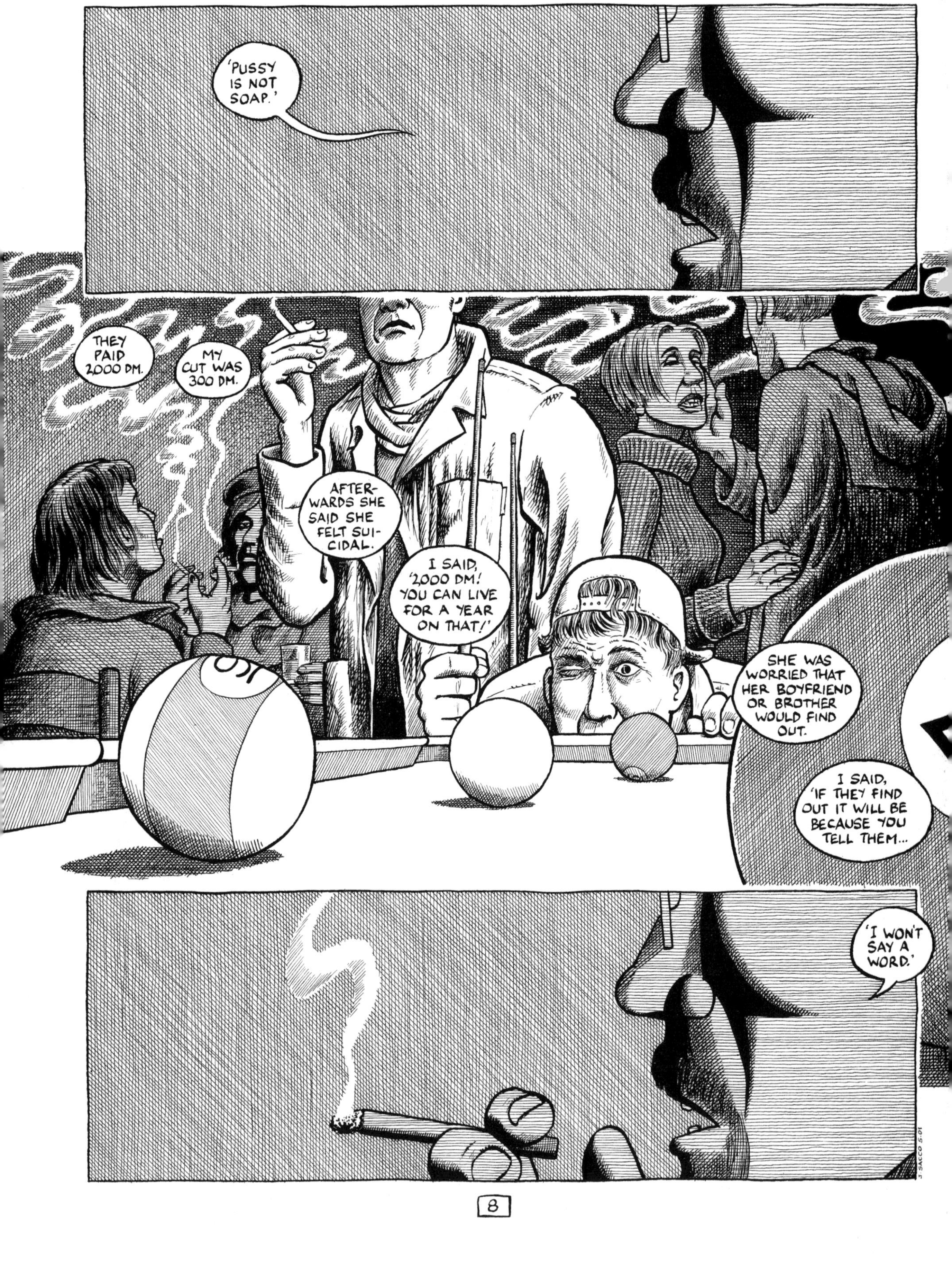
'PUSSY IS NOT SOAP.'
THEY PAID 2000 DM.
MY CUT WAS 300 DM.
AFTERWARDS SHE SAID SHE FELT SUICIDAL.
I SAID, '2000 DM! YOU CAN LIVE FOR A YEAR ON THAT!'
SHE WAS WORRIED THAT HER BOYFRIEND OR BROTHER WOULD FIND OUT.
I SAID, 'IF THEY FIND OUT IT WILL BE BECAUSE YOU TELL THEM...
'I WON'T SAY A WORD.'
J. SACCO 5.01

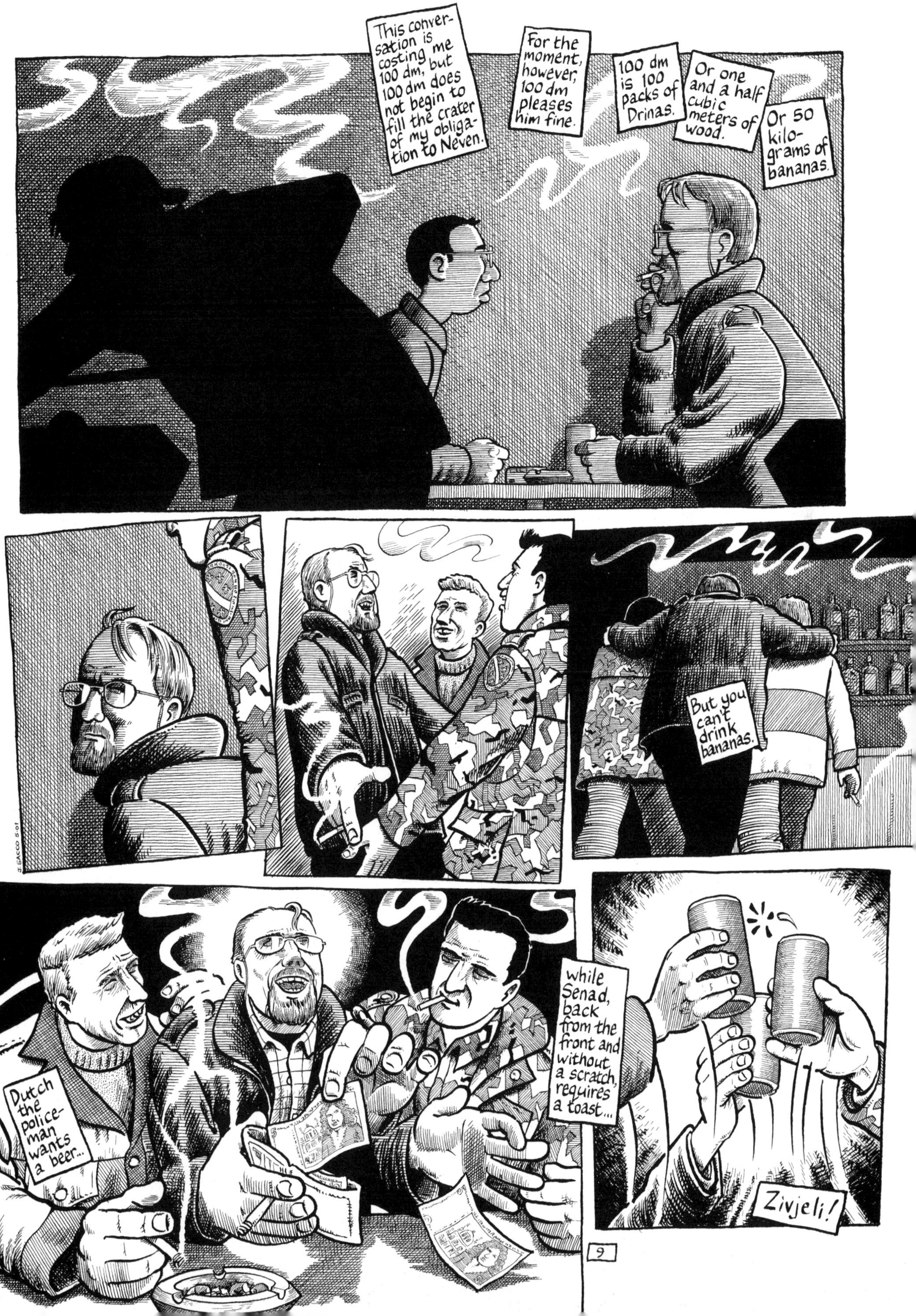

This conversation is costing me 100 dm, but 100 dm does not begin to fill the crater of my obligation to Neven.
For the moment, however, 100 dm pleases him fine.
100 dm is 100 packs of Drinas.
Or one and a half cubic meters of wood.
Or 50 kilograms of bananas.
But you can't drink bananas.
Dutch the policeman wants a beer...
while Senad, back from the front and without a scratch, requires a toast...
Zivjeli!

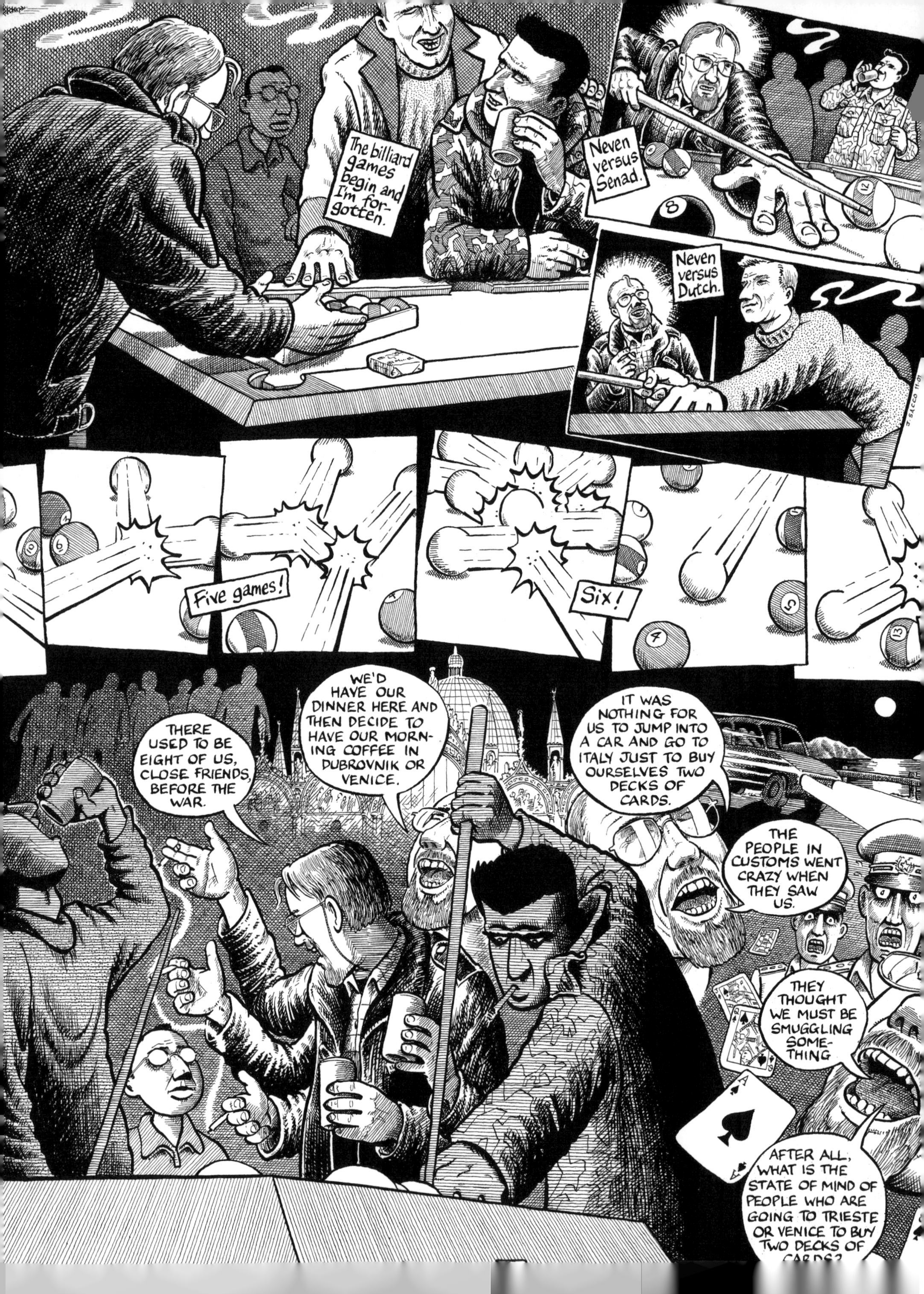
The billiard games begin and I'm forgotten.
Neven versus Senad.
Neven versus Dutch.
J. SACCO 11-01
Five games!
Six!
THERE USED TO BE EIGHT OF US, CLOSE FRIENDS, BEFORE THE WAR.
WE'D HAVE OUR DINNER HERE AND THEN DECIDE TO HAVE OUR MORNING COFFEE IN DUBROVNIK OR VENICE.
IT WAS NOTHING FOR US TO JUMP INTO A CAR AND GO TO ITALY JUST TO BUY OURSELVES TWO DECKS OF CARDS.
THE PEOPLE IN CUSTOMS WENT CRAZY WHEN THEY SAW US.
THEY THOUGHT WE MUST BE SMUGGLING SOMETHING
AFTER ALL, WHAT IS THE STATE OF MIND OF PEOPLE WHO ARE GOING TO TRIESTE OR VENICE TO BUY TWO DECKS OF CARDS?

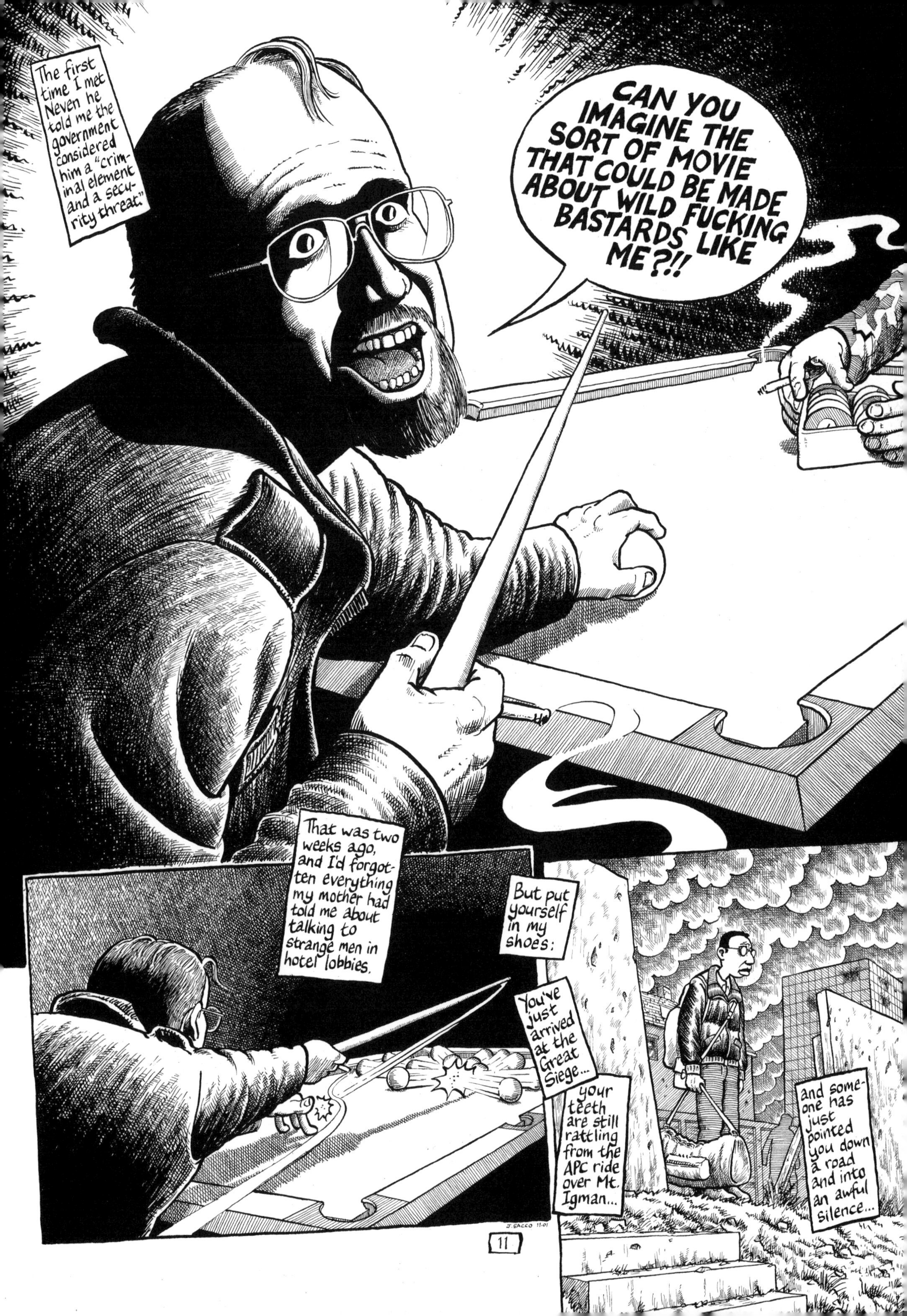
The first time I met Neven he told me the government considered him a "criminal element and a security threat."
CAN YOU IMAGINE THE SORT OF MOVIE THAT COULD BE MADE ABOUT WILD FUCKING BASTARDS LIKE ME?!!
That was two weeks ago, and I'd forgotten everything my mother had told me about talking to strange men in hotel lobbies.
But put yourself in my shoes:
You've just arrived at the Great Siege...
your teeth are still rattling from the APC ride over Mt. Igman...
and someone has just pointed you down a road and into an awful silence...
J. SACCO 11.01

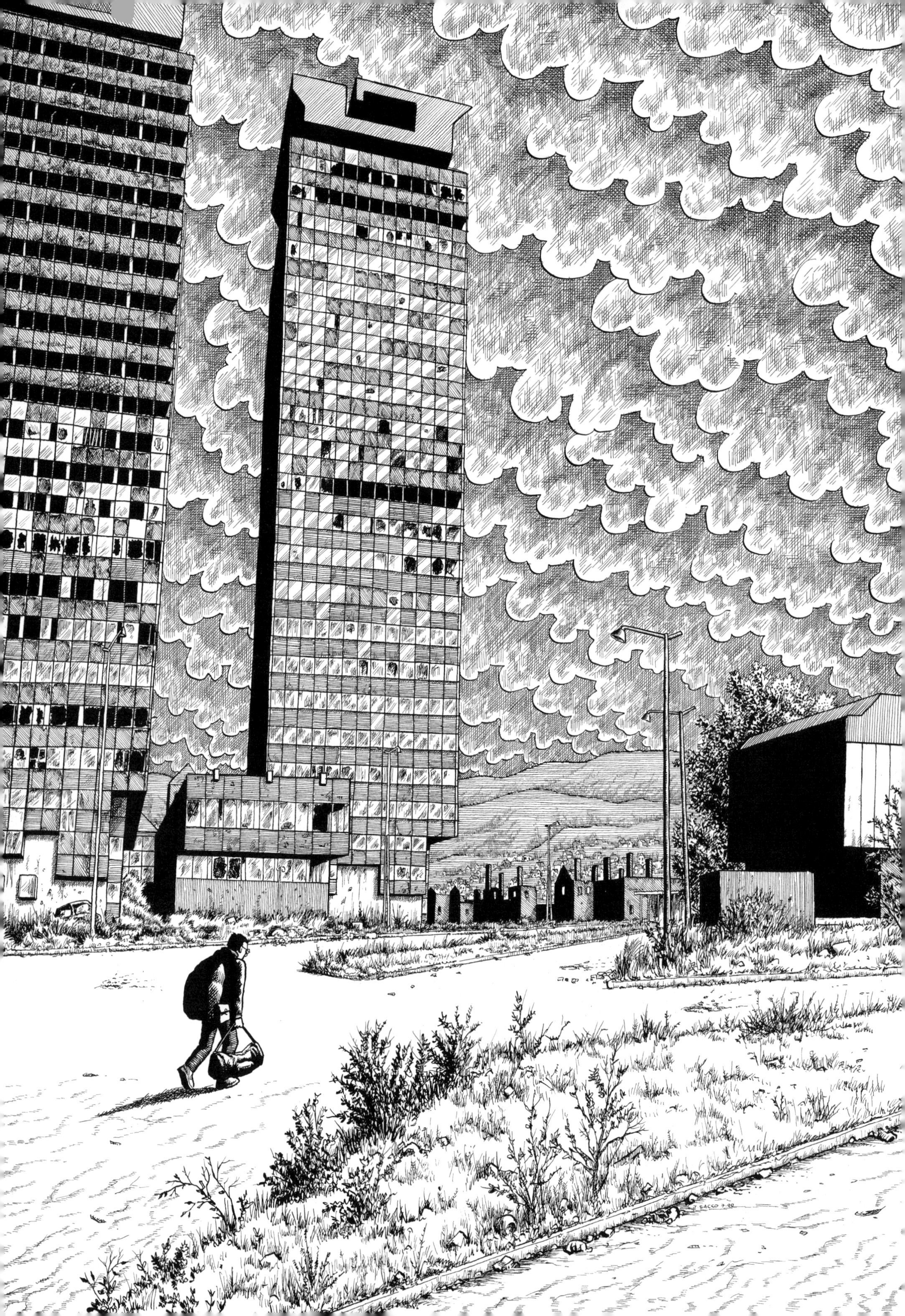
J. SACCO 7.00

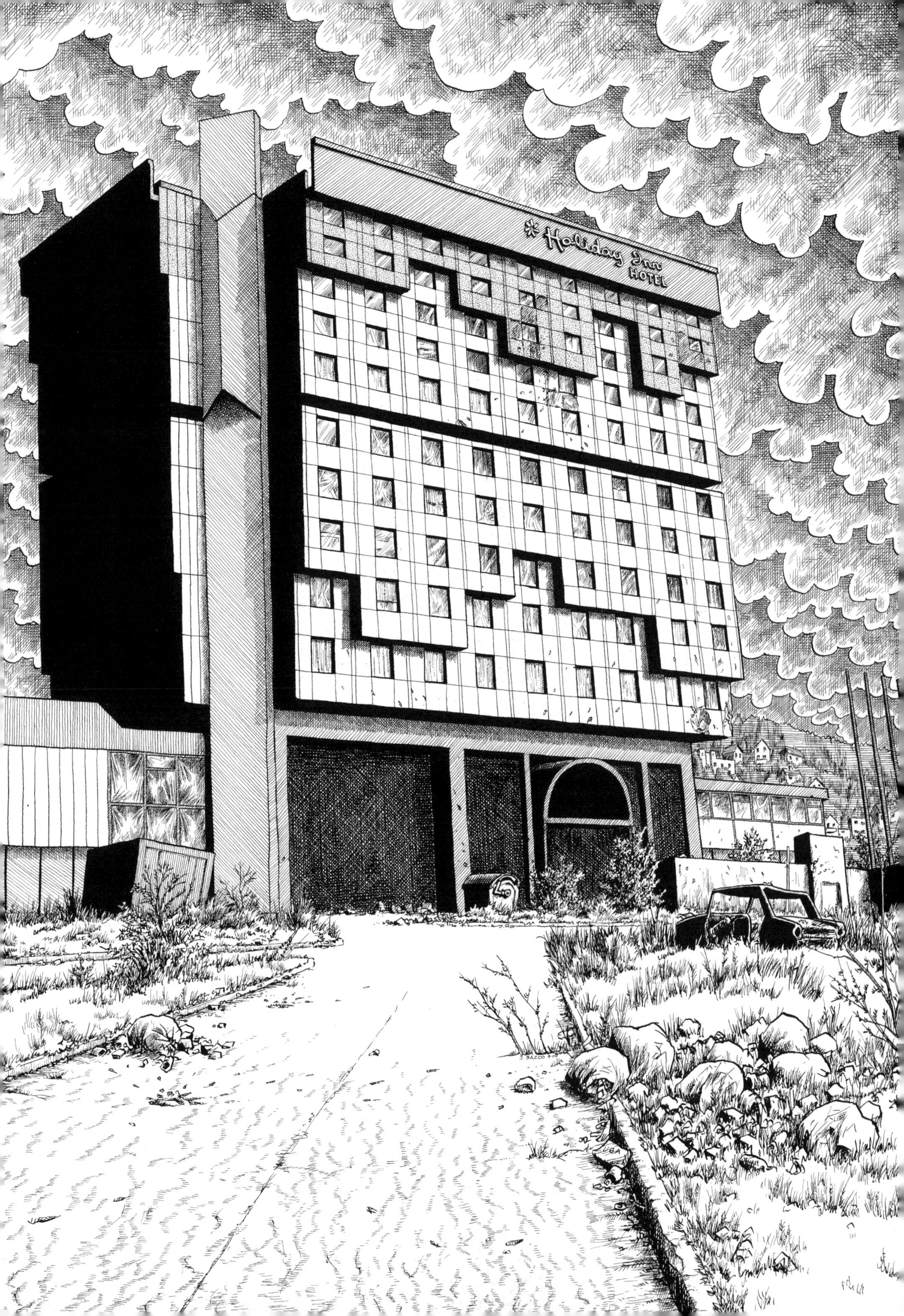
Holiday Inn
HOTEL

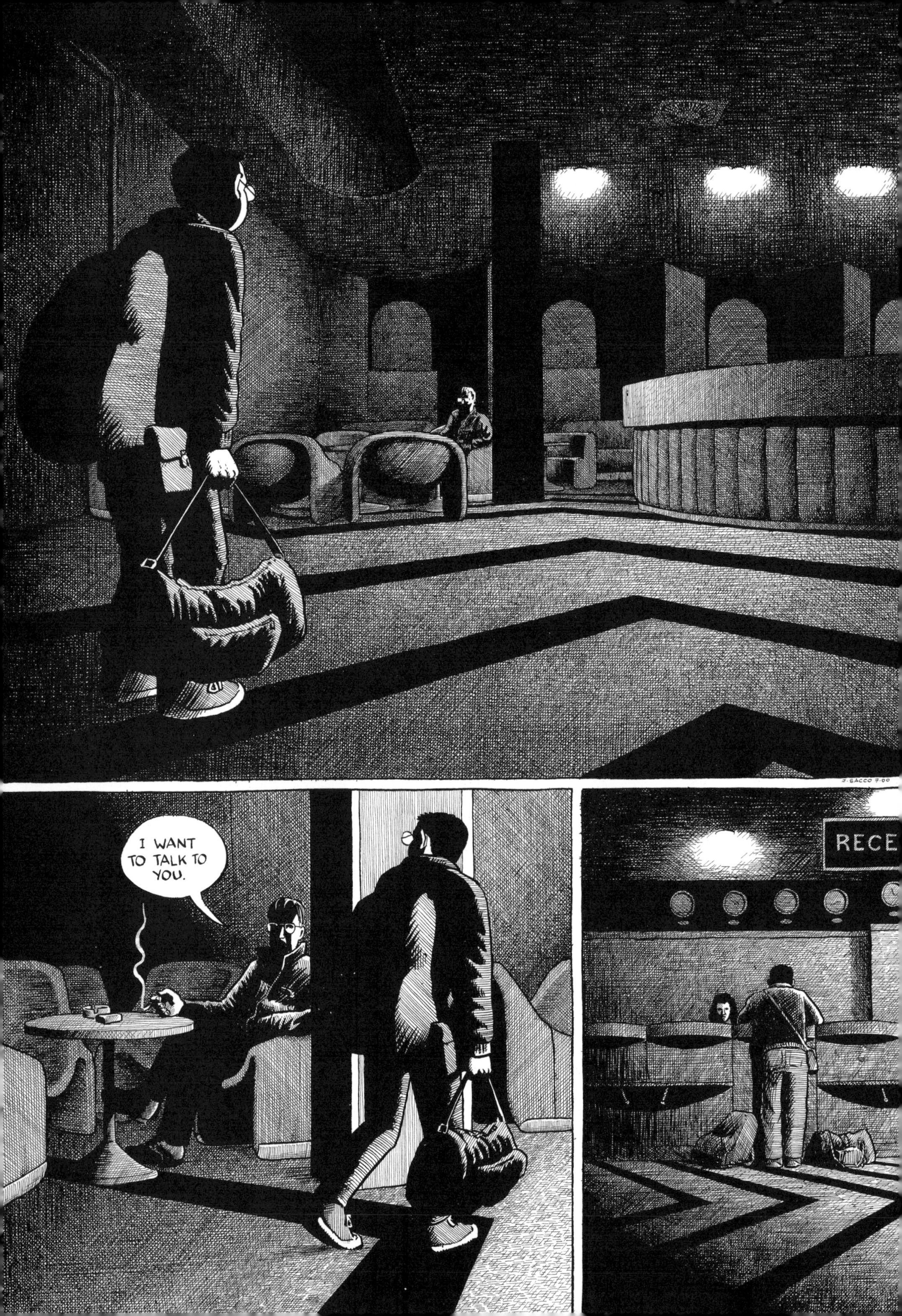
J. SACCO 7.00
I WANT TO TALK TO YOU.
RECE

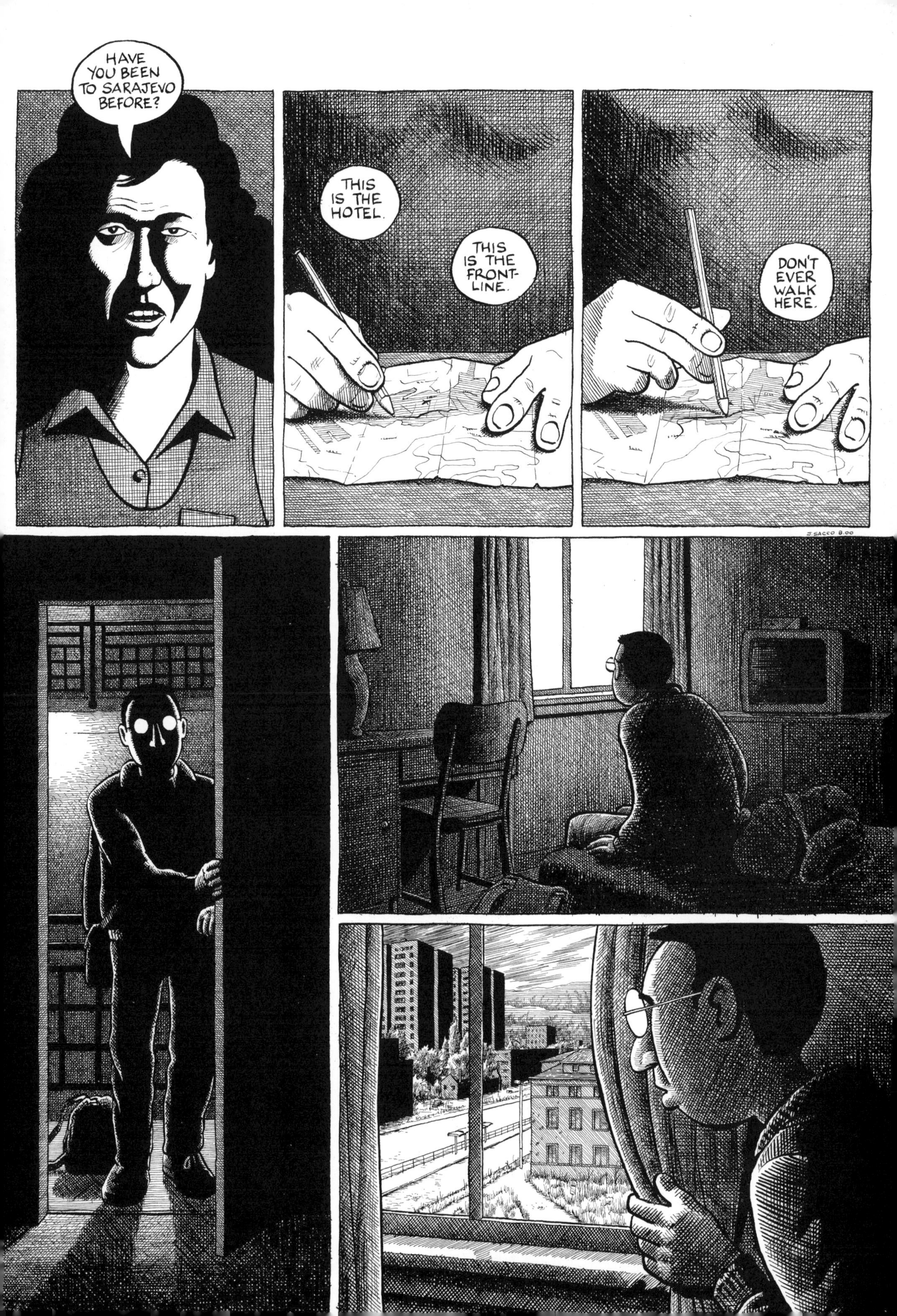
HAVE YOU BEEN TO SARAJEVO BEFORE?
THIS IS THE HOTEL.
THIS IS THE FRONT-LINE.
DON'T EVER WALK HERE.
J. SACCO 8.00

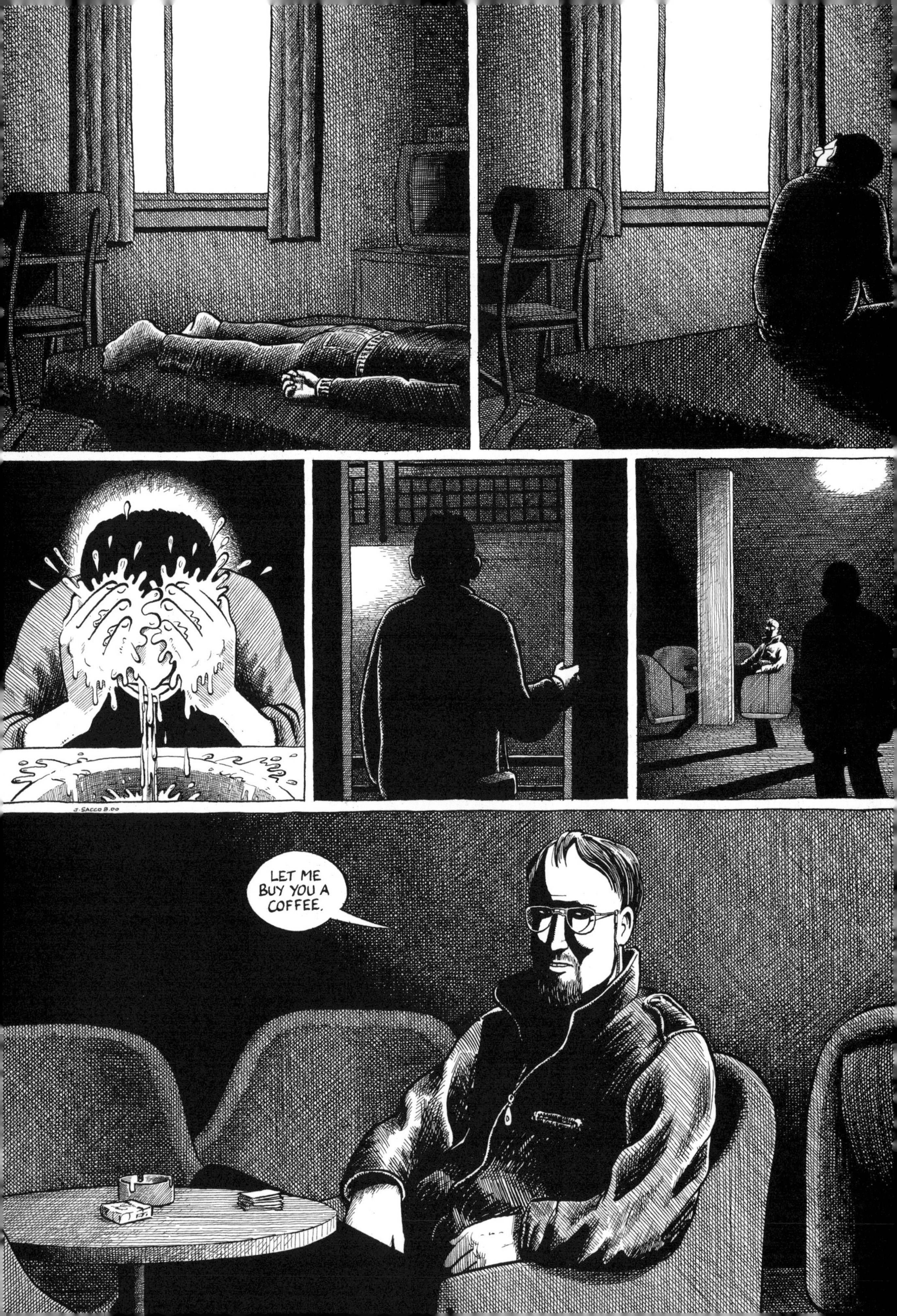
J. SACCO 8.00
LET ME BUY YOU A COFFEE.

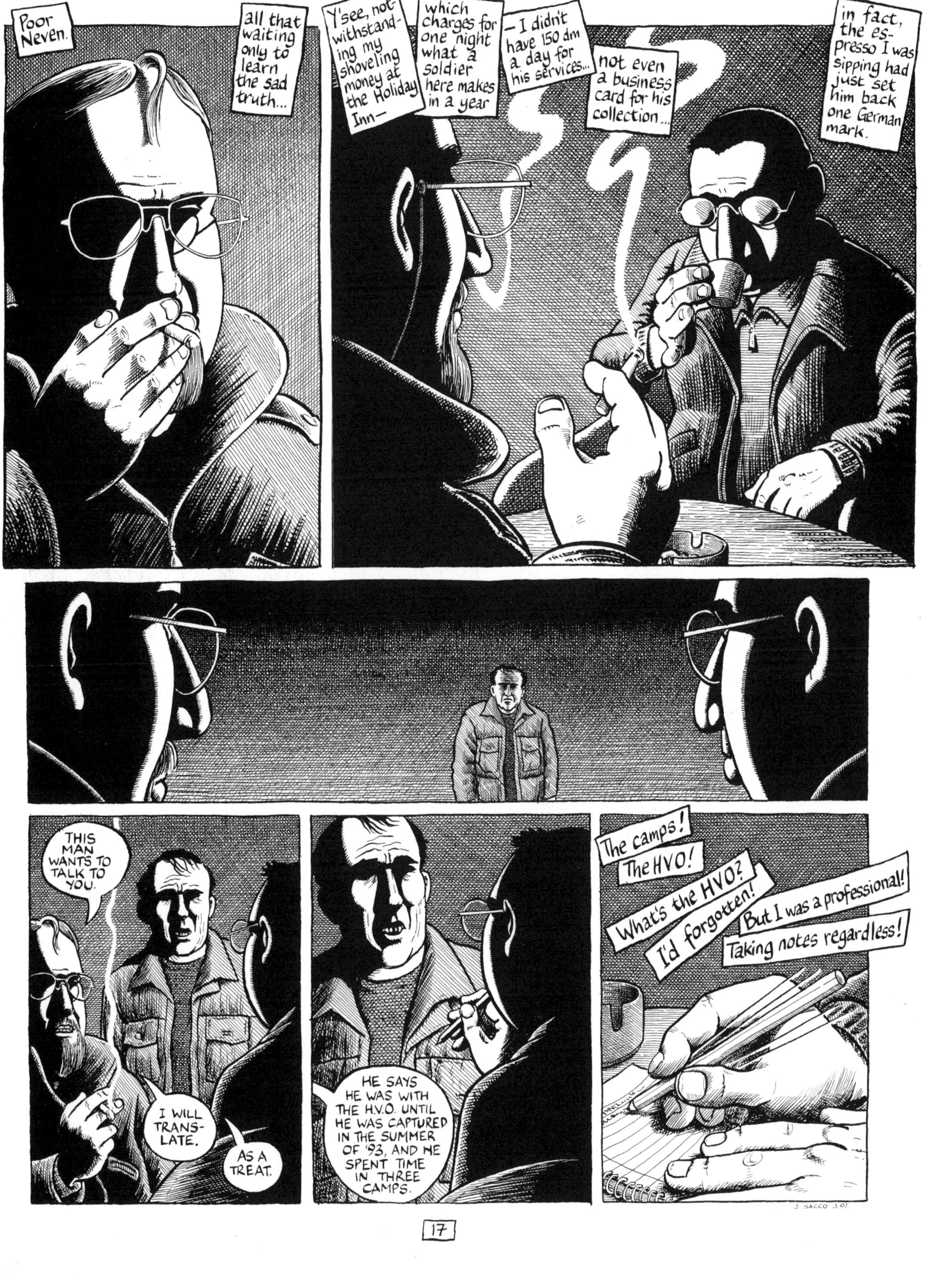
Poor Neven.
all that waiting only to learn the sad truth...
Y'see, notwithstanding my shoveling money at the Holiday Inn—
which charges for one night what a soldier here makes in a year
—I didn't have 150 dm a day for his services...
not even a business card for his collection...
in fact, the espresso I was sipping had just set him back one German mark.
THIS MAN WANTS TO TALK TO YOU.
I WILL TRANSLATE.
AS A TREAT.
HE SAYS HE WAS WITH THE H.V.O. UNTIL HE WAS CAPTURED IN THE SUMMER OF '93, AND HE SPENT TIME IN THREE CAMPS.
The camps!
The HVO!
What's the HVO?
I'd forgotten!
But I was a professional!
Taking notes regardless!
J. SACCO 3.01

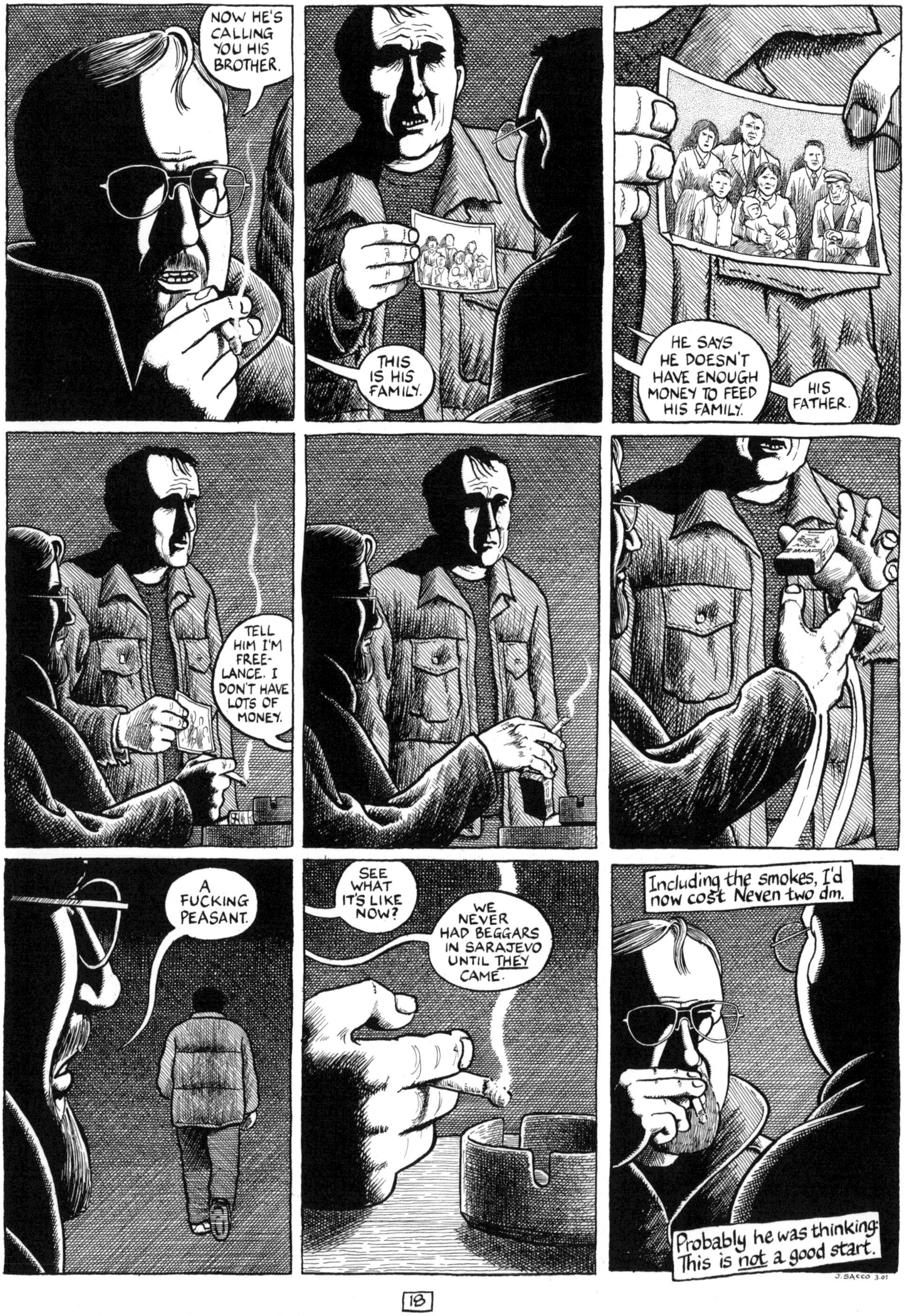
NOW HE'S CALLING YOU HIS BROTHER.
THIS IS HIS FAMILY.
HE SAYS HE DOESN'T HAVE ENOUGH MONEY TO FEED HIS FAMILY.
HIS FATHER.
TELL HIM I'M FREE-LANCE. I DON'T HAVE LOTS OF MONEY.
A FUCKING PEASANT.
SEE WHAT IT'S LIKE NOW?
WE NEVER HAD BEGGARS IN SARAJEVO UNTIL THEY CAME.
Including the smokes, I'd now cost Neven two dm.
Probably he was thinking: This is not a good start.
J. SACCO 3.01

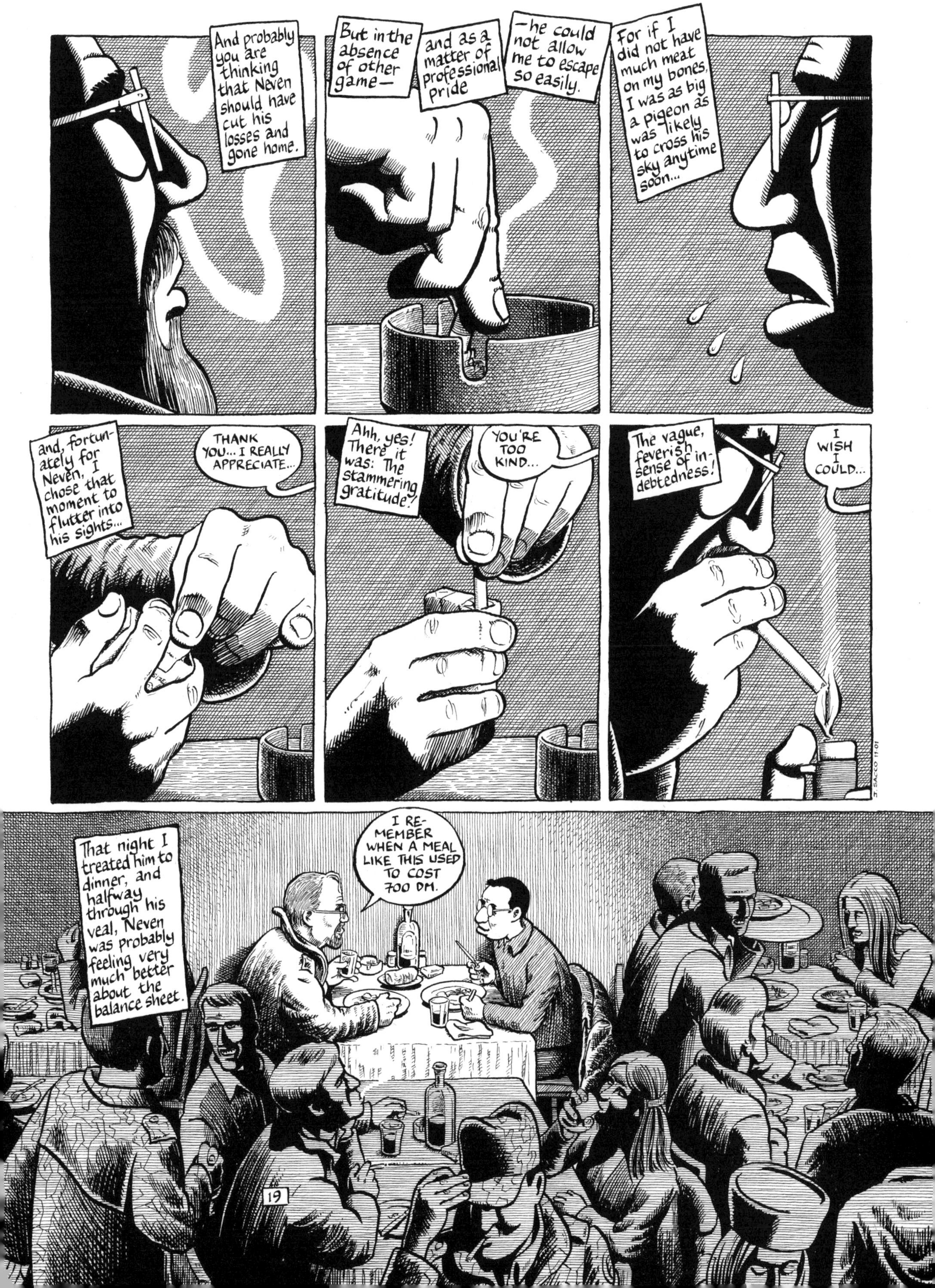
And probably you are thinking that Neven should have cut his losses and gone home.
But in the absence of other game—
and as a matter of professional pride
—he could not allow me to escape so easily.
For if I did not have much meat on my bones, I was as big a pigeon as was likely to cross his sky anytime soon...
and, fortunately for Neven, I chose that moment to flutter into his sights...
THANK YOU... I REALLY APPRECIATE...
Ahh, yes! There it was: The stammering gratitude!
YOU'RE TOO KIND...
The vague, feverish sense of indebtedness!
I WISH I COULD...
That night I treated him to dinner, and halfway through his veal, Neven was probably feeling very much better about the balance sheet.
I REMEMBER WHEN A MEAL LIKE THIS USED TO COST 700 DM.

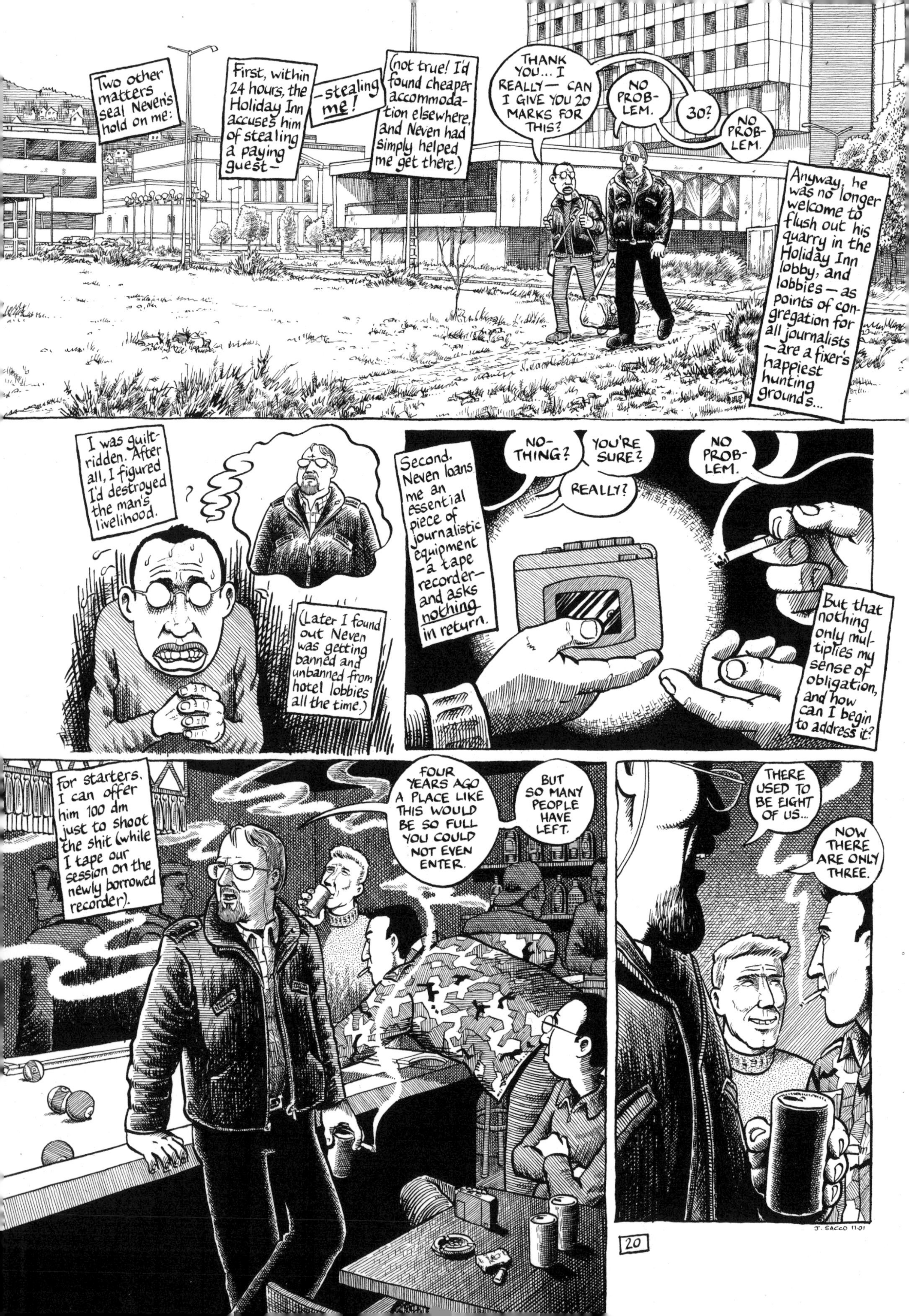
Two other matters seal Neven's hold on me:
First, within 24 hours, the Holiday Inn accuses him of stealing a paying guest–
–stealing me!
(not true! I'd found cheaper accommodation elsewhere, and Neven had simply helped me get there.)
THANK YOU... I REALLY— CAN I GIVE YOU 20 MARKS FOR THIS?
NO PROBLEM.
30?
NO PROBLEM.
Anyway, he was no longer welcome to flush out his quarry in the Holiday Inn lobby, and lobbies—as points of congregation for all journalists—are a fixer's happiest hunting grounds...
I was guilt-ridden. After all, I figured I'd destroyed the man's livelihood.
(Later I found out Neven was getting banned and unbanned from hotel lobbies all the time.)
Second, Neven loans me an essential piece of journalistic equipment—a tape recorder—and asks nothing in return.
NOTHING?
YOU'RE SURE?
REALLY?
NO PROBLEM.
But that nothing only multiplies my sense of obligation, and how can I begin to address it?
For starters, I can offer him 100 dm just to shoot the shit (while I tape our session on the newly borrowed recorder).
FOUR YEARS AGO A PLACE LIKE THIS WOULD BE SO FULL YOU COULD NOT EVEN ENTER.
BUT SO MANY PEOPLE HAVE LEFT.
THERE USED TO BE EIGHT OF US...
NOW THERE ARE ONLY THREE.
J. SACCO 11·01

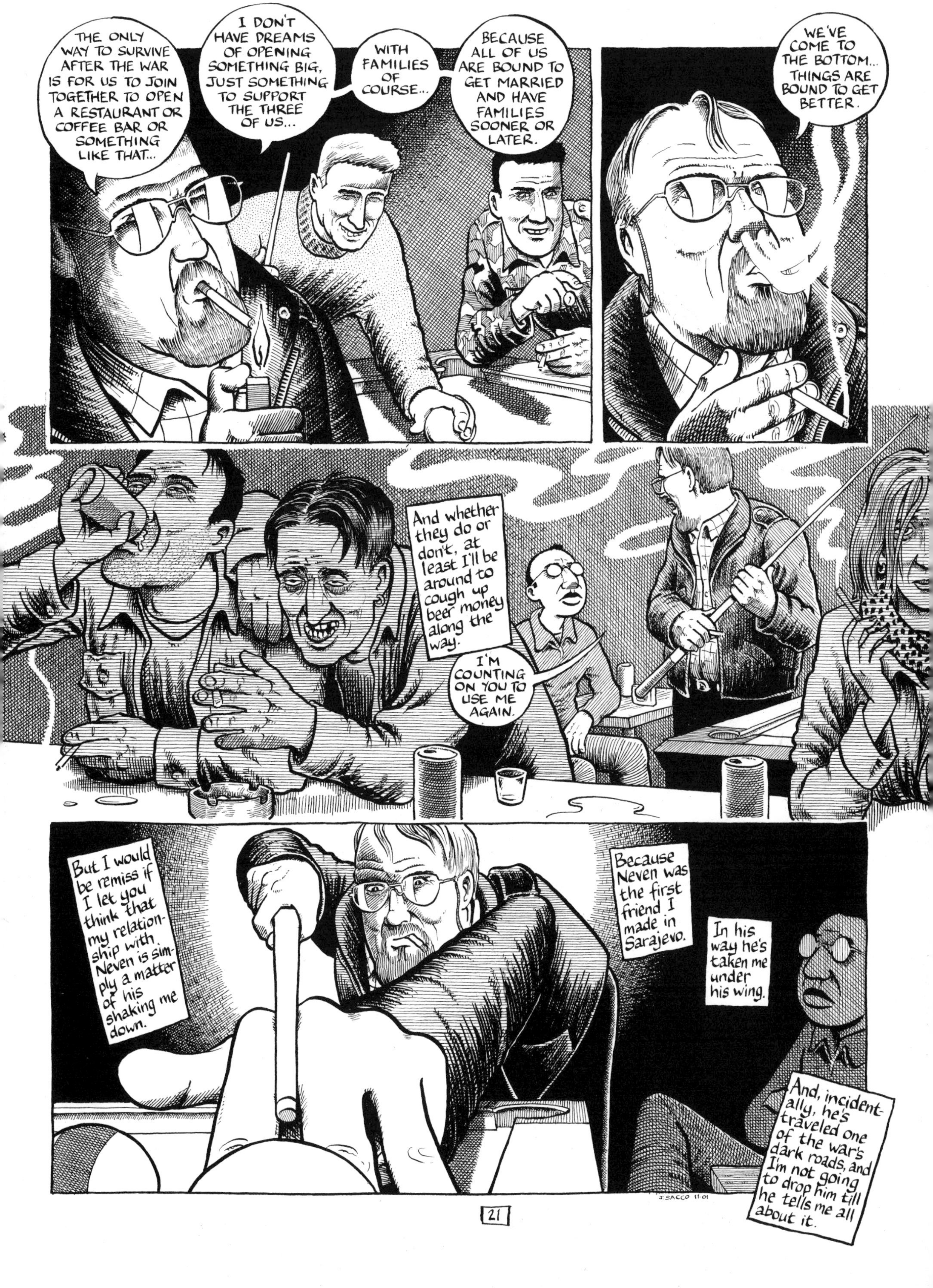
THE ONLY WAY TO SURVIVE AFTER THE WAR IS FOR US TO JOIN TOGETHER TO OPEN A RESTAURANT OR COFFEE BAR OR SOMETHING LIKE THAT...
I DON'T HAVE DREAMS OF OPENING SOMETHING BIG, JUST SOMETHING TO SUPPORT THE THREE OF US...
WITH FAMILIES OF COURSE...
BECAUSE ALL OF US ARE BOUND TO GET MARRIED AND HAVE FAMILIES SOONER OR LATER.
WE'VE COME TO THE BOTTOM... THINGS ARE BOUND TO GET BETTER.
And whether they do or don't, at least I'll be around to cough up beer money along the way.
I'M COUNTING ON YOU TO USE ME AGAIN.
But I would be remiss if I let you think that my relationship with Neven is simply a matter of his shaking me down.
Because Neven was the first friend I made in Sarajevo.
In his way he's taken me under his wing.
And, incidentally, he's traveled one of the war's dark roads, and I'm not going to drop him till he tells me all about it.
J. SACCO 11-01

1984

Put yourself in Neven's shoes.

J. SACCO 11-01

You've done your stint in the Yugoslav People's Army. You were rated a weapons specialist, trained as a sniper.

Back in civilian clothes, you've got some business to take care of. Your brother—you describe him as "a wild sort of guy whose screws were a little bit loose"—crossed the wrong people in Los Angeles and got whacked. You're going to retrace his movements. They begin in Paris.

You get sidetracked there, mixed up with some tough guys from Britain, the States, South Africa, Belgium...

You participate in some illicit activities... carjackings... "a bank robbery or two"...

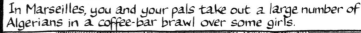

In Marseilles, you and your pals take out a large number of Algerians in a coffee-bar brawl over some girls.

Your gang is noticed and invited to join a larger enterprise.

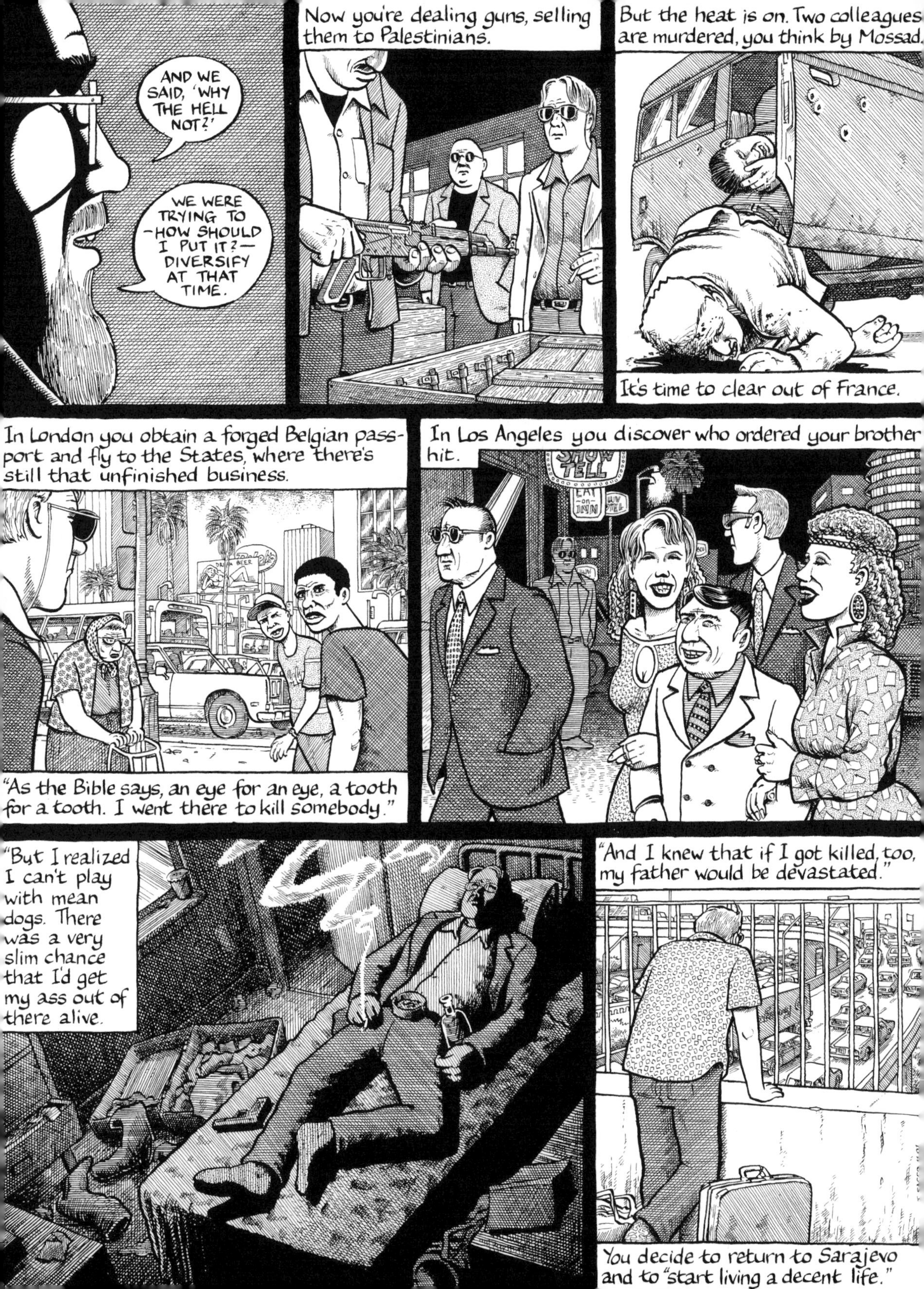
AND WE SAID, 'WHY THE HELL NOT?'
WE WERE TRYING TO —HOW SHOULD I PUT IT?— DIVERSIFY AT THAT TIME.
Now you're dealing guns, selling them to Palestinians.
But the heat is on. Two colleagues are murdered, you think by Mossad.
It's time to clear out of France.
In London you obtain a forged Belgian passport and fly to the States, where there's still that unfinished business.
"As the Bible says, an eye for an eye, a tooth for a tooth. I went there to kill somebody."
In Los Angeles you discover who ordered your brother hit.
SHOW TELL
"But I realized I can't play with mean dogs. There was a very slim chance that I'd get my ass out of there alive.
"And I knew that if I got killed, too, my father would be devastated."
You decide to return to Sarajevo and to "start living a decent life."

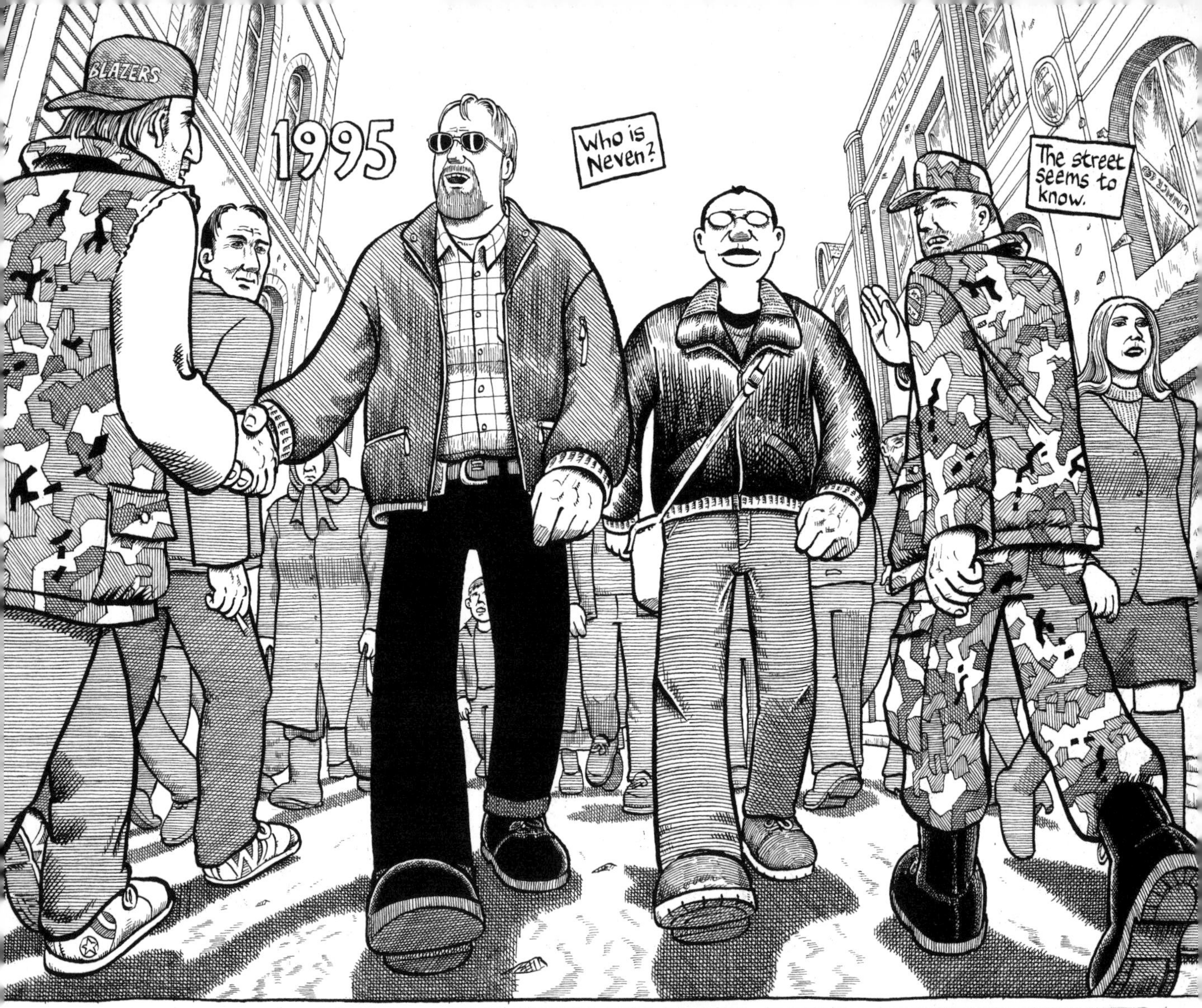
BLAZERS
1995
Who is Neven?
The street seems to know.

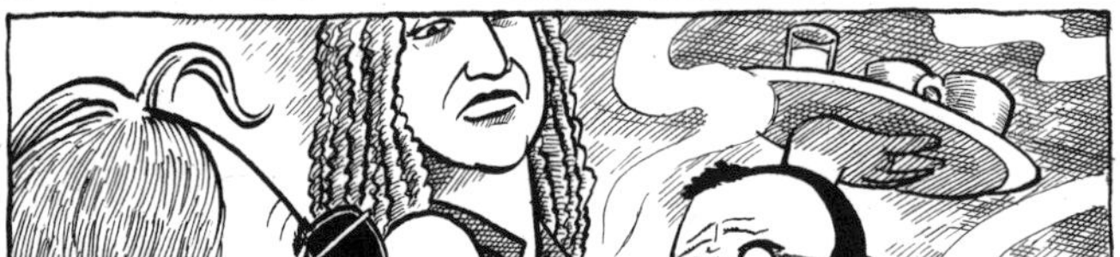
With Neven, I'm like a teenager on his first few dates— a little enthralled, a little infatuated perhaps, maybe a little in love, and what is love but a transaction...
THE COFFEE IS TWO MARKS.
I am vulnerable, understand me. It is war, for Christ's sake, and now that I've got myself into it, I need a hug, a support group, someone to carry me gently over the rubble...

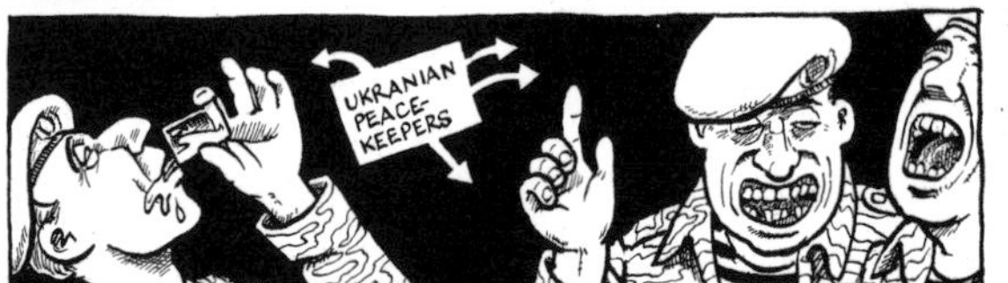
UKRANIAN PEACE-KEEPERS
And woe is me when I reach out to take hold of Neven's skirt and find he is not there...
YELTSIN?
WHAT YOU THINK OF YELTSIN?
ARM WRESTLE?
ARM WRESTLE?
J. SACCO 12-01

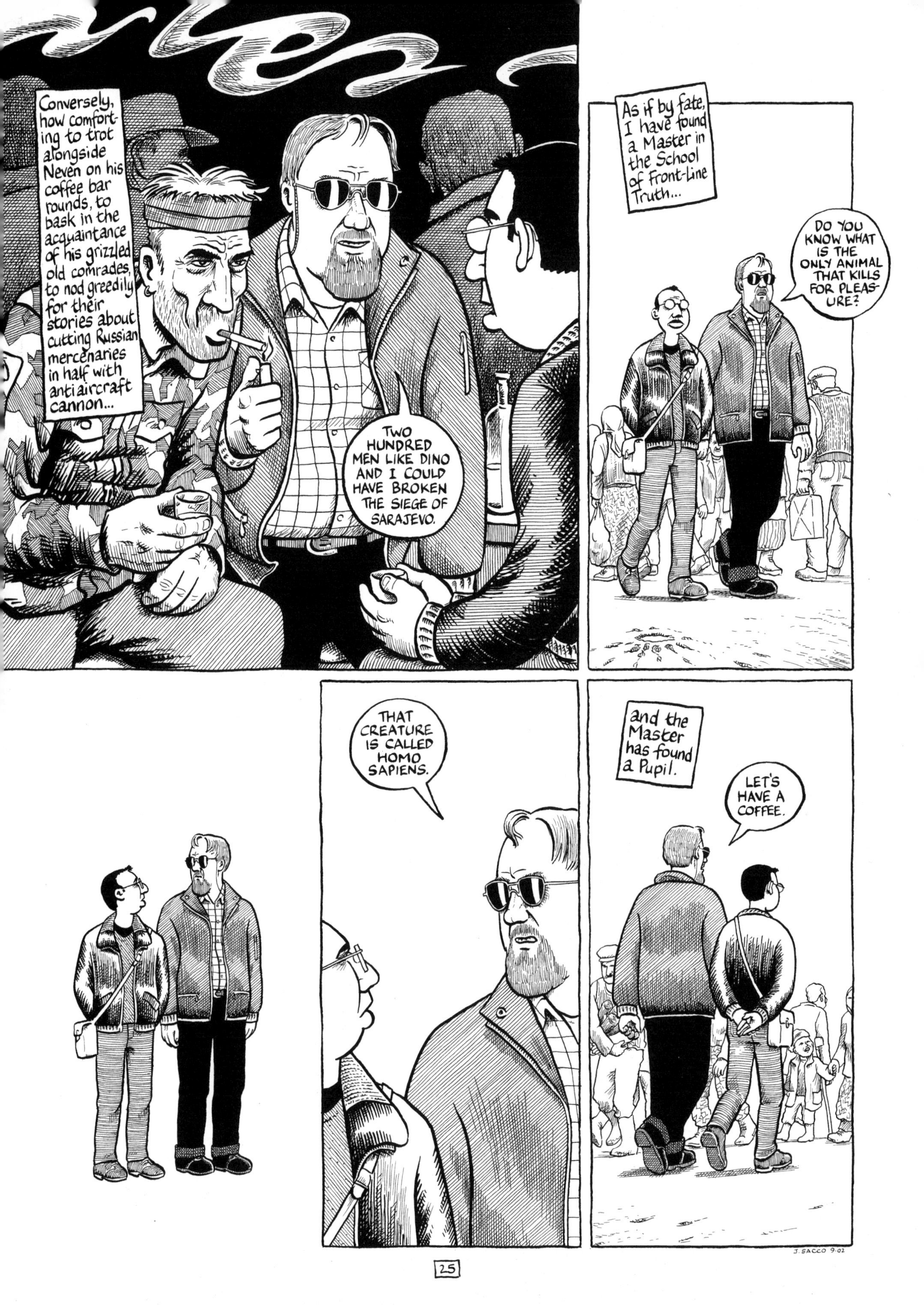

Conversely, how comforting to trot alongside Neven on his coffee bar rounds, to bask in the acquaintance of his grizzled old comrades, to nod greedily for their stories about cutting Russian mercenaries in half with antiaircraft cannon...
TWO HUNDRED MEN LIKE DINO AND I COULD HAVE BROKEN THE SIEGE OF SARAJEVO.
As if by fate, I have found a Master in the School of Front-Line Truth...
DO YOU KNOW WHAT IS THE ONLY ANIMAL THAT KILLS FOR PLEASURE?
THAT CREATURE IS CALLED HOMO SAPIENS.
and the Master has found a Pupil.
LET'S HAVE A COFFEE.
J. SACCO 9·02

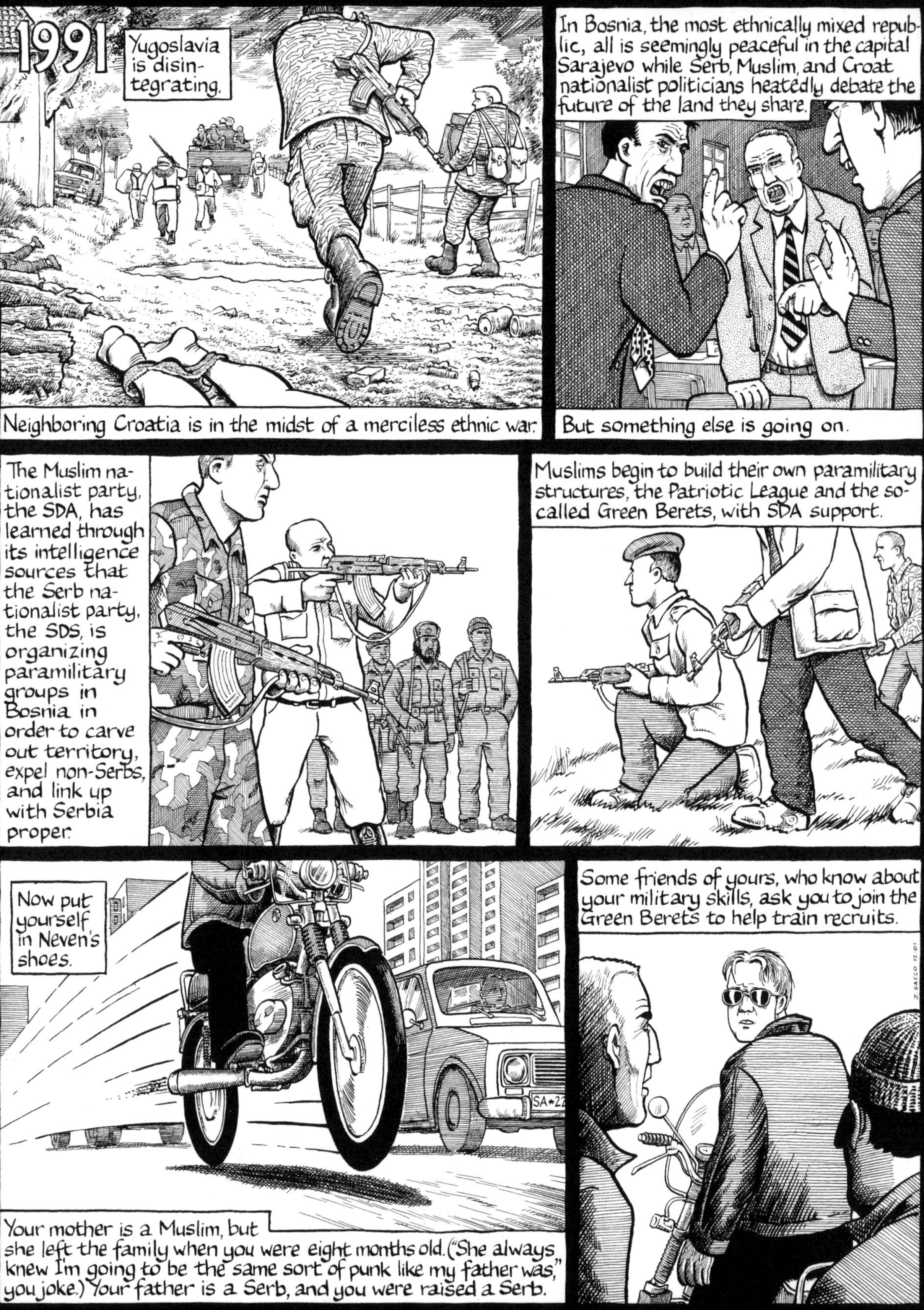
1991
Yugoslavia is disintegrating.
Neighboring Croatia is in the midst of a merciless ethnic war.
In Bosnia, the most ethnically mixed republic, all is seemingly peaceful in the capital Sarajevo while Serb, Muslim, and Croat nationalist politicians heatedly debate the future of the land they share.
But something else is going on.
The Muslim nationalist party, the SDA, has learned through its intelligence sources that the Serb nationalist party, the SDS, is organizing paramilitary groups in Bosnia in order to carve out territory, expel non-Serbs, and link up with Serbia proper.
Muslims begin to build their own paramilitary structures, the Patriotic League and the so-called Green Berets, with SDA support.
Now put yourself in Neven's shoes.
Your mother is a Muslim, but she left the family when you were eight months old. ("She always knew I'm going to be the same sort of punk like my father was," you joke.) Your father is a Serb, and you were raised a Serb.
Some friends of yours, who know about your military skills, ask you to join the Green Berets to help train recruits.

I ASKED MYSELF A QUESTION...

ON WHOSE SIDE AM I?

BEING A SERB, YOU KNOW.

AND I DECIDED TO STAKE MY CARDS WITH BOSNIA. I REALLY DON'T KNOW WHY.

BECAUSE I ALWAYS THOUGHT OF MYSELF AS A SERB NATIONALIST.

I'M A NATIONALIST IN THE SENSE THAT I LOVE MY NATION...

BUT I DON'T HATE ANYBODY ELSE.

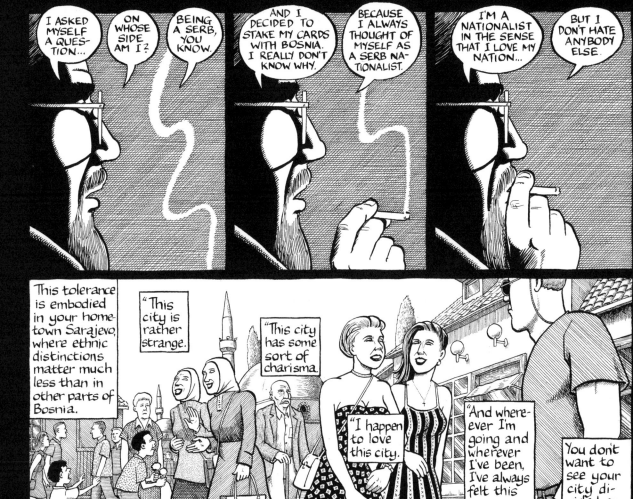

This tolerance is embodied in your home-town Sarajevo, where ethnic distinctions matter much less than in other parts of Bosnia.

"This city is rather strange.

"This city has some sort of charisma.

"I happen to love this city.

"And wherever I'm going and wherever I've been, I've always felt this urge to return."

You don't want to see your city divided or endangered. You join the Green Berets in September.

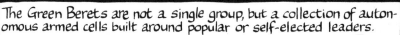

The Green Berets are not a single group, but a collection of autonomous armed cells built around popular or self-elected leaders.

CELO WAS THE SPITTING IMAGE OF A WILD GUY FROM SARAJEVO.

One of the most charismatic of these men is Ismet Bajramovic, who is known as Celo.

Born in 1966...

Ismet Bajramovic AKA Celo*

in 7th grade, after he punched his geography teacher in the face, his father told young Ismet he'd done the right thing, then beat up the boy...

he began dealing drugs while still in his teens...

invited to play for Sarajevo's soccer team, he was kicked out for beating up a teammate after his first practice.

WHEN HE WAS 19 HE WAS SENTENCED TO 11 YEARS IN PRISON FOR ATTEMPTED MURDER, RAPE, BREAKING AND ENTERING, BLAH BLAH BLAH...

OF THAT I BELIEVE ONLY THE CHARGE OF ATTEMPTED MURDER.

HE WAS SIMPLY TOO GOOD-LOOKING FOR RAPE.

Later Bajramovic would claim he'd had more than 300 women, that some had even asked him to take their virginity.

According to his own account, in prison Bajramovic earned the respect of the guards and warden by thrashing a problem convict.

Subsequently, the self-declared "strongest and most popular prisoner" was called upon to resolve disputes between inmates.

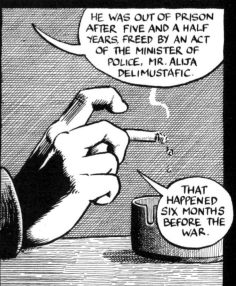

HE WAS OUT OF PRISON AFTER FIVE AND A HALF YEARS, FREED BY AN ACT OF THE MINISTER OF POLICE, MR. ALIJA DELIMUSTAFIC.

THAT HAPPENED SIX MONTHS BEFORE THE WAR.

28

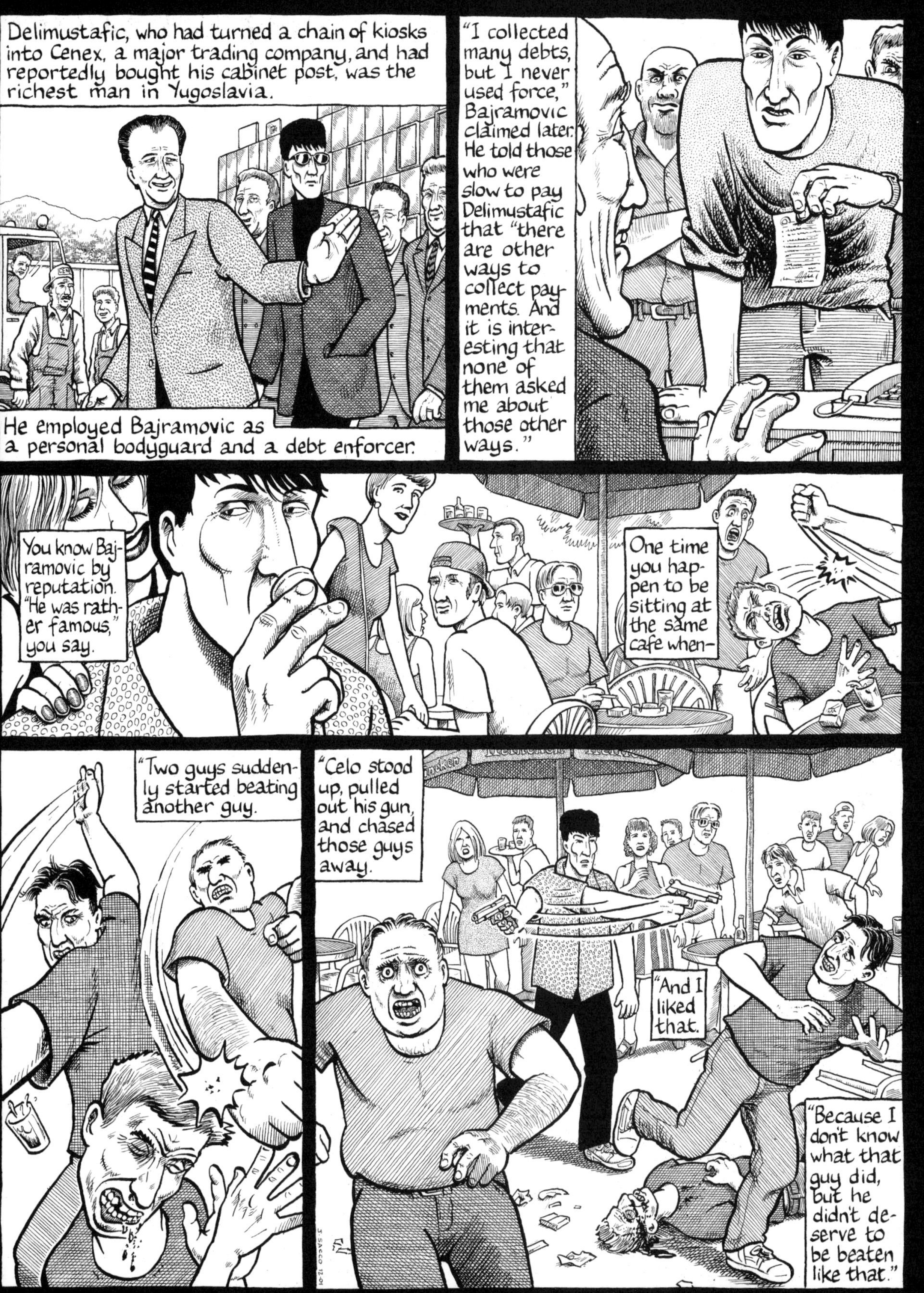
Delimustafic, who had turned a chain of kiosks into Cenex, a major trading company, and had reportedly bought his cabinet post, was the richest man in Yugoslavia.
He employed Bajramovic as a personal bodyguard and a debt enforcer.
"I collected many debts, but I never used force," Bajramovic claimed later. He told those who were slow to pay Delimustafic that "there are other ways to collect payments. And it is interesting that none of them asked me about those other ways."
You know Bajramovic by reputation. "He was rather famous," you say.
One time you happen to be sitting at the same cafe when-
"Two guys suddenly started beating another guy.
"Celo stood up, pulled out his gun, and chased those guys away.
"And I liked that.
"Because I don't know what that guy did, but he didn't deserve to be beaten like that."
J. SACCO 12-01

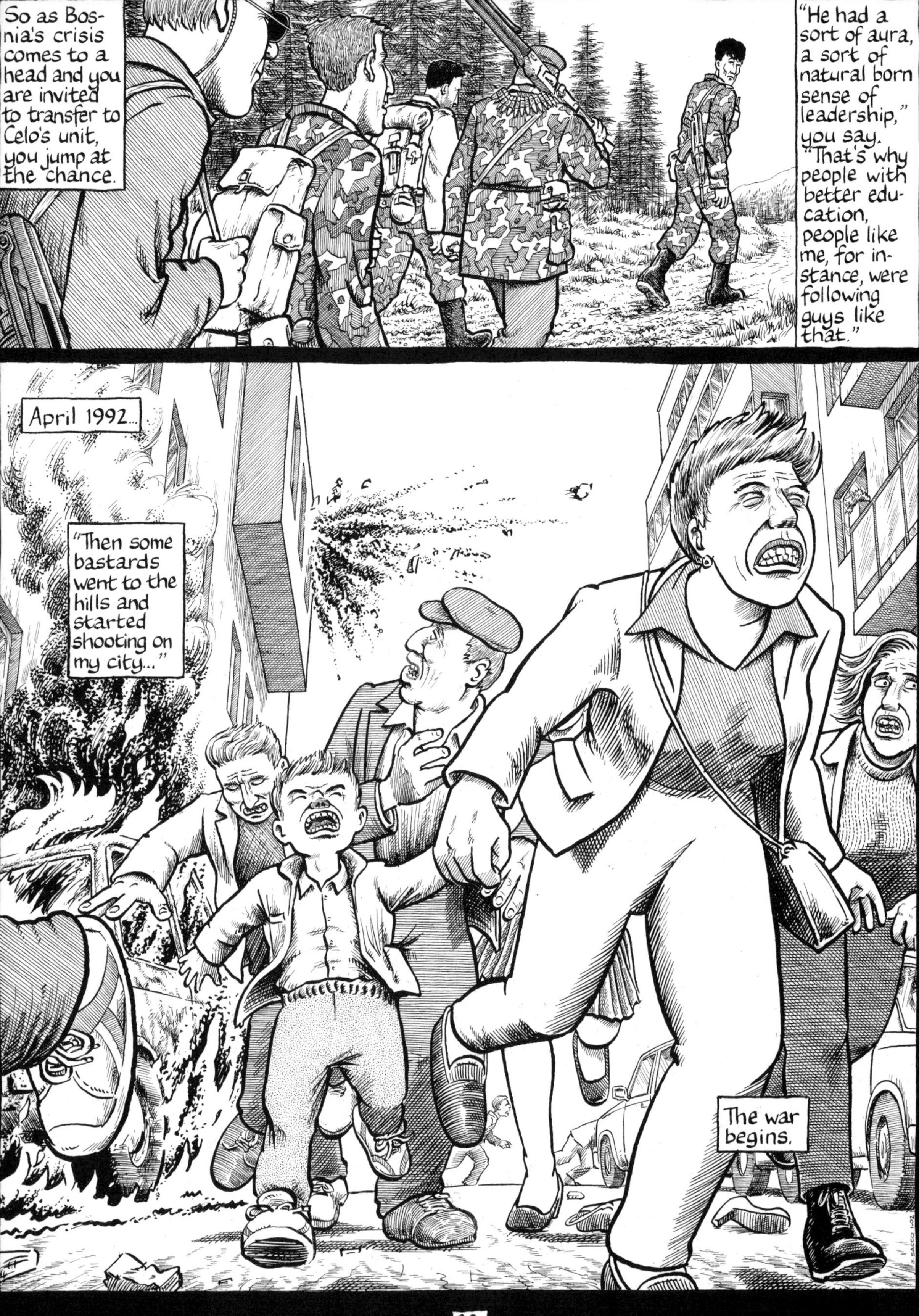
So as Bosnia's crisis comes to a head and you are invited to transfer to Celo's unit, you jump at the chance.
"He had a sort of aura, a sort of natural born sense of leadership," you say. "That's why people with better education, people like me, for instance, were following guys like that."
April 1992...
"Then some bastards went to the hills and started shooting on my city..."
The war begins.

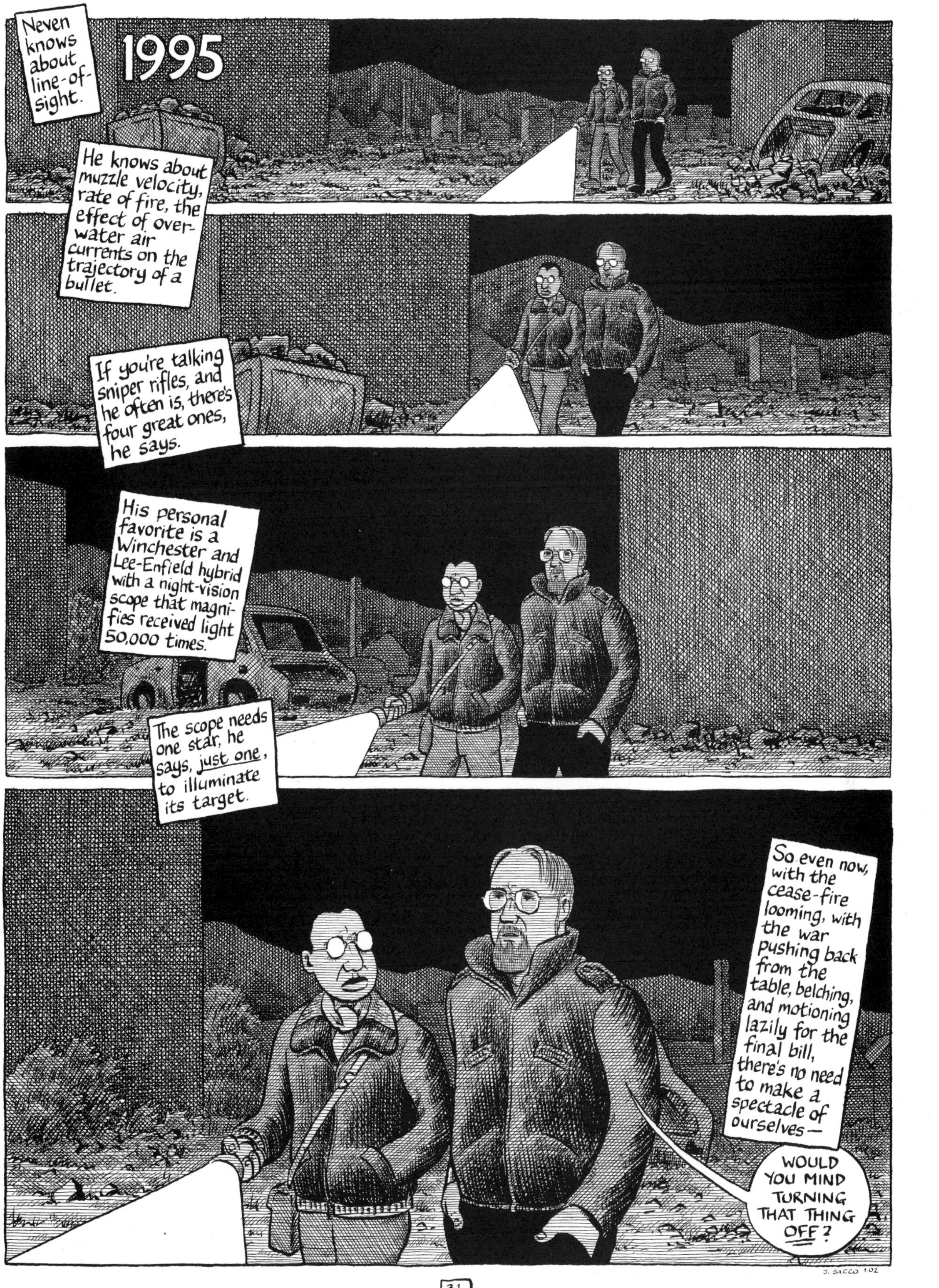
Neven knows about line-of-sight.
1995
He knows about muzzle velocity, rate of fire, the effect of over-water air currents on the trajectory of a bullet.
If you're talking sniper rifles, and he often is, there's four great ones, he says.
His personal favorite is a Winchester and Lee-Enfield hybrid with a night-vision scope that magni-fies received light 50,000 times.
The scope needs one star, he says, just one, to illuminate its target.
So even now, with the cease-fire looming, with the war pushing back from the table, belching, and motioning lazily for the final bill, there's no need to make a spectacle of ourselves—
WOULD YOU MIND TURNING THAT THING OFF?
J. SACCO 1.02

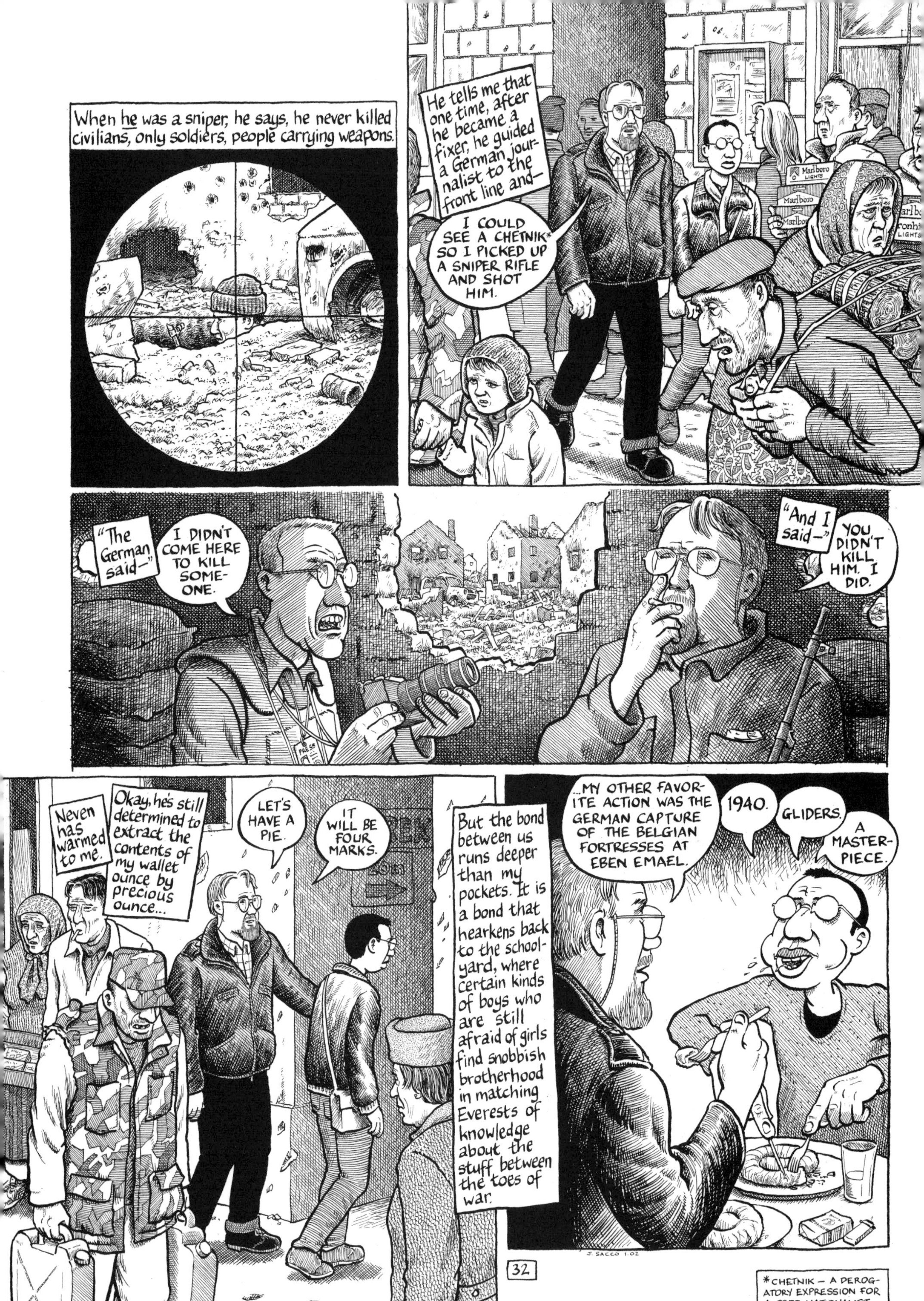

When he was a sniper, he says, he never killed civilians, only soldiers, people carrying weapons.
He tells me that one time, after he became a fixer, he guided a German journalist to the front line and—
I COULD SEE A CHETNIK* SO I PICKED UP A SNIPER RIFLE AND SHOT HIM.
Marlboro LIGHTS
"The German said—"
I DIDN'T COME HERE TO KILL SOMEONE.
PRESS
"And I said—"
YOU DIDN'T KILL HIM. I DID.
Neven has warmed to me.
Okay, he's still determined to extract the contents of my wallet ounce by precious ounce...
LET'S HAVE A PIE.
IT WILL BE FOUR MARKS.
But the bond between us runs deeper than my pockets. It is a bond that hearkens back to the schoolyard, where certain kinds of boys who are still afraid of girls find snobbish brotherhood in matching Everests of knowledge about the stuff between the toes of war.
...MY OTHER FAVORITE ACTION WAS THE GERMAN CAPTURE OF THE BELGIAN FORTRESSES AT EBEN EMAEL.
1940.
GLIDERS.
A MASTERPIECE.
J. SACCO 1.02

*CHETNIK — A DEROGATORY EXPRESSION FOR A SERB NATIONALIST

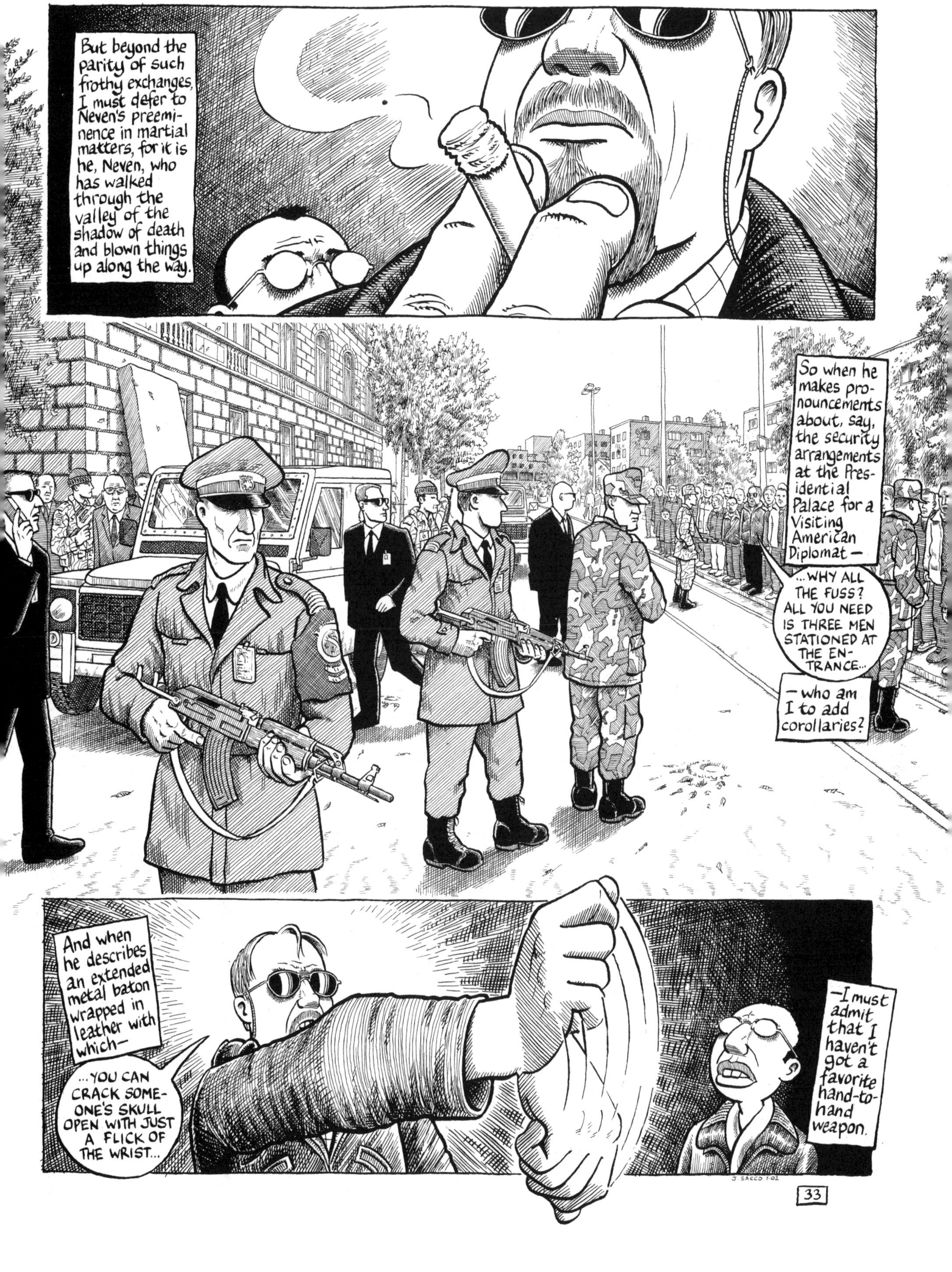
But beyond the parity of such frothy exchanges, I must defer to Neven's preeminence in martial matters, for it is he, Neven, who has walked through the valley of the shadow of death and blown things up along the way.
So when he makes pronouncements about, say, the security arrangements at the Presidential Palace for a Visiting American Diplomat —
...WHY ALL THE FUSS? ALL YOU NEED IS THREE MEN STATIONED AT THE ENTRANCE...
— who am I to add corollaries?
And when he describes an extended metal baton wrapped in leather with which—
...YOU CAN CRACK SOMEONE'S SKULL OPEN WITH JUST A FLICK OF THE WRIST...
—I must admit that I haven't got a favorite hand-to-hand weapon.
J. SACCO 1.02

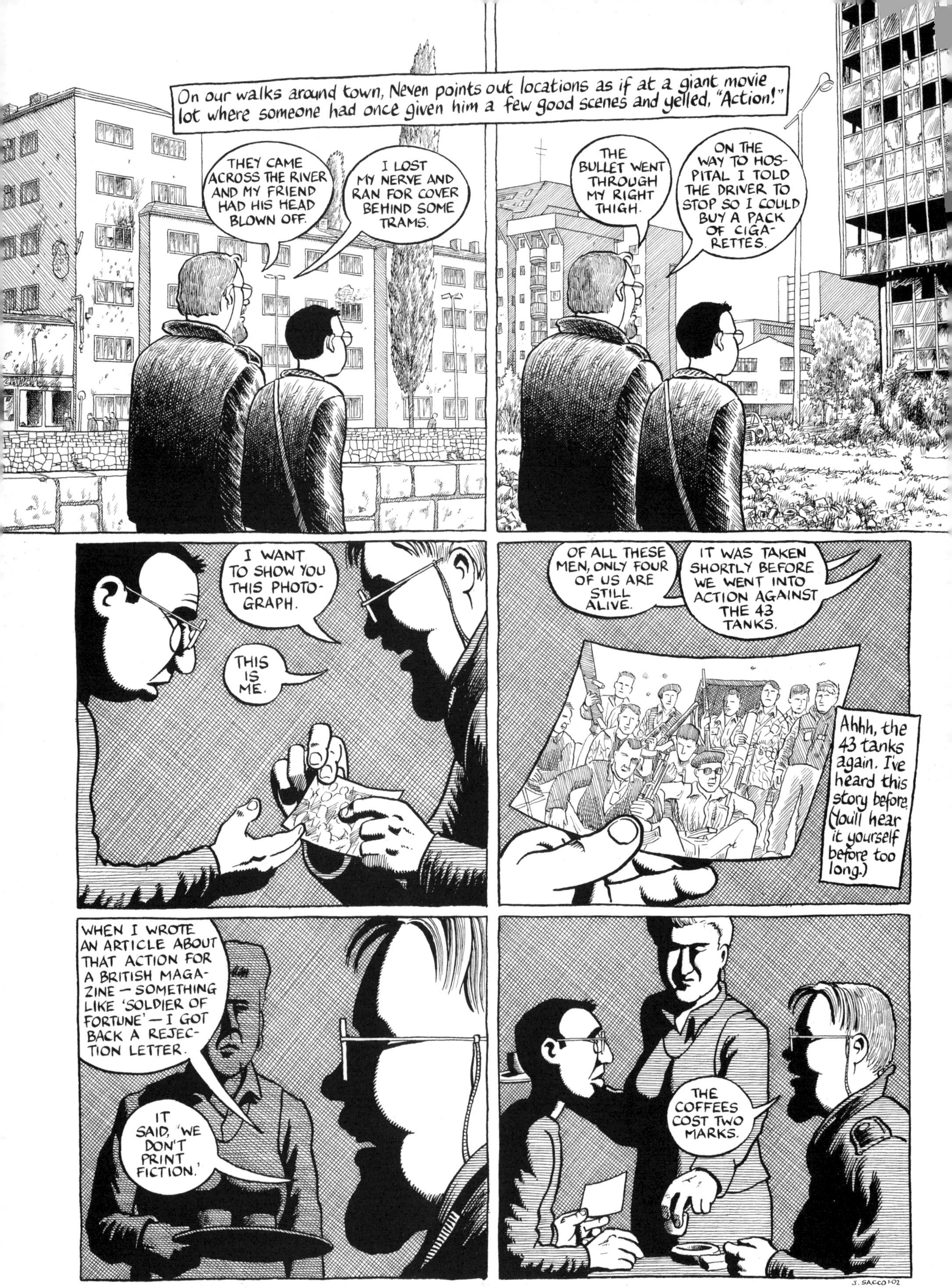
On our walks around town, Neven points out locations as if at a giant movie lot where someone had once given him a few good scenes and yelled, "Action!"
THEY CAME ACROSS THE RIVER AND MY FRIEND HAD HIS HEAD BLOWN OFF.
I LOST MY NERVE AND RAN FOR COVER BEHIND SOME TRAMS.
THE BULLET WENT THROUGH MY RIGHT THIGH.
ON THE WAY TO HOS-PITAL I TOLD THE DRIVER TO STOP SO I COULD BUY A PACK OF CIGA-RETTES.
I WANT TO SHOW YOU THIS PHOTO-GRAPH.
THIS IS ME.
OF ALL THESE MEN, ONLY FOUR OF US ARE STILL ALIVE.
IT WAS TAKEN SHORTLY BEFORE WE WENT INTO ACTION AGAINST THE 43 TANKS.
Ahhh, the 43 tanks again. I've heard this story before. (You'll hear it yourself before too long.)
WHEN I WROTE AN ARTICLE ABOUT THAT ACTION FOR A BRITISH MAGA-ZINE — SOMETHING LIKE 'SOLDIER OF FORTUNE' — I GOT BACK A REJEC-TION LETTER.
IT SAID, 'WE DON'T PRINT FICTION.'
THE COFFEES COST TWO MARKS.
J. SACCO '02

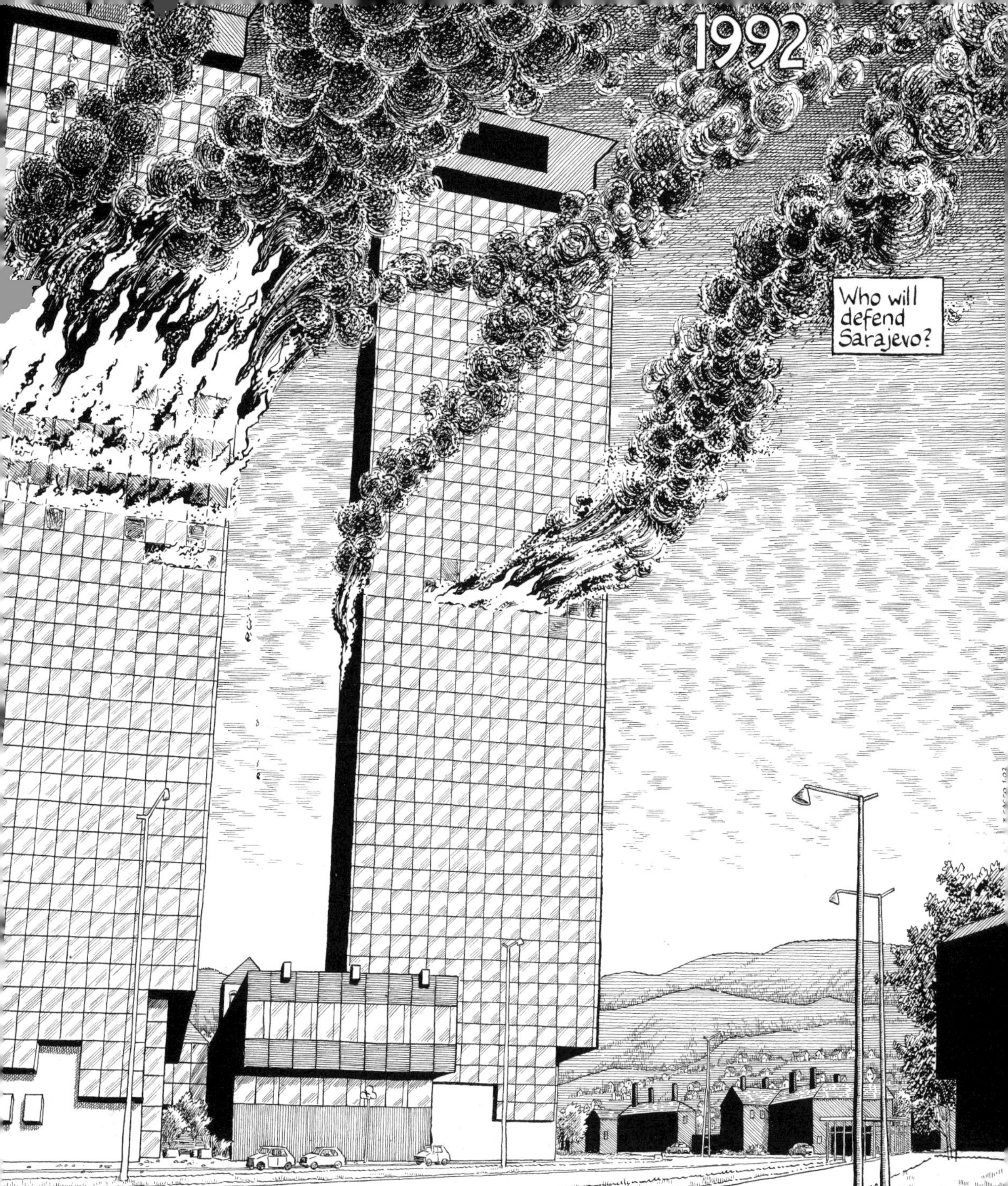
1992
Who will defend Sarajevo?

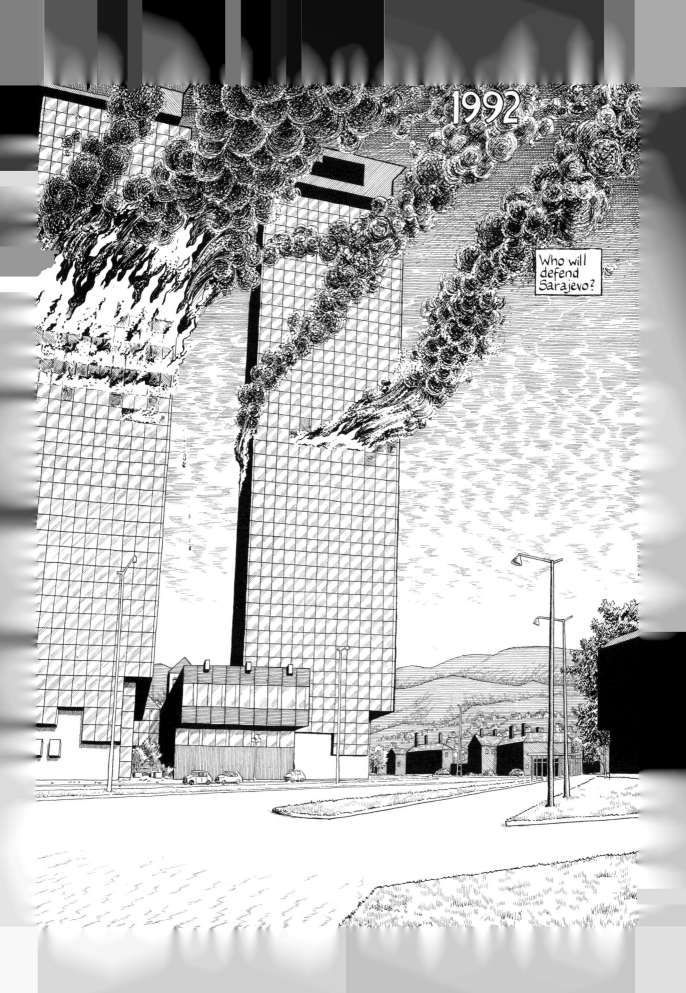

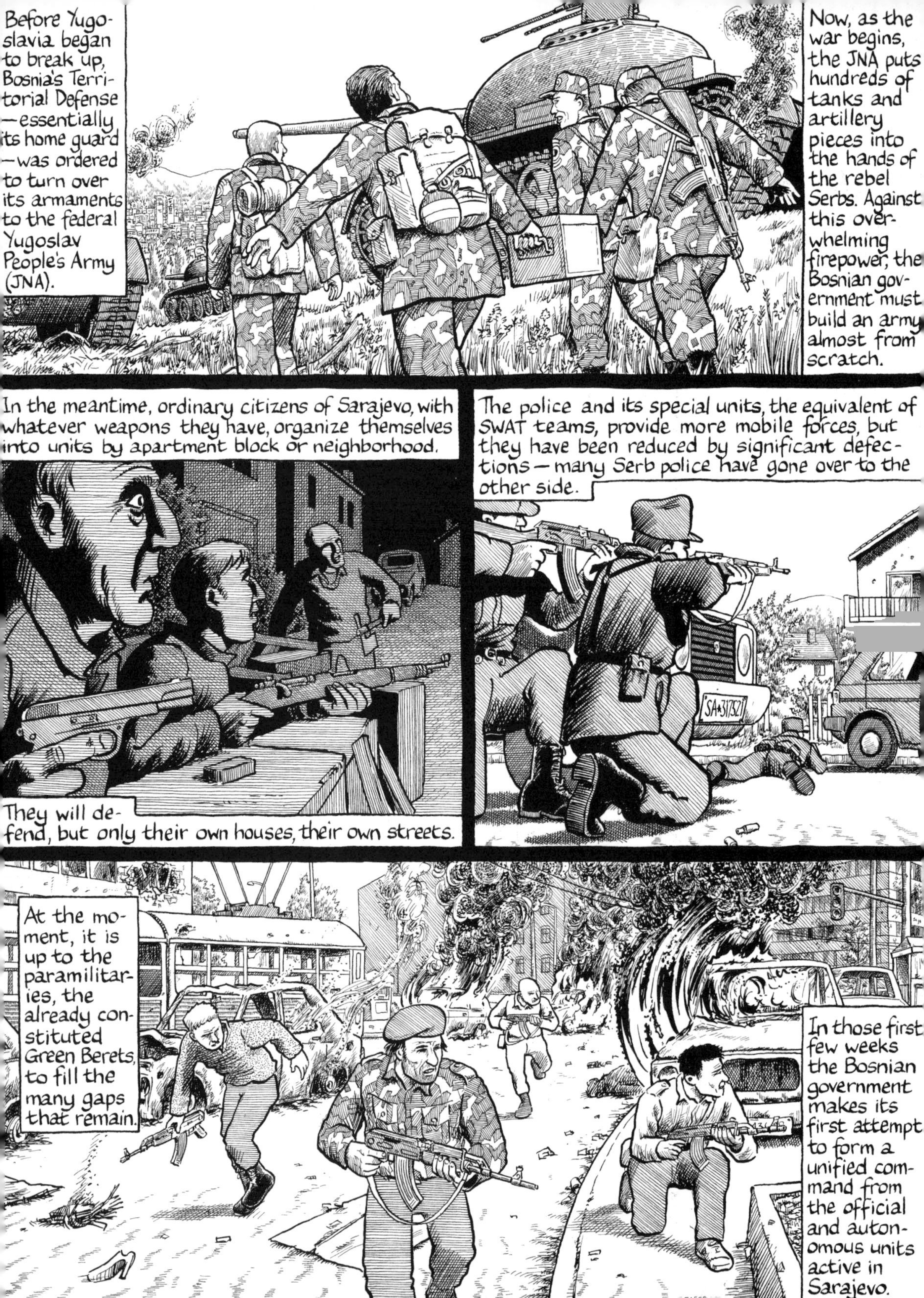

Before Yugoslavia began to break up, Bosnia's Territorial Defense —essentially its home guard —was ordered to turn over its armaments to the federal Yugoslav People's Army (JNA).
Now, as the war begins, the JNA puts hundreds of tanks and artillery pieces into the hands of the rebel Serbs. Against this overwhelming firepower, the Bosnian government must build an army almost from scratch.
In the meantime, ordinary citizens of Sarajevo, with whatever weapons they have, organize themselves into units by apartment block or neighborhood.
They will defend, but only their own houses, their own streets.
The police and its special units, the equivalent of SWAT teams, provide more mobile forces, but they have been reduced by significant defections — many Serb police have gone over to the other side.
At the moment, it is up to the paramilitaries, the already constituted Green Berets, to fill the many gaps that remain.
In those first few weeks the Bosnian government makes its first attempt to form a unified command from the official and autonomous units active in Sarajevo.

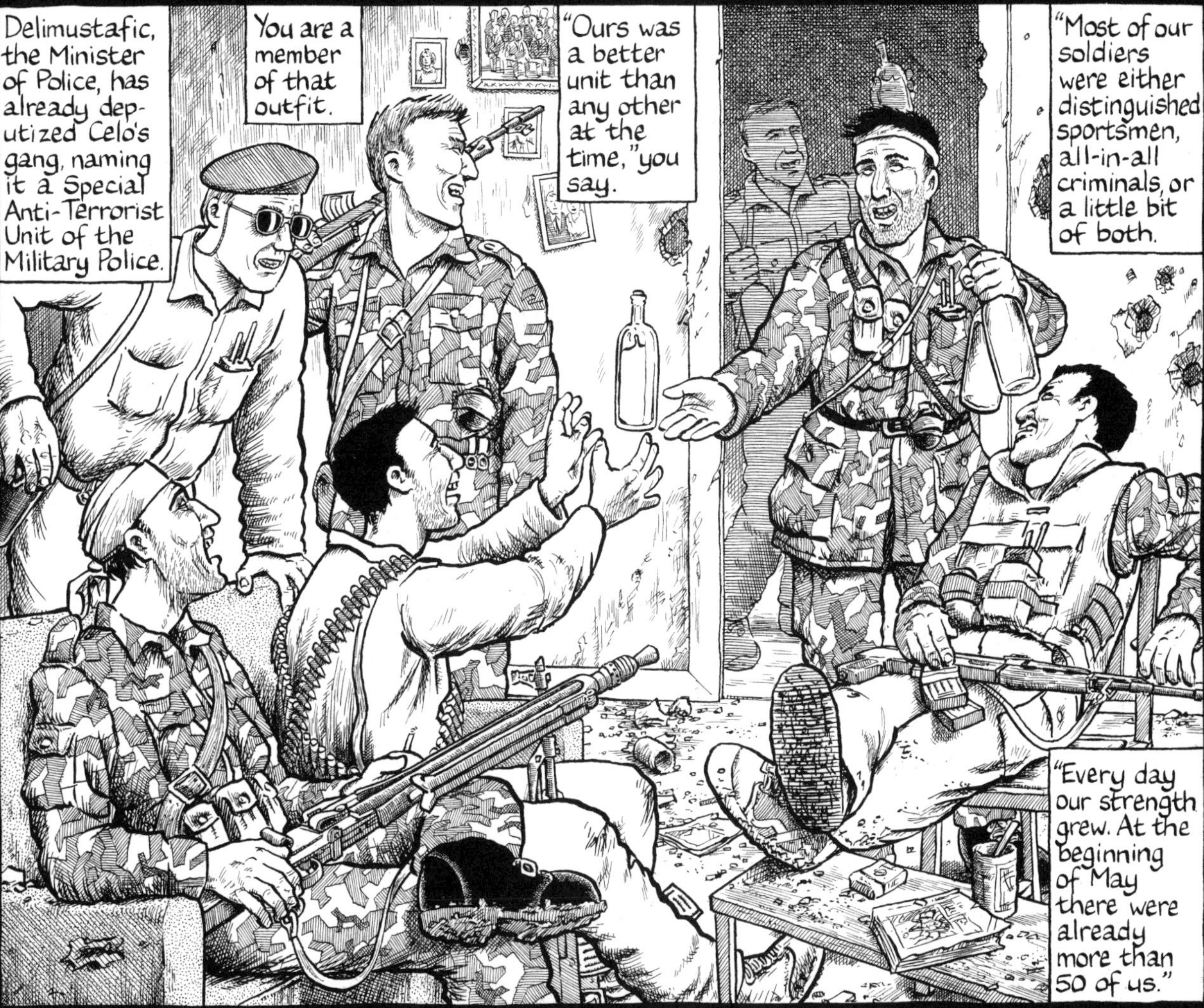
Delimustafic, the Minister of Police, has already dep-utized Celo's gang, naming it a Special Anti-Terrorist Unit of the Military Police.
You are a member of that outfit.
"Ours was a better unit than any other at the time," you say.
"Most of our soldiers were either distinguished sportsmen, all-in-all criminals, or a little bit of both.
"Every day our strength grew. At the beginning of May there were already more than 50 of us."

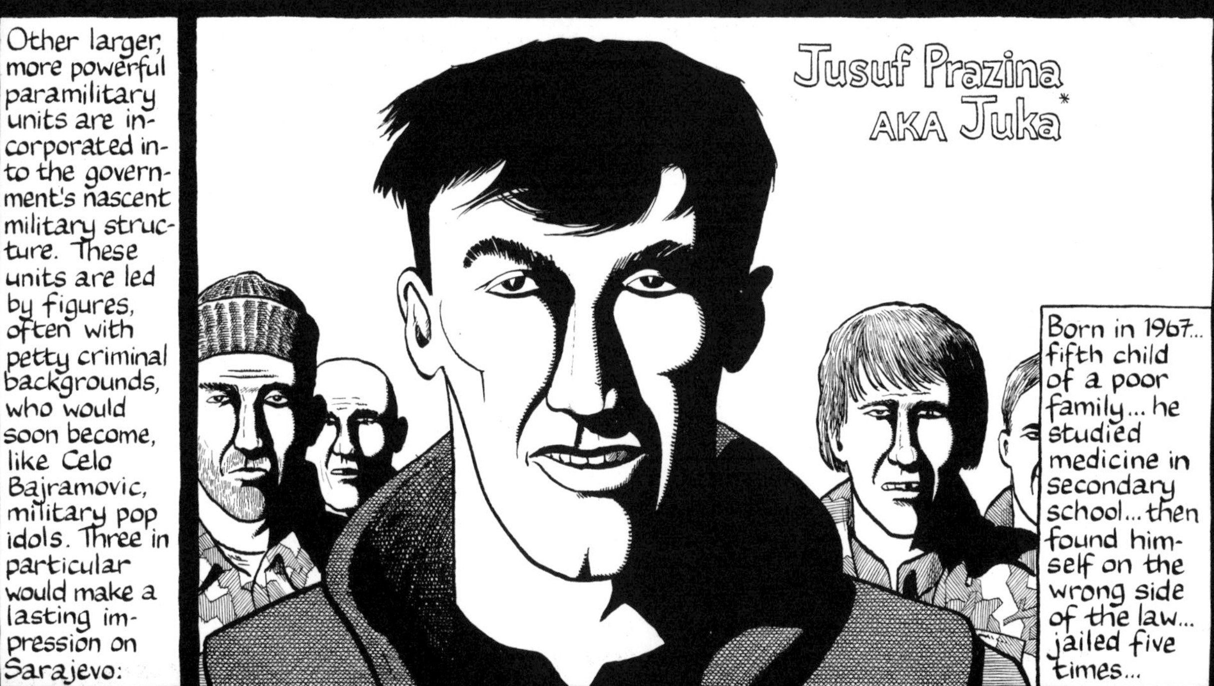
Other larger, more powerful paramilitary units are in-corporated in-to the govern-ment's nascent military struc-ture. These units are led by figures, often with petty criminal backgrounds, who would soon become, like Celo Bajramovic, military pop idols. Three in particular would make a lasting im-pression on Sarajevo:
Jusuf Prazina AKA Juka*
Born in 1967... fifth child of a poor family... he studied medicine in secondary school... then found him-self on the wrong side of the law... jailed five times...

*PRONOUNCED "YUKA"

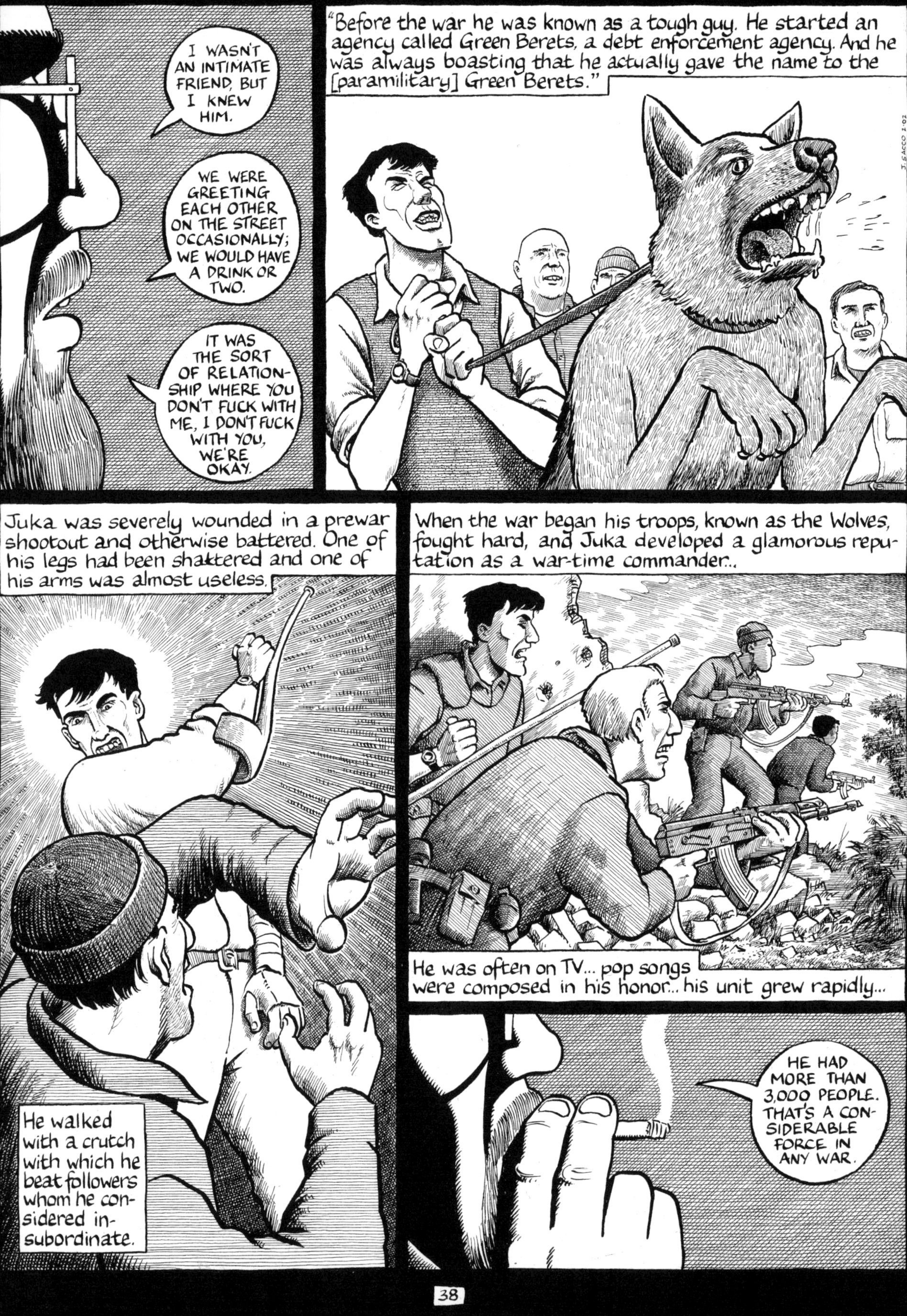
I WASN'T AN INTIMATE FRIEND, BUT I KNEW HIM.
WE WERE GREETING EACH OTHER ON THE STREET OCCASIONALLY; WE WOULD HAVE A DRINK OR TWO.
IT WAS THE SORT OF RELATIONSHIP WHERE YOU DON'T FUCK WITH ME, I DON'T FUCK WITH YOU, WE'RE OKAY.
"Before the war he was known as a tough guy. He started an agency called Green Berets, a debt enforcement agency. And he was always boasting that he actually gave the name to the [paramilitary] Green Berets."
Juka was severely wounded in a prewar shootout and otherwise battered. One of his legs had been shattered and one of his arms was almost useless.
He walked with a crutch with which he beat followers whom he considered insubordinate.
When the war began his troops, known as the Wolves, fought hard, and Juka developed a glamorous reputation as a war-time commander...
He was often on TV... pop songs were composed in his honor... his unit grew rapidly...
HE HAD MORE THAN 3,000 PEOPLE. THAT'S A CONSIDERABLE FORCE IN ANY WAR.

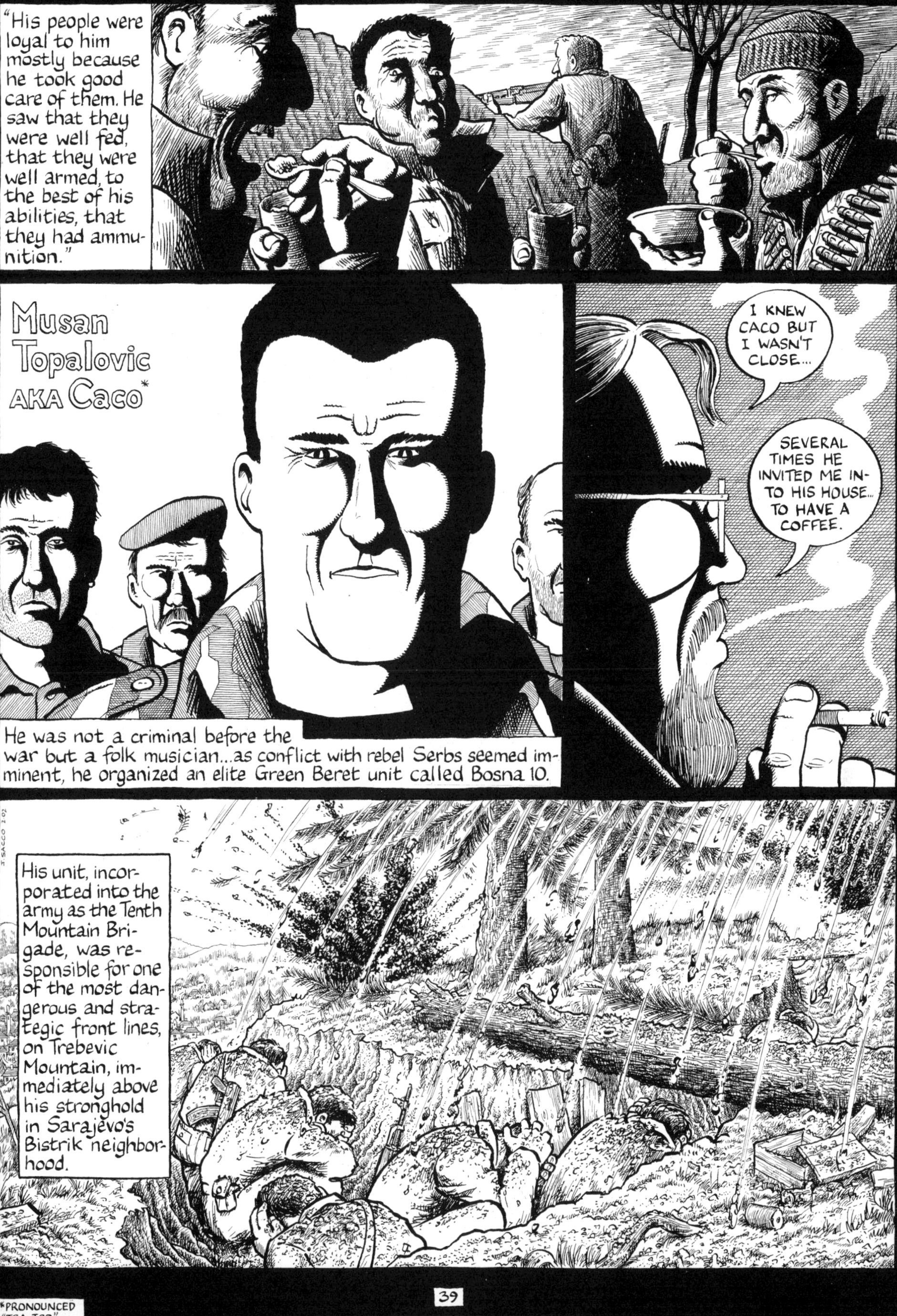
"His people were loyal to him mostly because he took good care of them. He saw that they were well fed, that they were well armed, to the best of his abilities, that they had ammunition."
Musan Topalovic AKA Caco*
I KNEW CACO BUT I WASN'T CLOSE...
SEVERAL TIMES HE INVITED ME INTO HIS HOUSE... TO HAVE A COFFEE.
He was not a criminal before the war but a folk musician...as conflict with rebel Serbs seemed imminent, he organized an elite Green Beret unit called Bosna 10.
His unit, incorporated into the army as the Tenth Mountain Brigade, was responsible for one of the most dangerous and strategic front lines, on Trebevic Mountain, immediately above his stronghold in Sarajevo's Bistrik neighborhood.

*PRONOUNCED "TSA-TSO"

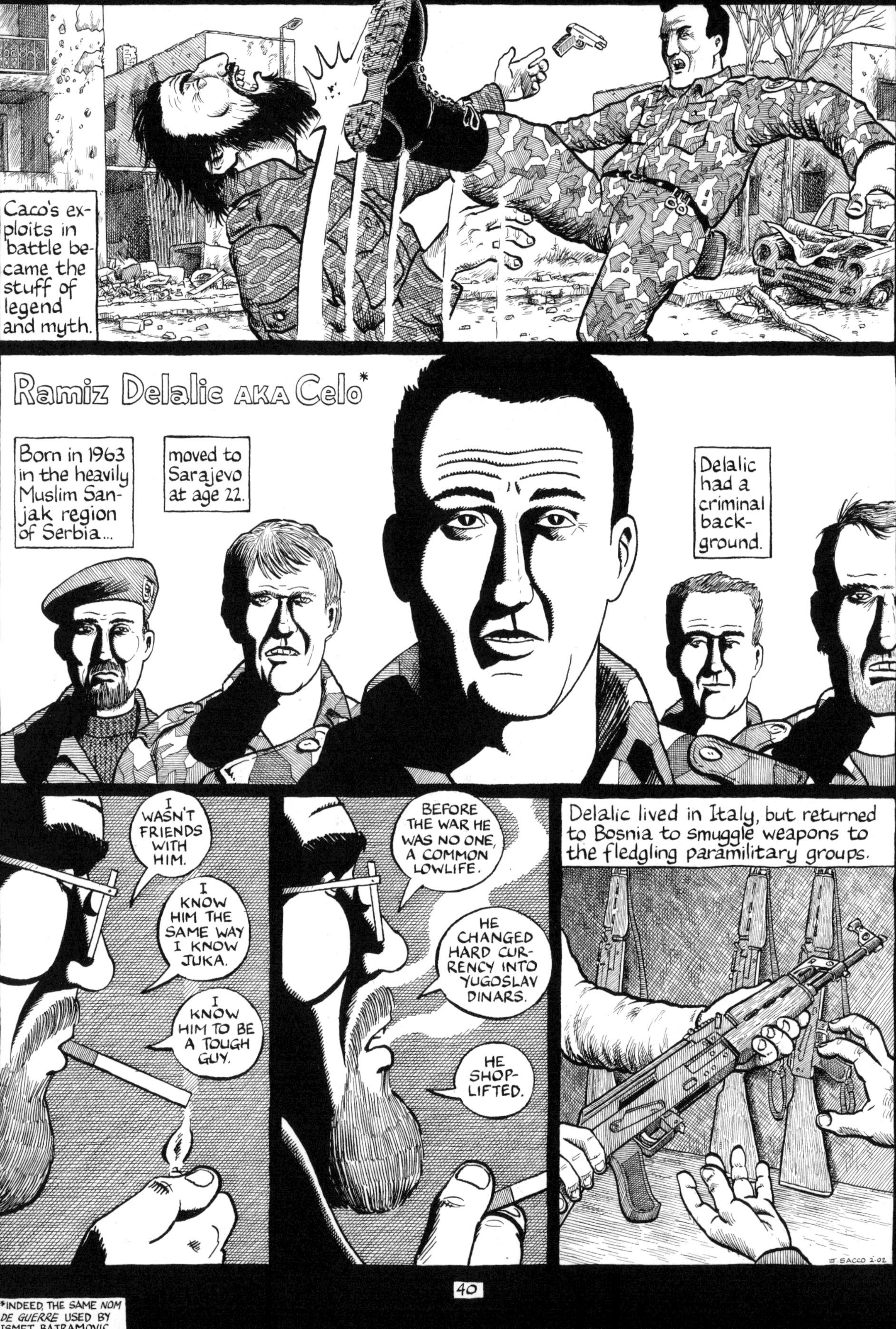
Caco's exploits in battle became the stuff of legend and myth.
Ramiz Delalic AKA Celo*
Born in 1963 in the heavily Muslim Sanjak region of Serbia...
moved to Sarajevo at age 22.
Delalic had a criminal background.
I WASN'T FRIENDS WITH HIM.
I KNOW HIM THE SAME WAY I KNOW JUKA.
I KNOW HIM TO BE A TOUGH GUY.
BEFORE THE WAR HE WAS NO ONE, A COMMON LOWLIFE.
HE CHANGED HARD CURRENCY INTO YUGOSLAV DINARS.
HE SHOPLIFTED.
Delalic lived in Italy, but returned to Bosnia to smuggle weapons to the fledgling paramilitary groups.
J. SACCO 2.02

*INDEED, THE SAME *NOM DE GUERRE* USED BY ISMET BAJRAMOVIC

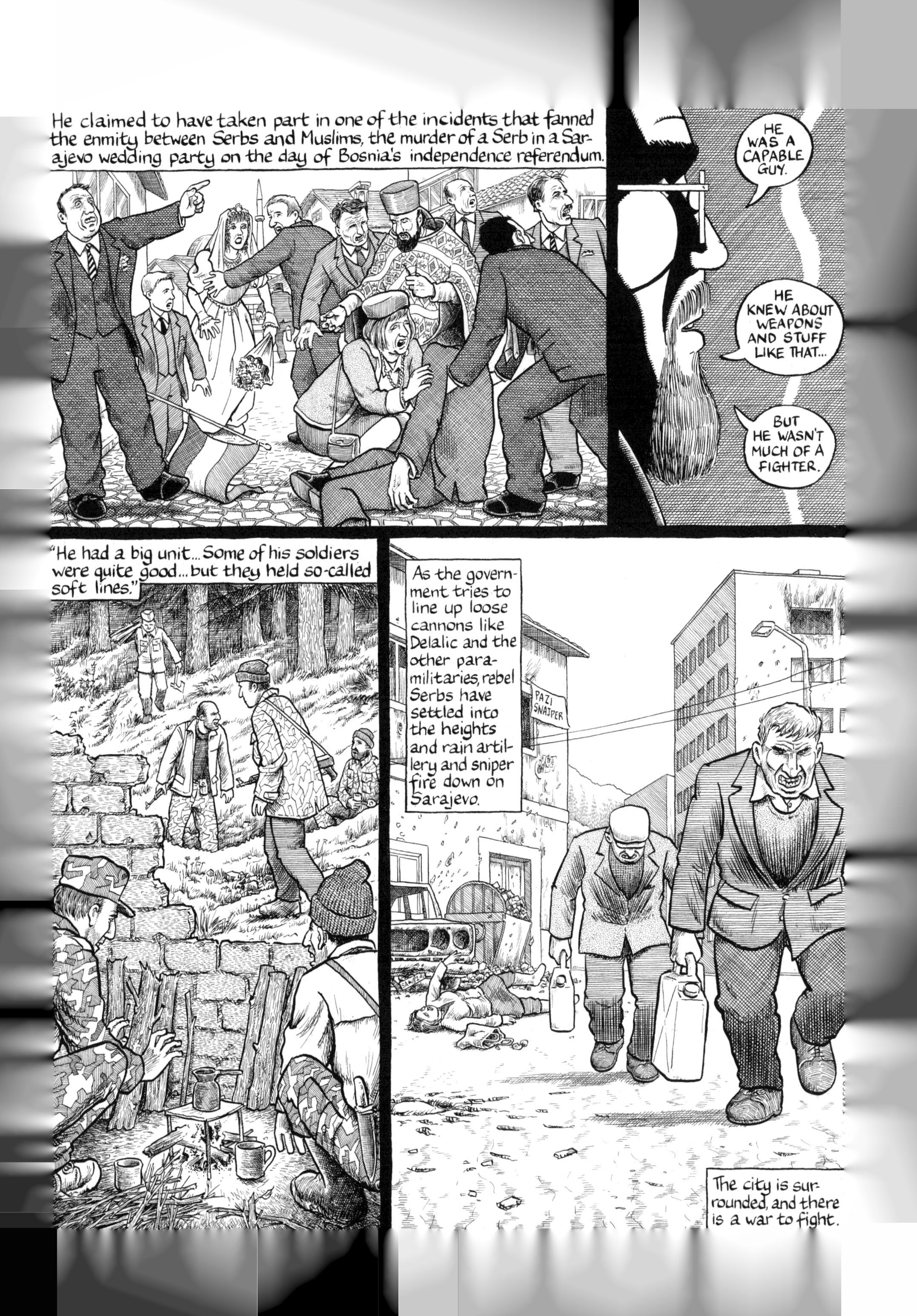
He claimed to have taken part in one of the incidents that fanned the enmity between Serbs and Muslims, the murder of a Serb in a Sarajevo wedding party on the day of Bosnia's independence referendum.
HE WAS A CAPABLE GUY.
HE KNEW ABOUT WEAPONS AND STUFF LIKE THAT...
BUT HE WASN'T MUCH OF A FIGHTER.
"He had a big unit... Some of his soldiers were quite good... but they held so-called soft lines."
As the government tries to line up loose cannons like Delalic and the other paramilitaries, rebel Serbs have settled into the heights and rain artillery and sniper fire down on Sarajevo.
PAZI SNAJPER
The city is surrounded, and there is a war to fight.

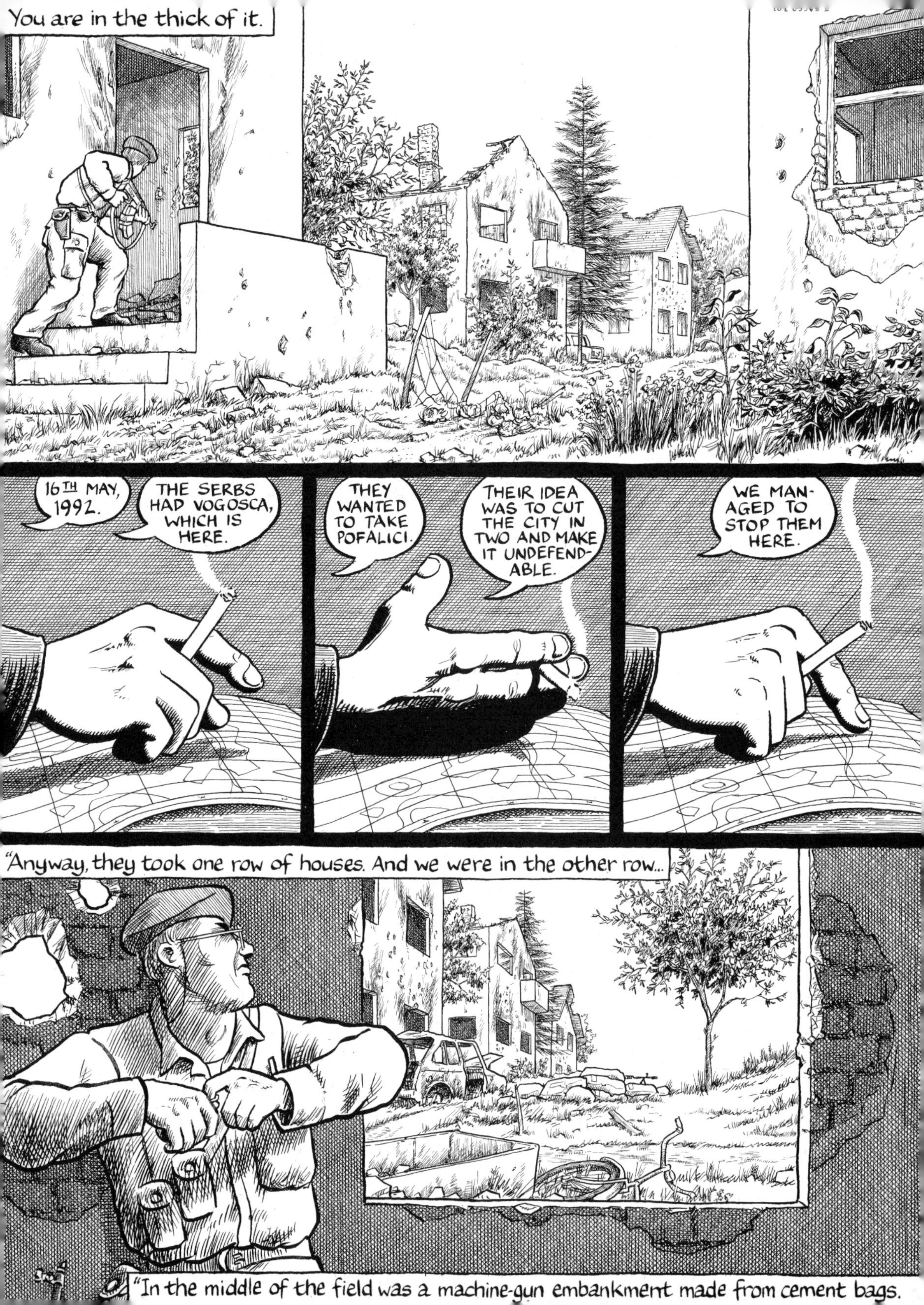
You are in the thick of it.
16TH MAY, 1992.
THE SERBS HAD VOGOSCA, WHICH IS HERE.
THEY WANTED TO TAKE POFALICI.
THEIR IDEA WAS TO CUT THE CITY IN TWO AND MAKE IT UNDEFEND-ABLE.
WE MAN-AGED TO STOP THEM HERE.
"Anyway, they took one row of houses. And we were in the other row...
"In the middle of the field was a machine-gun embankment made from cement bags.

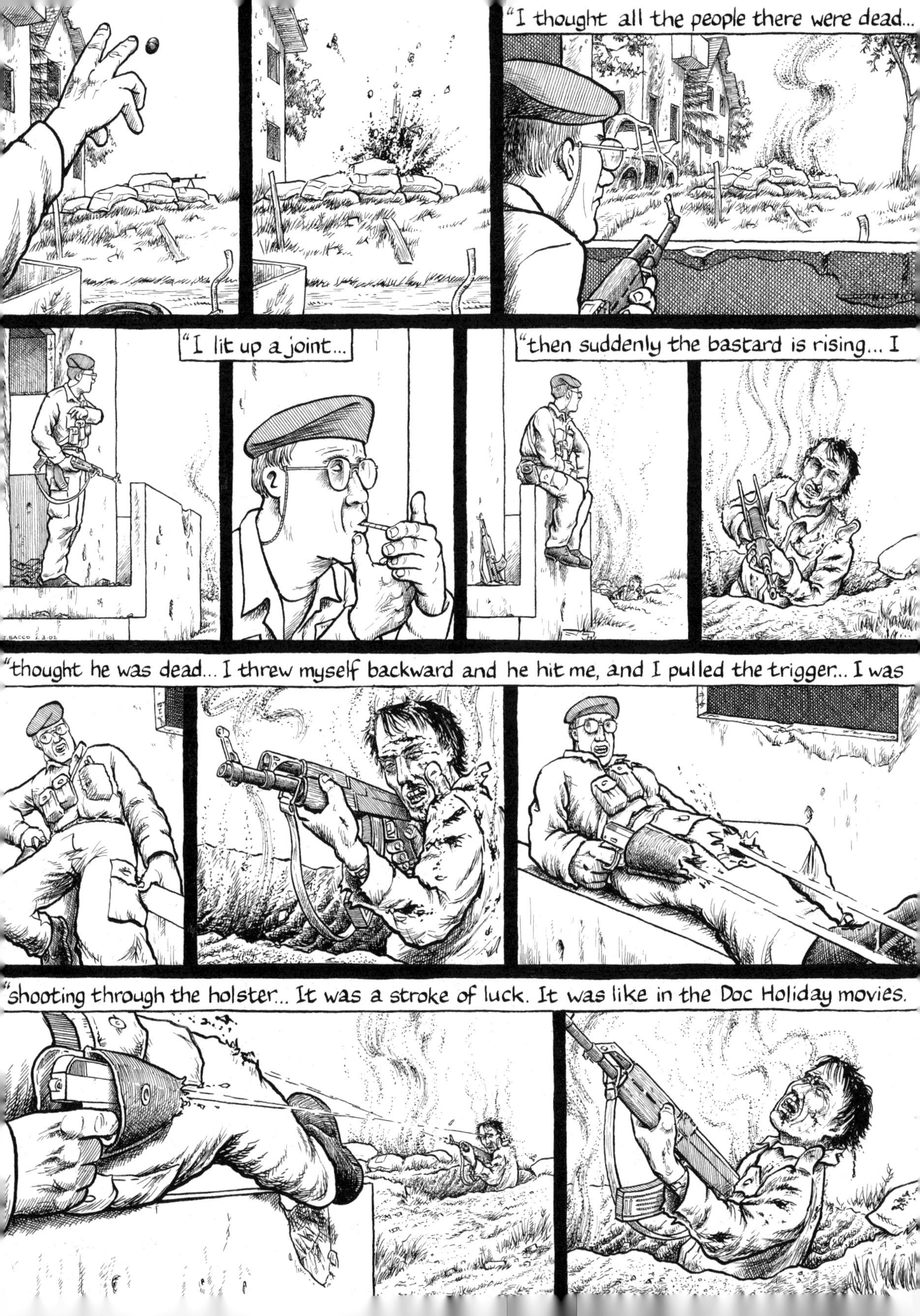
"I thought all the people there were dead...
"I lit up a joint...
"then suddenly the bastard is rising... I
"thought he was dead... I threw myself backward and he hit me, and I pulled the trigger... I was
"shooting through the holster... It was a stroke of luck. It was like in the Doc Holiday movies.

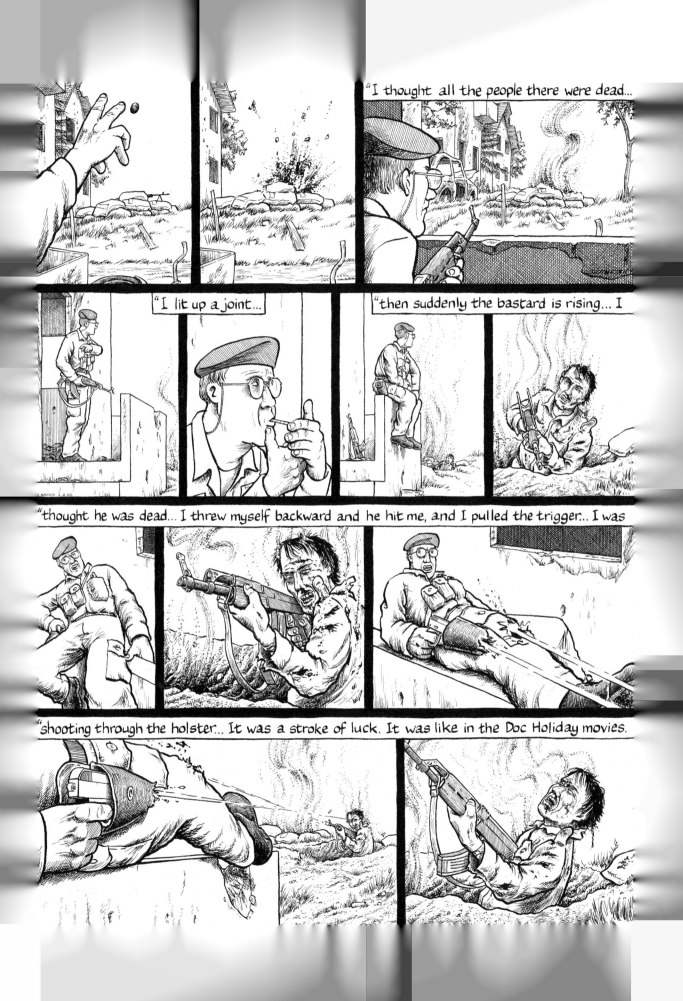

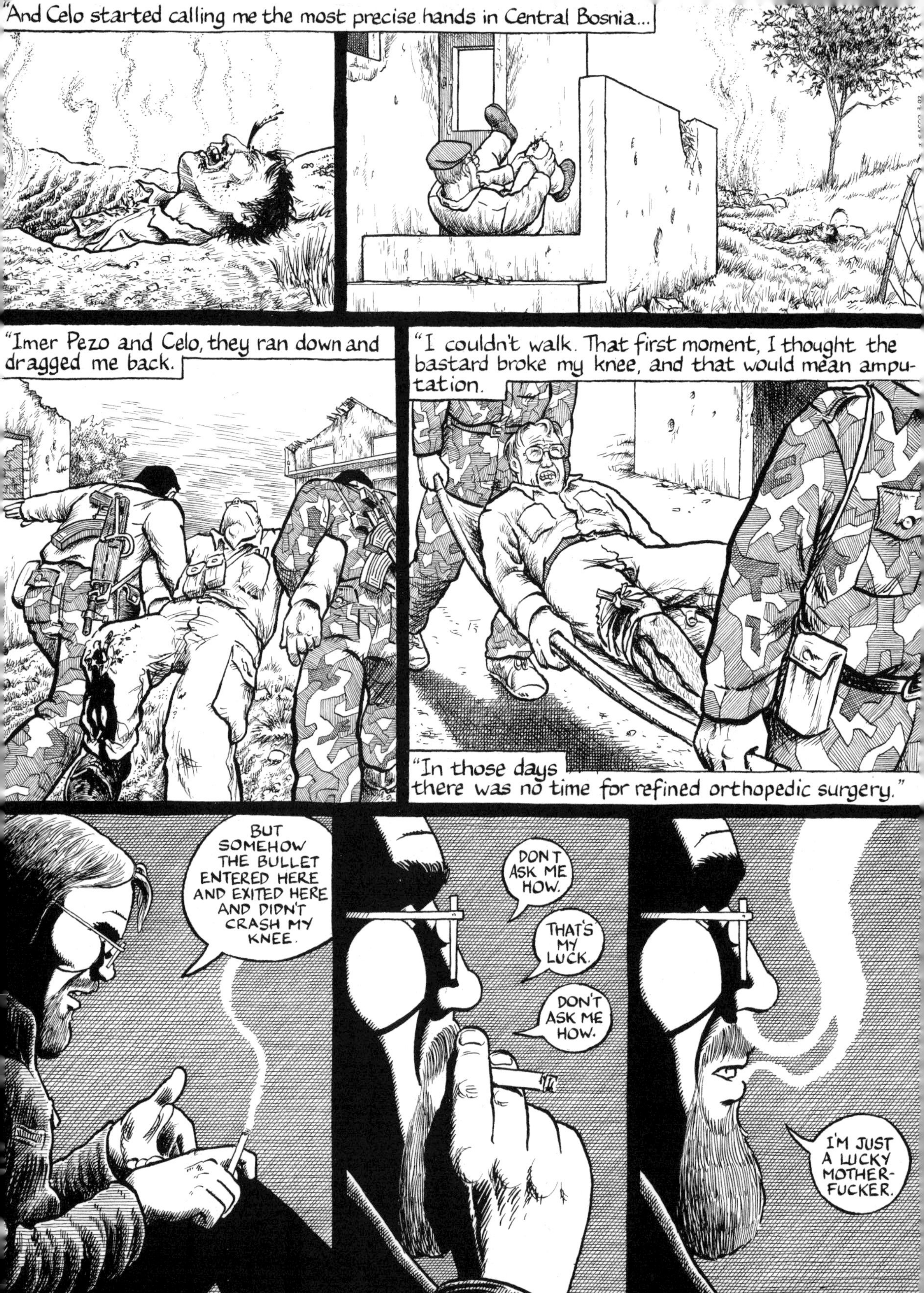
"And Celo started calling me the most precise hands in Central Bosnia...
"Imer Pezo and Celo, they ran down and dragged me back.
"I couldn't walk. That first moment, I thought the bastard broke my knee, and that would mean amputation.
"In those days there was no time for refined orthopedic surgery."
BUT SOMEHOW THE BULLET ENTERED HERE AND EXITED HERE AND DIDN'T CRASH MY KNEE.
DON'T ASK ME HOW.
THAT'S MY LUCK.
DON'T ASK ME HOW.
I'M JUST A LUCKY MOTHER-FUCKER.

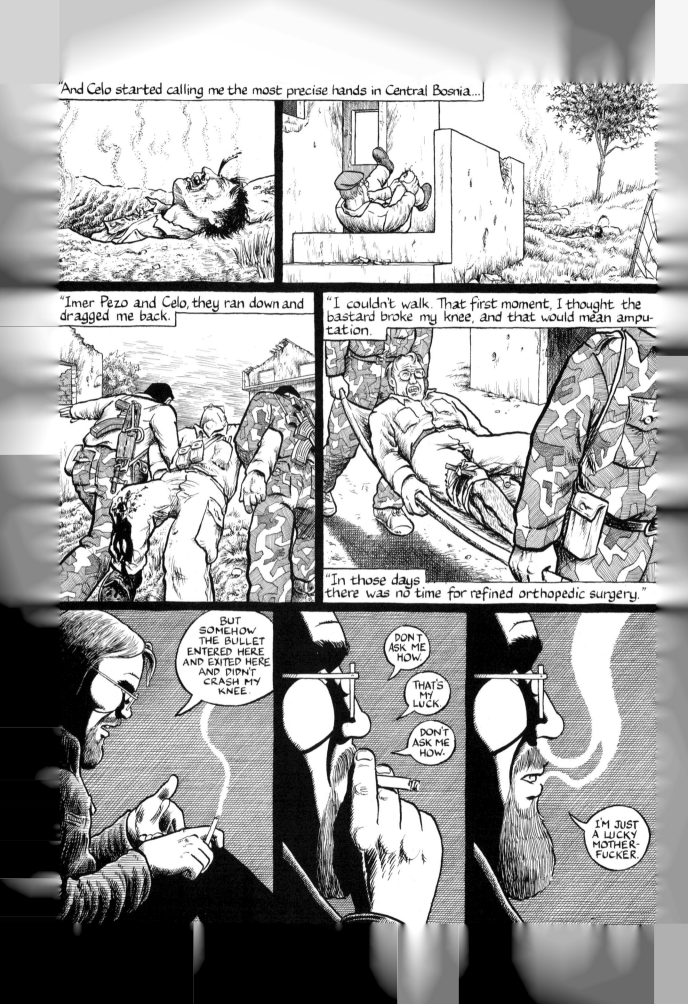

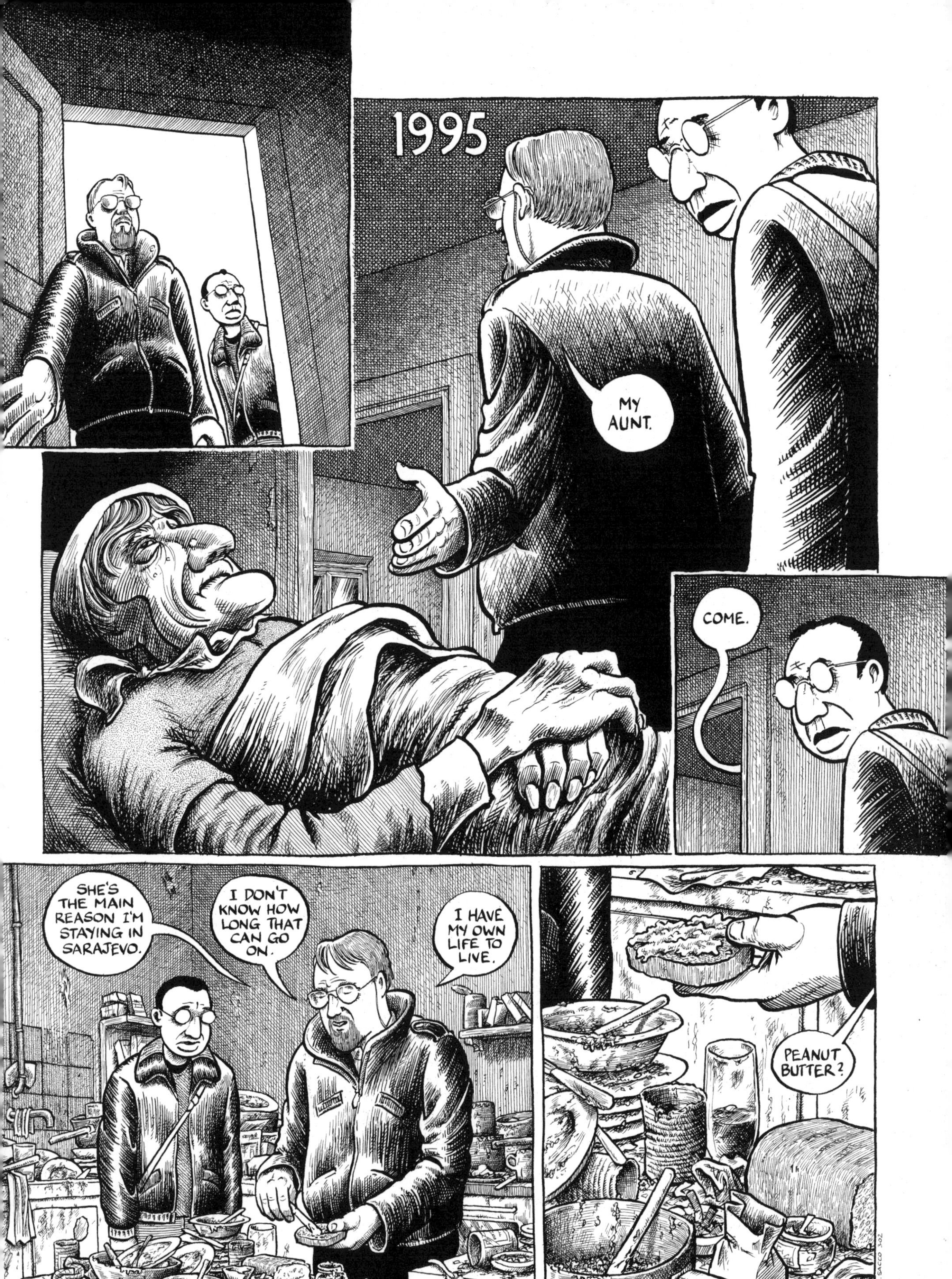
1995
MY AUNT.
COME.
SHE'S THE MAIN REASON I'M STAYING IN SARAJEVO.
I DON'T KNOW HOW LONG THAT CAN GO ON.
I HAVE MY OWN LIFE TO LIVE.
PEANUT BUTTER?

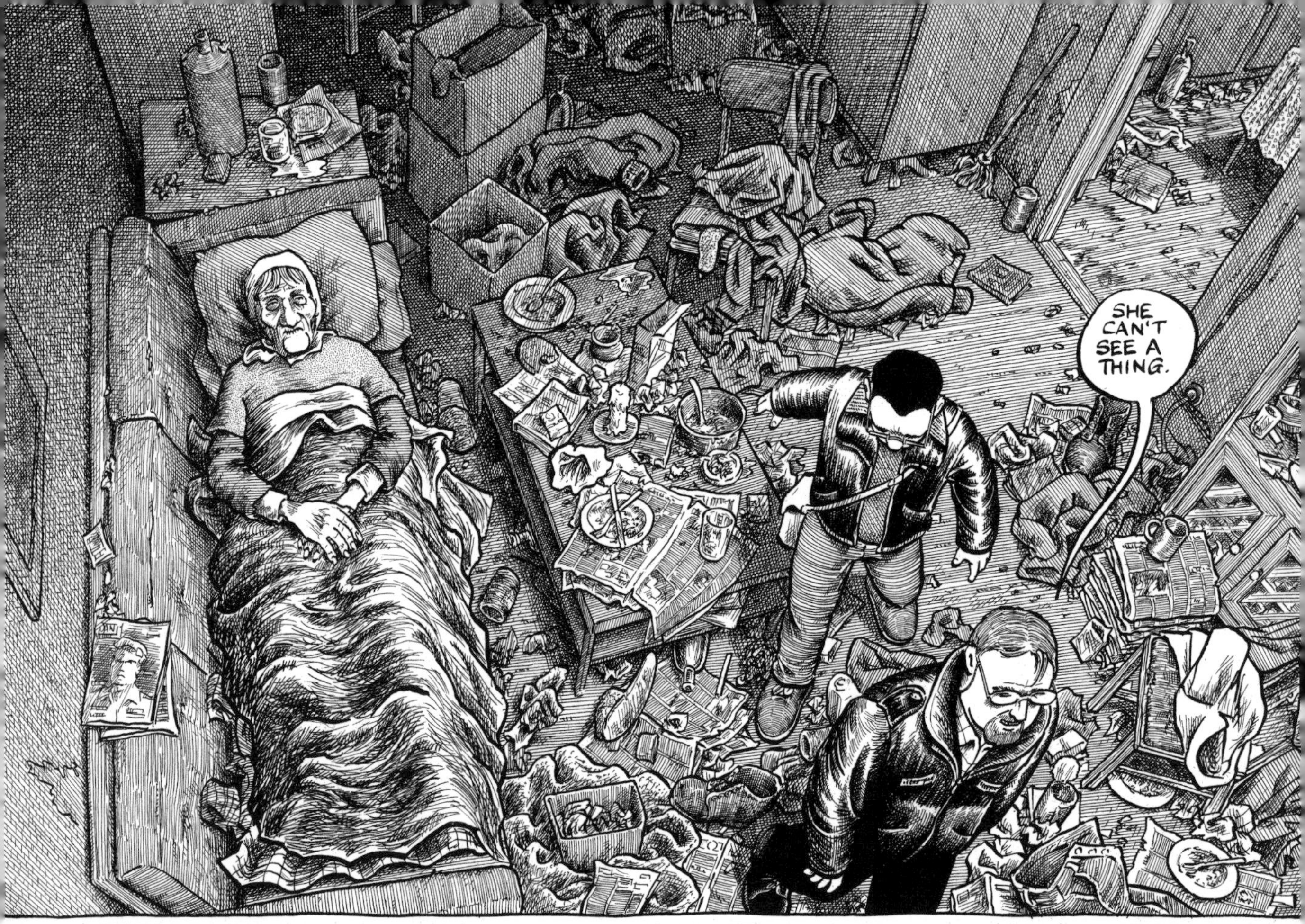
SHE CAN'T SEE A THING.

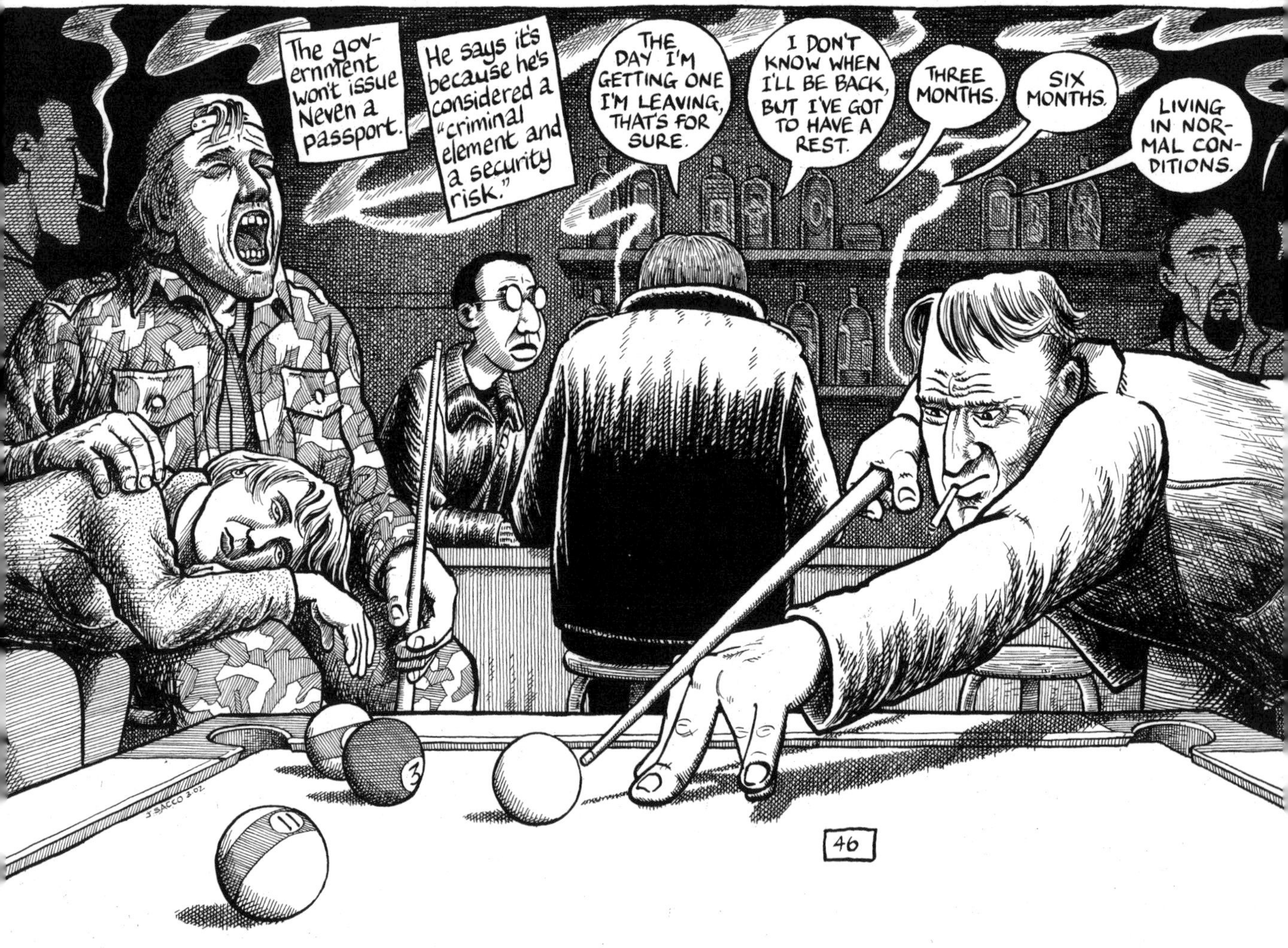
The government won't issue Neven a passport.
He says it's because he's considered a "criminal element and a security risk."
THE DAY I'M GETTING ONE I'M LEAVING, THAT'S FOR SURE.
I DON'T KNOW WHEN I'LL BE BACK, BUT I'VE GOT TO HAVE A REST.
THREE MONTHS.
SIX MONTHS.
LIVING IN NORMAL CONDITIONS.
J. SACCO 3.02

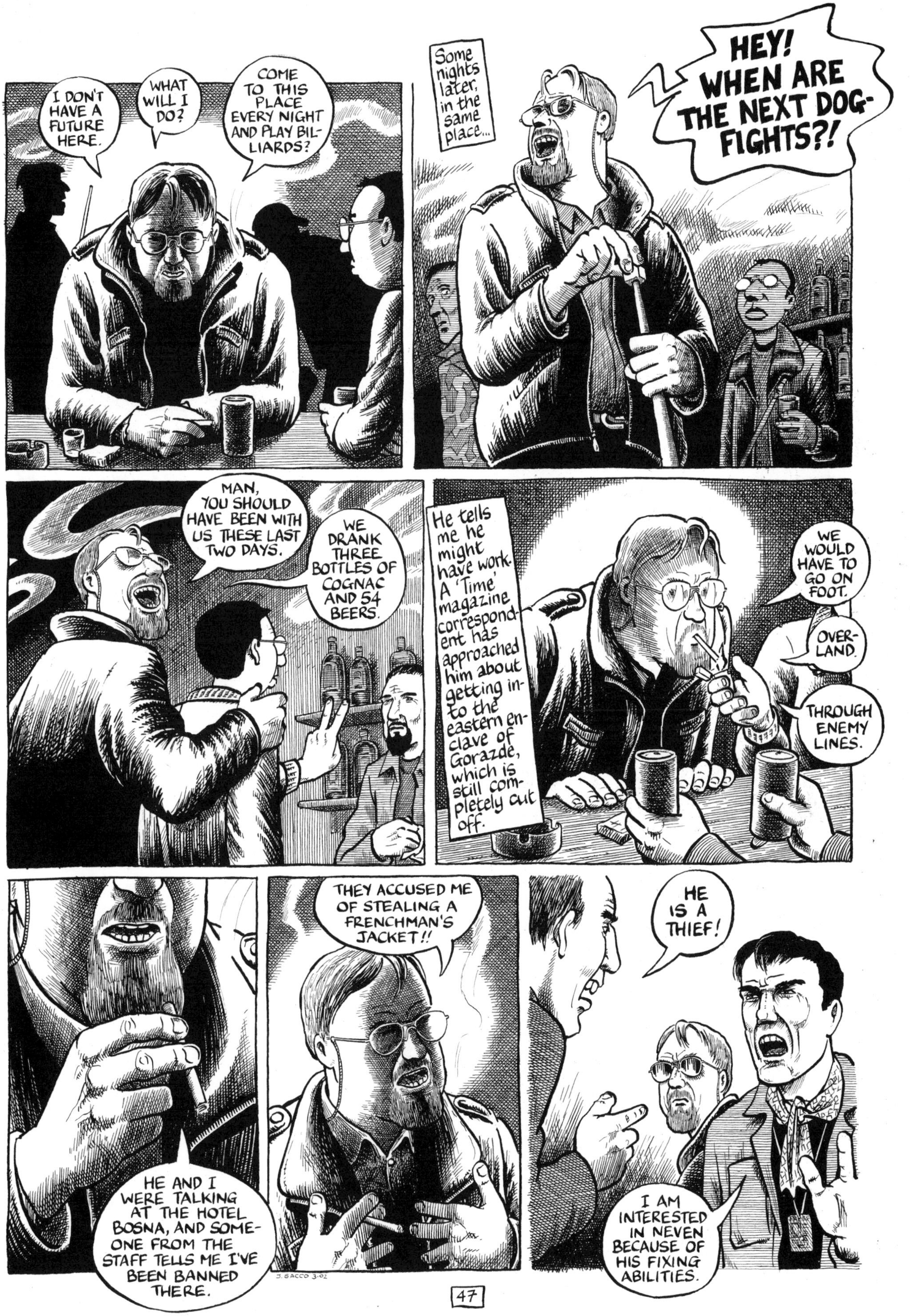

I DON'T HAVE A FUTURE HERE.
WHAT WILL I DO?
COME TO THIS PLACE EVERY NIGHT AND PLAY BILLIARDS?
Some nights later, in the same place...
HEY! WHEN ARE THE NEXT DOG-FIGHTS?!
MAN, YOU SHOULD HAVE BEEN WITH US THESE LAST TWO DAYS.
WE DRANK THREE BOTTLES OF COGNAC AND 54 BEERS.
He tells me he might have work. A 'Time' magazine correspondent has approached him about getting into the eastern enclave of Gorazde, which is still completely cut off.
WE WOULD HAVE TO GO ON FOOT.
OVER-LAND.
THROUGH ENEMY LINES.
HE AND I WERE TALKING AT THE HOTEL BOSNA, AND SOME-ONE FROM THE STAFF TELLS ME I'VE BEEN BANNED THERE.
THEY ACCUSED ME OF STEALING A FRENCHMAN'S JACKET!!
J. SACCO 3.02
HE IS A THIEF!
I AM INTERESTED IN NEVEN BECAUSE OF HIS FIXING ABILITIES.

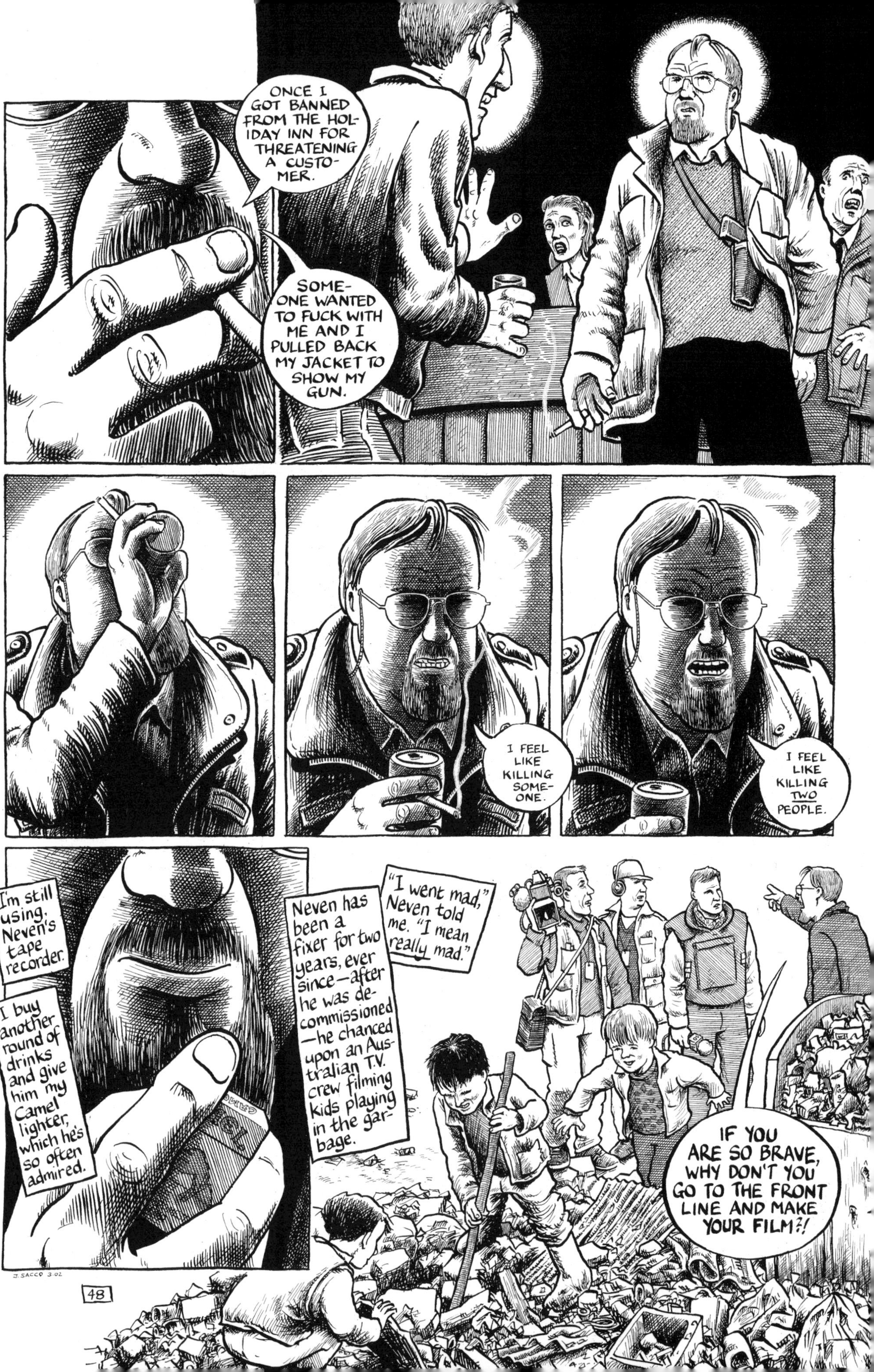

ONCE I GOT BANNED FROM THE HOLIDAY INN FOR THREATENING A CUSTOMER.
SOMEONE WANTED TO FUCK WITH ME AND I PULLED BACK MY JACKET TO SHOW MY GUN.
I FEEL LIKE KILLING SOMEONE.
I FEEL LIKE KILLING TWO PEOPLE.
I'm still using Neven's tape recorder.
I buy another round of drinks and give him my Camel lighter, which he's so often admired.
Neven has been a fixer for two years, ever since—after he was decommissioned—he chanced upon an Australian T.V. crew filming kids playing in the garbage.
"I went mad," Neven told me. "I mean really mad."
IF YOU ARE SO BRAVE, WHY DON'T YOU GO TO THE FRONT LINE AND MAKE YOUR FILM?!
J. SACCO 3.02

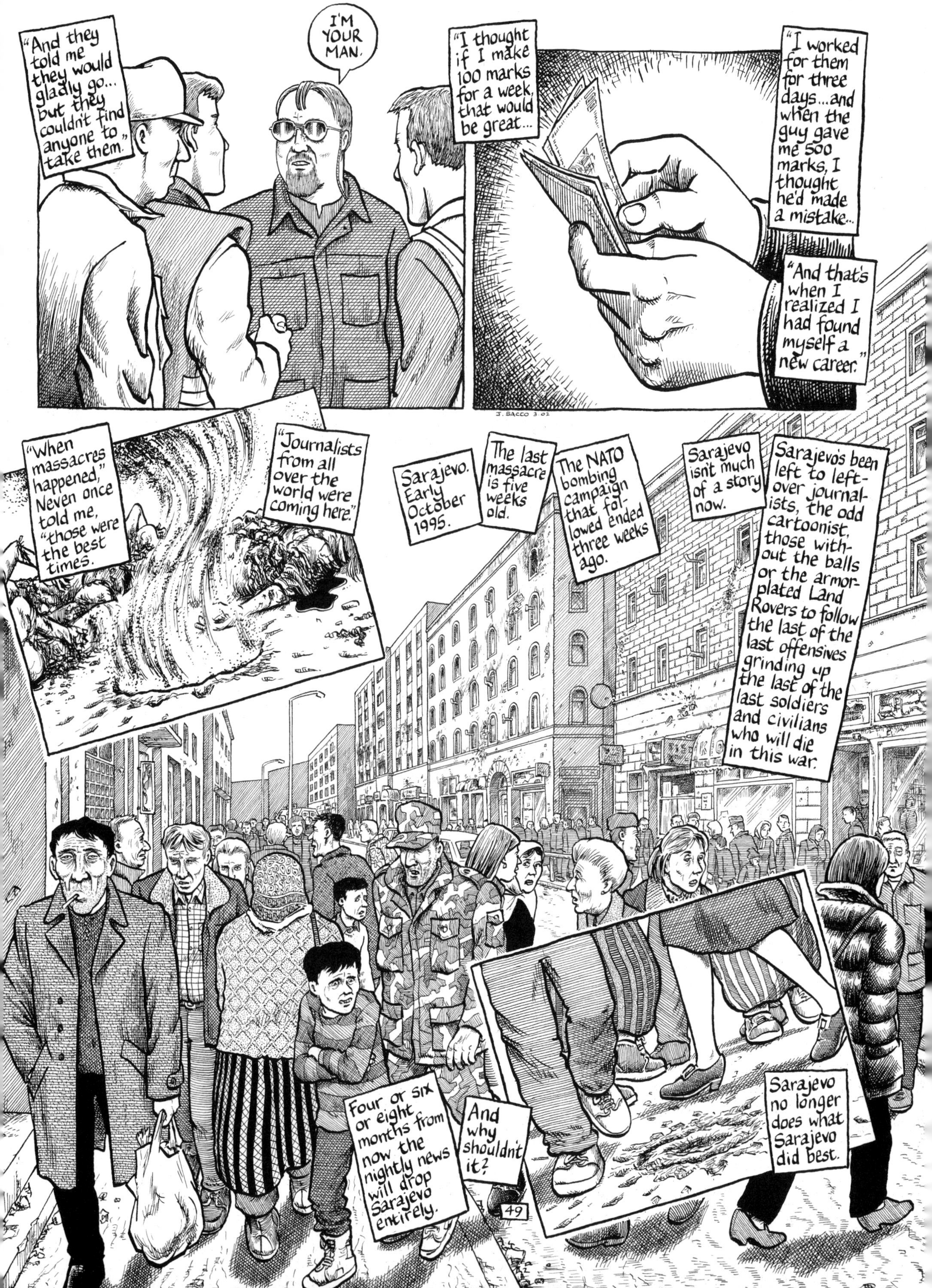
"And they told me they would gladly go... but they couldn't find anyone to take them."
I'M YOUR MAN.
"I thought if I make 100 marks for a week, that would be great...
"I worked for them for three days...and when the guy gave me 500 marks, I thought he'd made a mistake...
"And that's when I realized I had found myself a new career."
J. SACCO 3.02
"When massacres happened," Neven once told me, "those were the best times.
"Journalists from all over the world were coming here."
Sarajevo. Early October 1995.
The last massacre is five weeks old.
The NATO bombing campaign that followed ended three weeks ago.
Sarajevo isn't much of a story now.
Sarajevo's been left to left-over journalists, the odd cartoonist, those without the balls or the armor-plated Land Rovers to follow the last of the last offensives grinding up the last of the last soldiers and civilians who will die in this war.
Four or six or eight months from now the nightly news will drop Sarajevo entirely.
And why shouldn't it?
Sarajevo no longer does what Sarajevo did best.

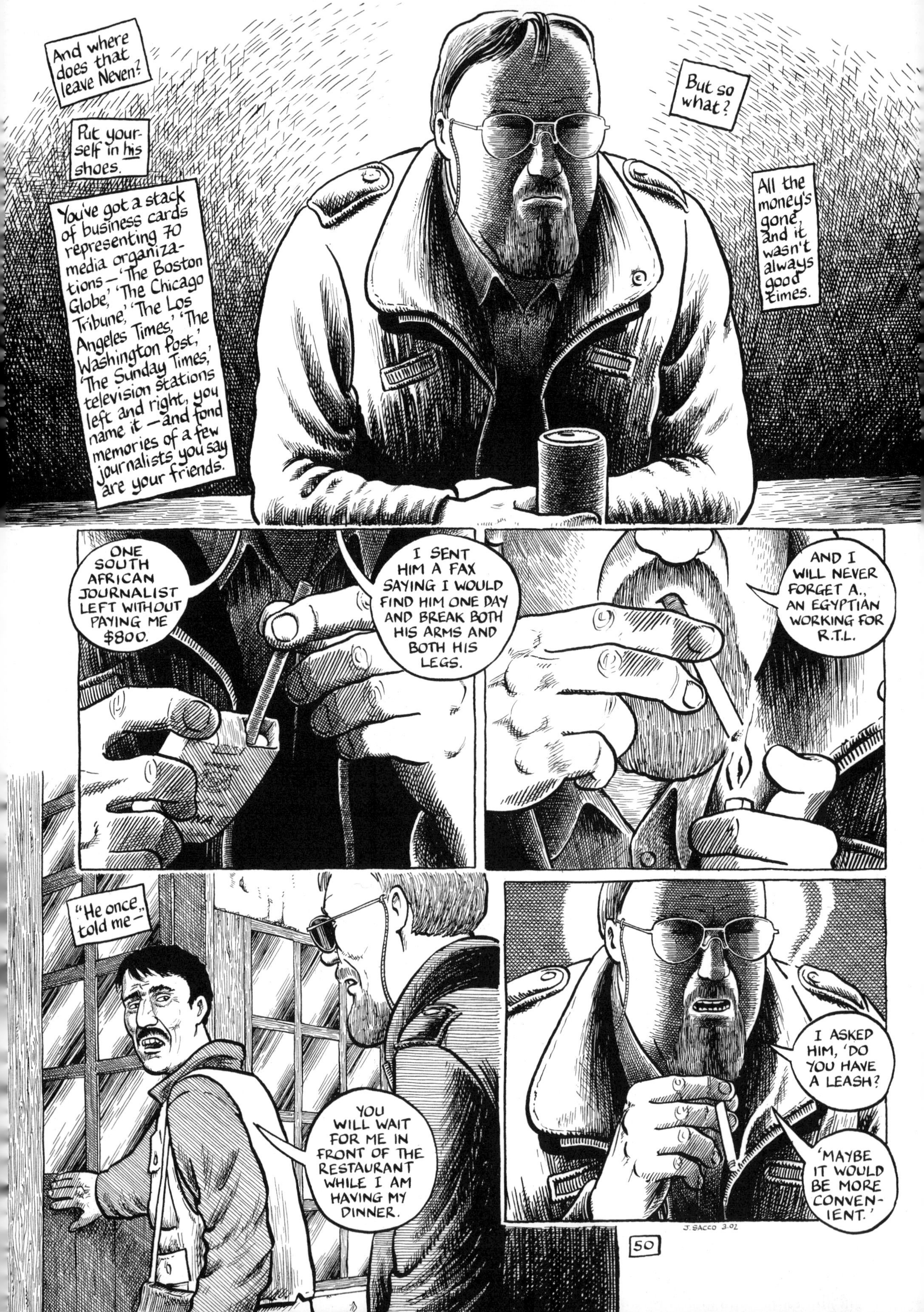

And where does that leave Neven?
Put yourself in his shoes.
You've got a stack of business cards representing 70 media organizations—'The Boston Globe,' 'The Chicago Tribune,' 'The Los Angeles Times,' 'The Washington Post,' 'The Sunday Times,' television stations left and right, you name it—and fond memories of a few journalists you say are your friends.
But so what?
All the money's gone, and it wasn't always good times.
ONE SOUTH AFRICAN JOURNALIST LEFT WITHOUT PAYING ME $800.
I SENT HIM A FAX SAYING I WOULD FIND HIM ONE DAY AND BREAK BOTH HIS ARMS AND BOTH HIS LEGS.
AND I WILL NEVER FORGET A., AN EGYPTIAN WORKING FOR R.T.L.
"He once told me—
YOU WILL WAIT FOR ME IN FRONT OF THE RESTAURANT WHILE I AM HAVING MY DINNER.
I ASKED HIM, 'DO YOU HAVE A LEASH?
'MAYBE IT WOULD BE MORE CONVENIENT.'
J. SACCO 3.02

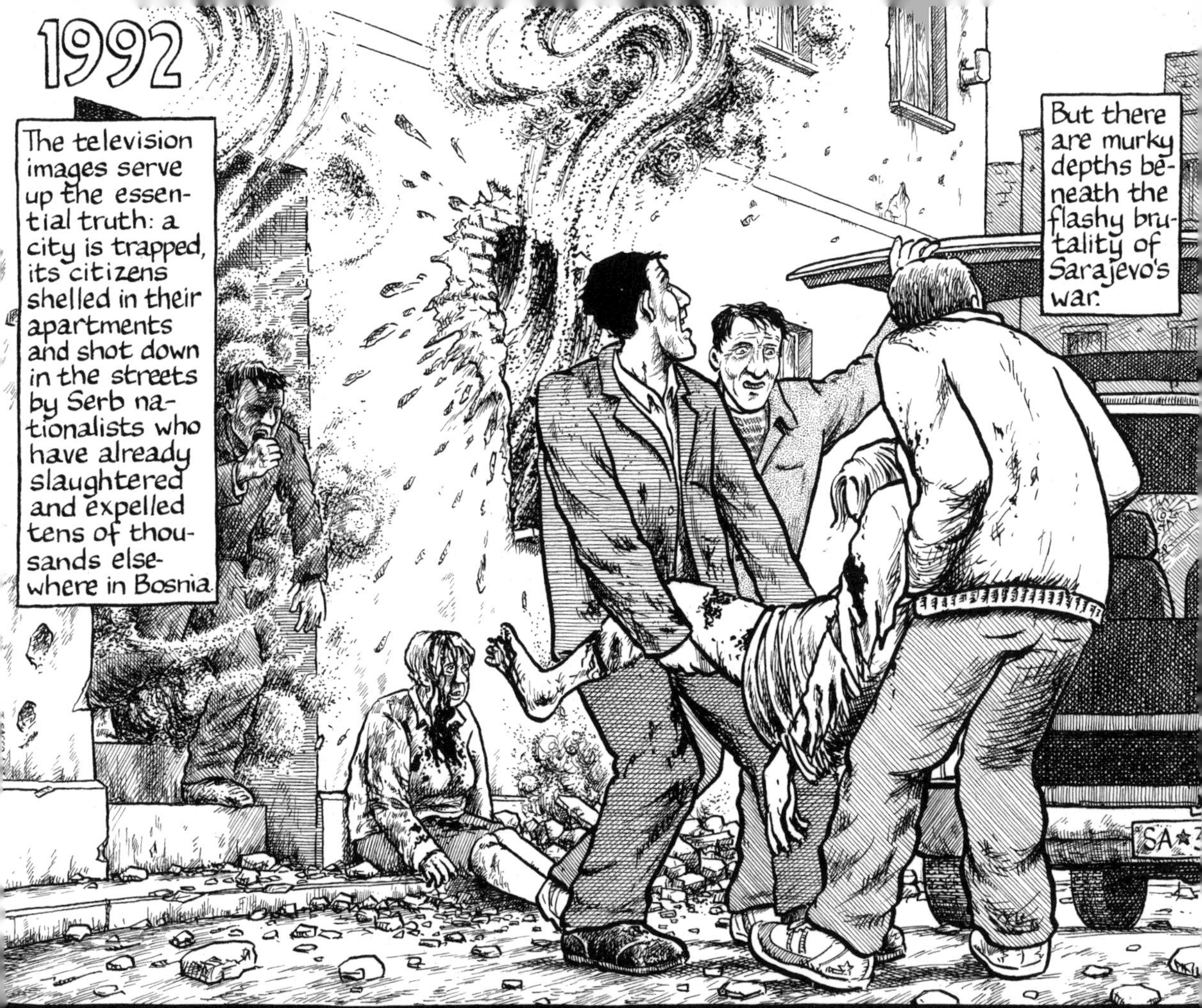
1992
The television images serve up the essential truth: a city is trapped, its citizens shelled in their apartments and shot down in the streets by Serb nationalists who have already slaughtered and expelled tens of thousands elsewhere in Bosnia.
But there are murky depths beneath the flashy brutality of Sarajevo's war.
SA

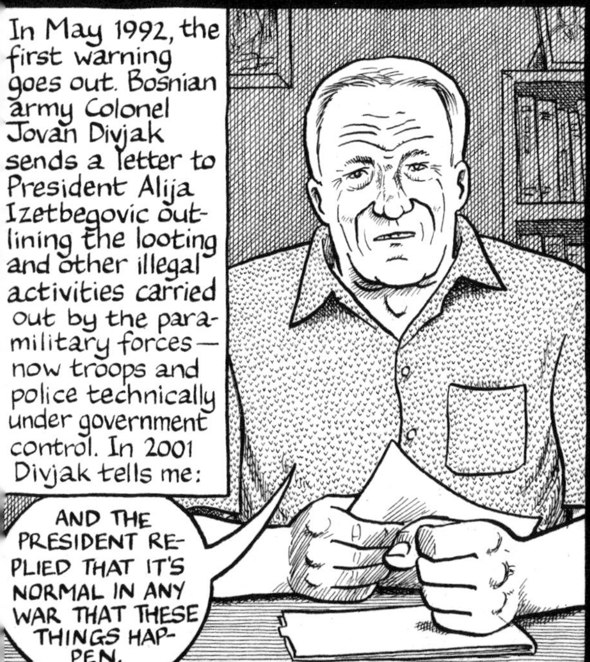
In May 1992, the first warning goes out. Bosnian army Colonel Jovan Divjak sends a letter to President Alija Izetbegovic outlining the looting and other illegal activities carried out by the paramilitary forces—now troops and police technically under government control. In 2001 Divjak tells me:
AND THE PRESIDENT REPLIED THAT IT'S NORMAL IN ANY WAR THAT THESE THINGS HAPPEN.

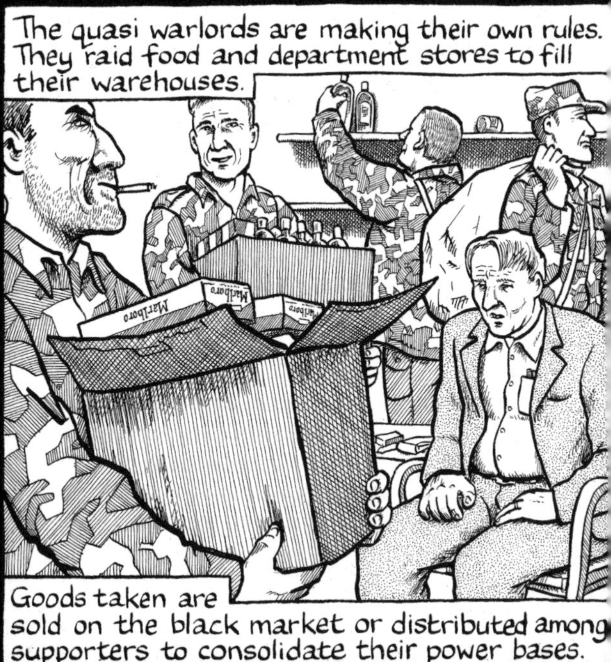
The quasi warlords are making their own rules. They raid food and department stores to fill their warehouses.
Marlboro
Marlboro
Marlboro
Goods taken are sold on the black market or distributed among supporters to consolidate their power bases.

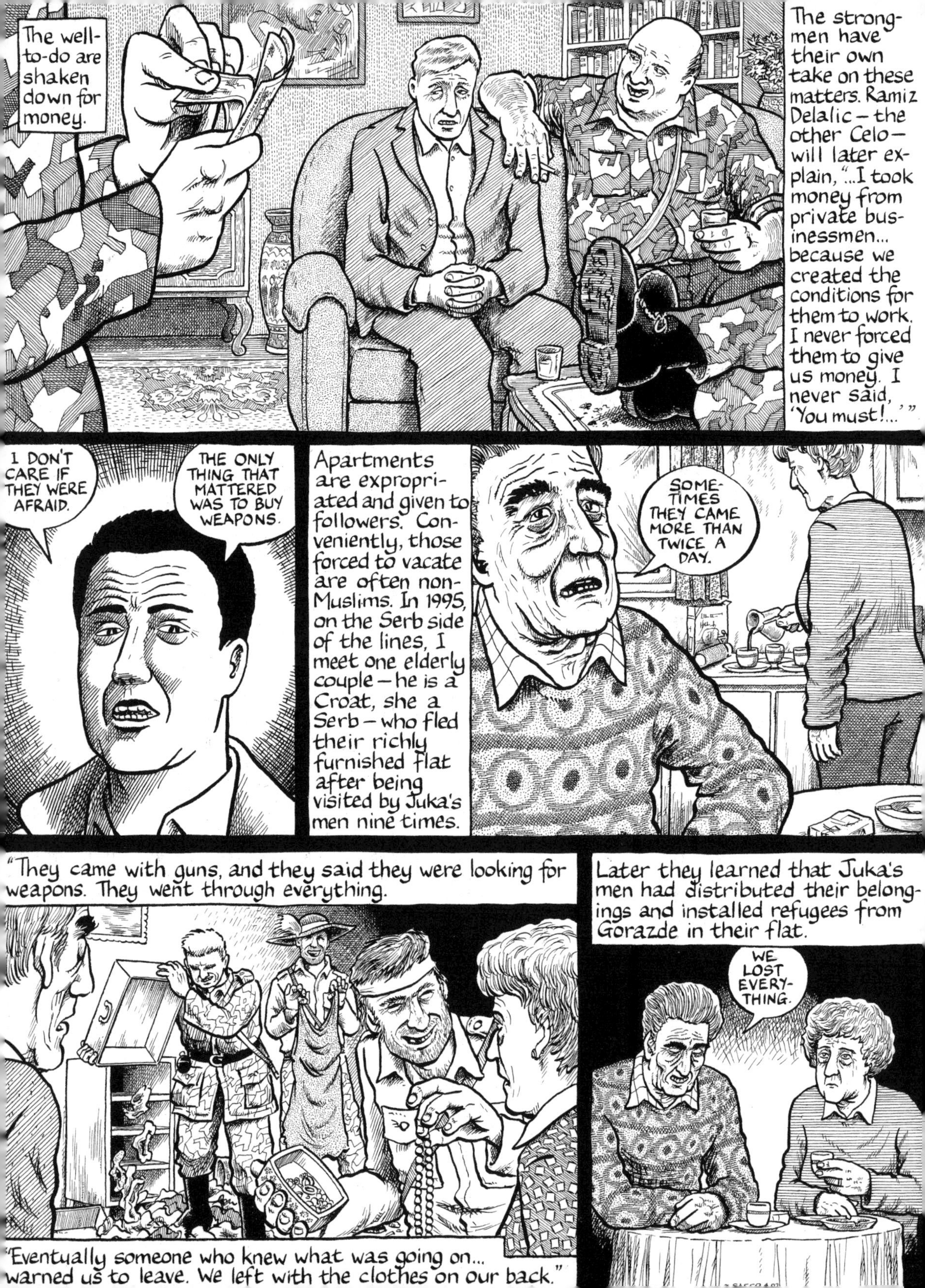
The well-to-do are shaken down for money.
The strongmen have their own take on these matters. Ramiz Delalic – the other Celo – will later explain, "...I took money from private businessmen... because we created the conditions for them to work. I never forced them to give us money. I never said, 'You must!...'"
I DON'T CARE IF THEY WERE AFRAID.
THE ONLY THING THAT MATTERED WAS TO BUY WEAPONS.
Apartments are expropriated and given to followers. Conveniently, those forced to vacate are often non-Muslims. In 1995, on the Serb side of the lines, I meet one elderly couple – he is a Croat, she a Serb – who fled their richly furnished flat after being visited by Juka's men nine times.
SOMETIMES THEY CAME MORE THAN TWICE A DAY.
"They came with guns, and they said they were looking for weapons. They went through everything.
"Eventually someone who knew what was going on... warned us to leave. We left with the clothes on our back."
Later they learned that Juka's men had distributed their belongings and installed refugees from Gorazde in their flat.
WE LOST EVERYTHING.

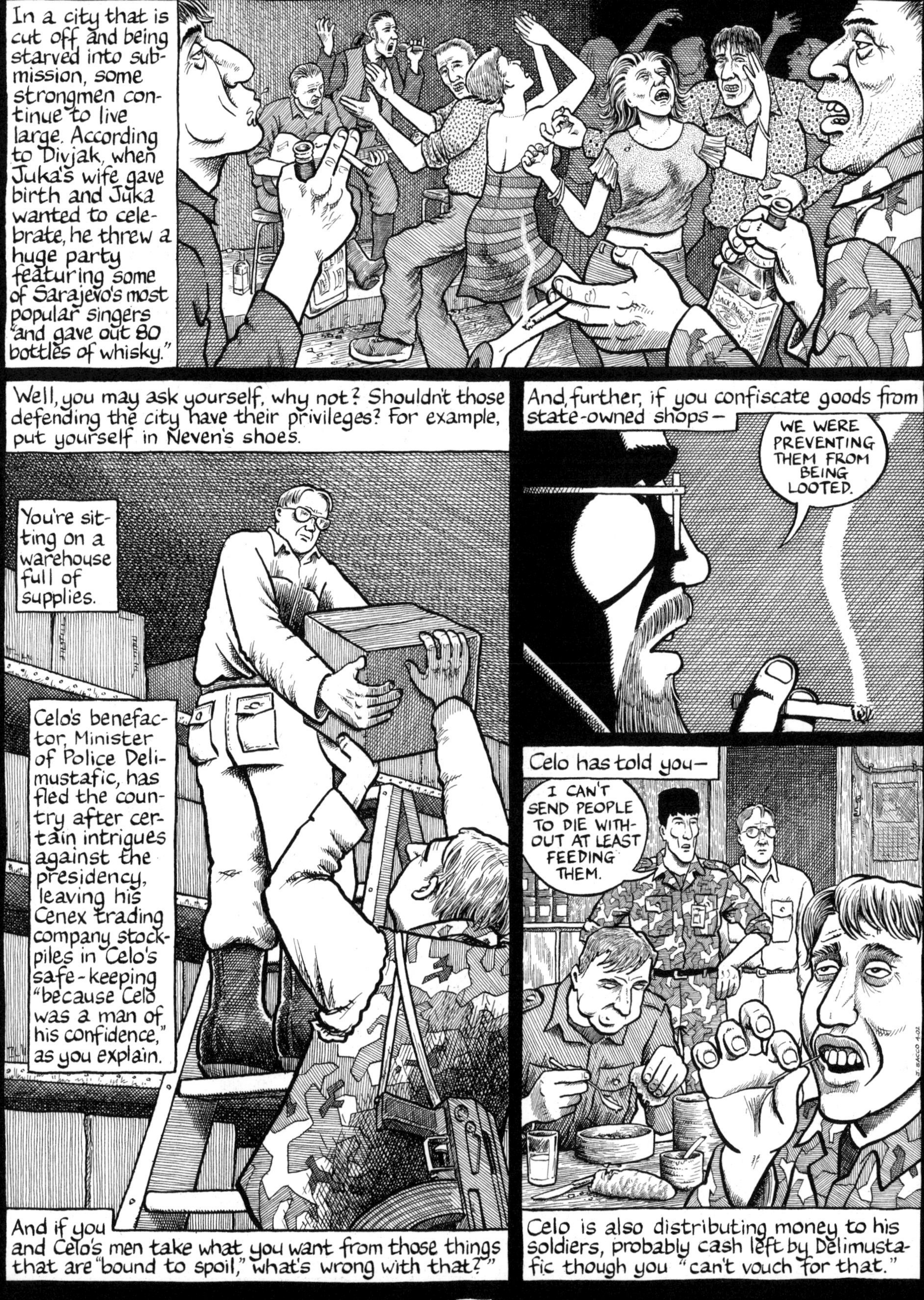
In a city that is cut off and being starved into submission, some strongmen continue to live large. According to Divjak, when Juka's wife gave birth and Juka wanted to celebrate, he threw a huge party featuring some of Sarajevo's most popular singers "and gave out 80 bottles of whisky."
Well, you may ask yourself, why not? Shouldn't those defending the city have their privileges? For example, put yourself in Neven's shoes.
You're sitting on a warehouse full of supplies.
Celo's benefactor, Minister of Police Delimustafic, has fled the country after certain intrigues against the presidency, leaving his Cenex trading company stockpiles in Celo's safe-keeping "because Celo was a man of his confidence," as you explain.
And if you and Celo's men take what you want from those things that are "bound to spoil," what's wrong with that?"
And, further, if you confiscate goods from state-owned shops—
WE WERE PREVENTING THEM FROM BEING LOOTED.
Celo has told you—
I CAN'T SEND PEOPLE TO DIE WITHOUT AT LEAST FEEDING THEM.
Celo is also distributing money to his soldiers, probably cash left by Delimustafic though you "can't vouch for that."

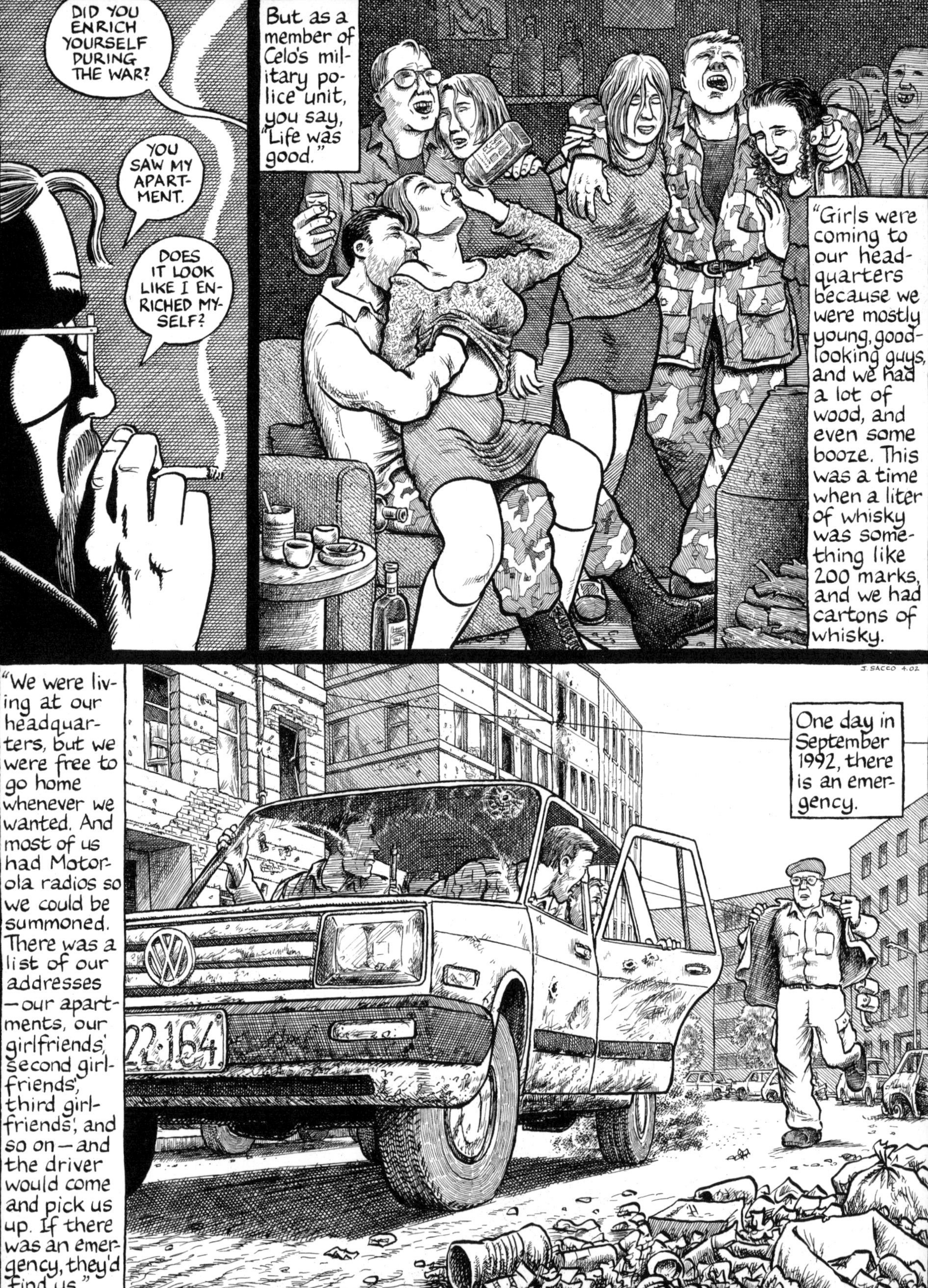
DID YOU ENRICH YOURSELF DURING THE WAR?
YOU SAW MY APARTMENT.
DOES IT LOOK LIKE I ENRICHED MYSELF?
But as a member of Celo's military police unit, you say, "Life was good."
"Girls were coming to our headquarters because we were mostly young, good-looking guys, and we had a lot of wood, and even some booze. This was a time when a liter of whisky was something like 200 marks, and we had cartons of whisky.
J. SACCO 4.02
"We were living at our headquarters, but we were free to go home whenever we wanted. And most of us had Motorola radios so we could be summoned. There was a list of our addresses—our apartments, our girlfriends', second girlfriends', third girlfriends', and so on—and the driver would come and pick us up. If there was an emergency, they'd find us."
One day in September 1992, there is an emergency.
22-164

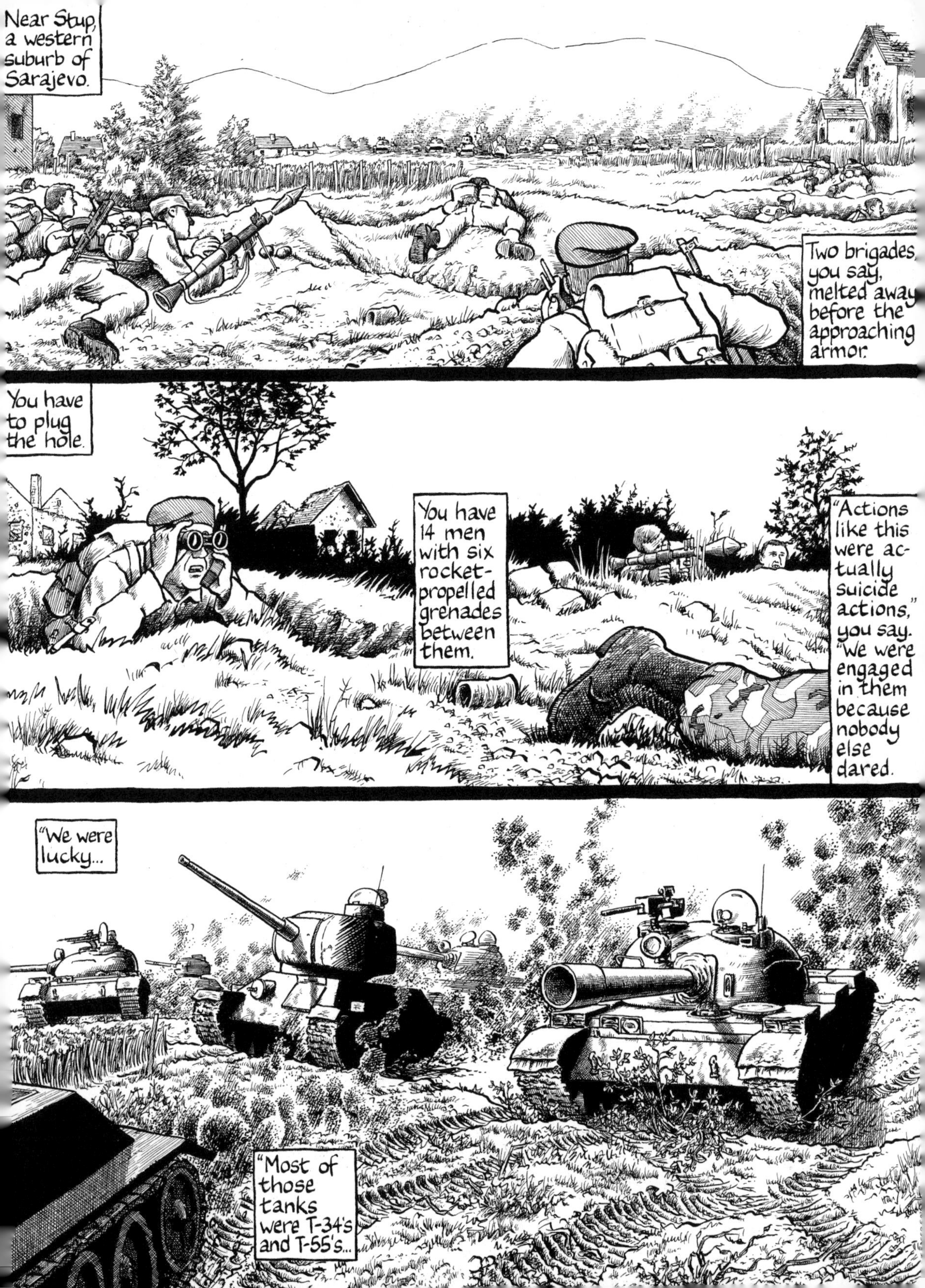

Near Stup, a western suburb of Sarajevo.
Two brigades, you say, melted away before the approaching armor.
You have to plug the hole.
You have 14 men with six rocket-propelled grenades between them.
"Actions like this were actually suicide actions," you say. "We were engaged in them because nobody else dared.
"We were lucky...
"Most of those tanks were T-34's and T-55's...

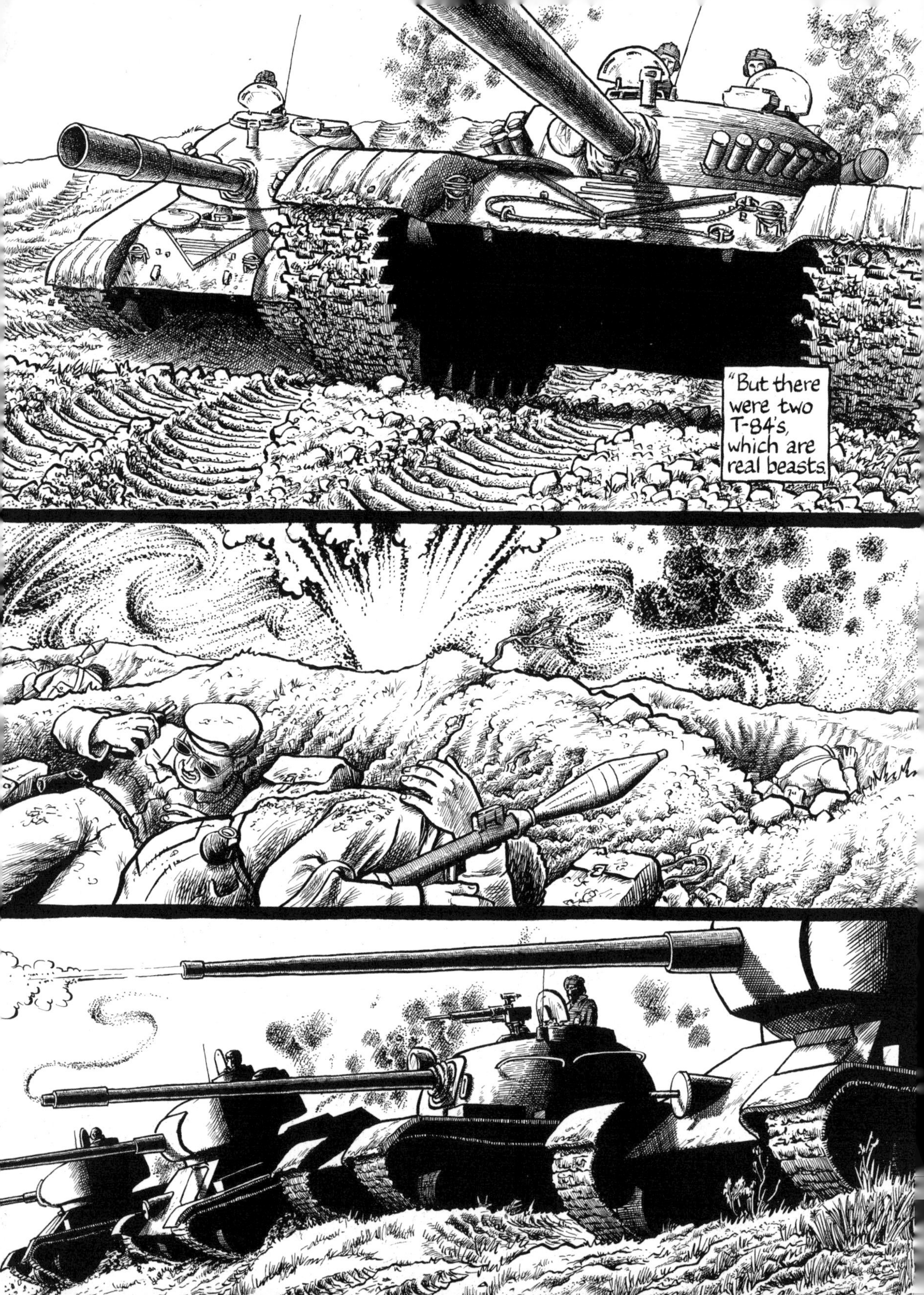
"But there were two T-84's, which are real beasts.

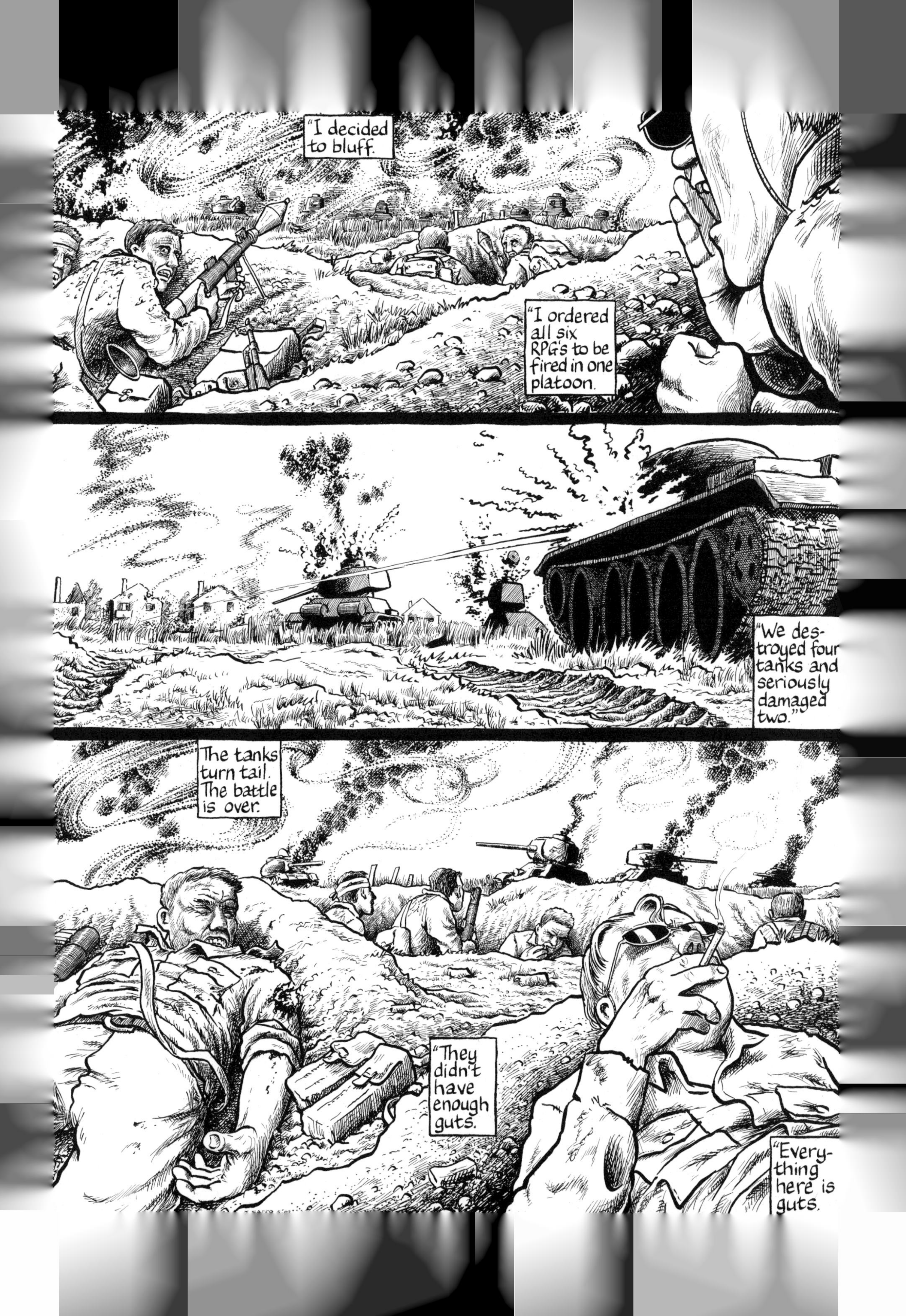
"I decided to bluff.
"I ordered all six RPG's to be fired in one platoon.
"We destroyed four tanks and seriously damaged two."
The tanks turn tail. The battle is over.
"They didn't have enough guts.
"Everything here is guts.

"Three of our guys were killed and each of us was wounded.

"When that action was over we couldn't withdraw because the body of one of my friends was in our front lines, and we had standing orders from Celo that all of us are coming back, dead or alive..."

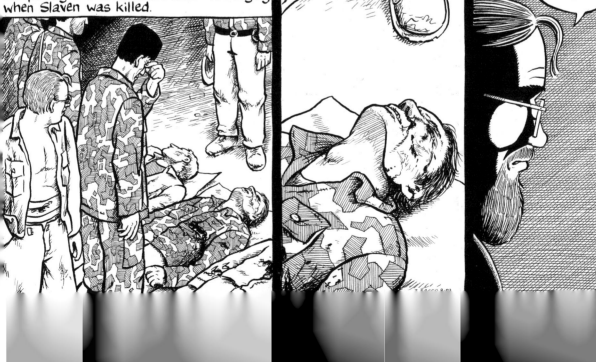

"And that cult of Celo is based on the fact that he's a cruel son of a bitch, which is completely untrue. Because I saw him crying when Slaven was killed.

"He was our favorite kid."

CAN WE TAKE A SHORT BREAK?

The days, the weeks pass. I have a circle of friends now. I know my way around. The cease-fire has arrived and holds my hand as I cross the street.

1995

One day I'm sitting with D., one of my new friends.

He was de-mobilized a couple of years back after being injured in an artillery bombardment.

Now he's a journalist.

Anyway, we're warming our bones in a bit of mid-Autumn cease-fire sun when—

café

LO

HEY, YOU CRAZY MOTHER-FUCKER!!

Neven!

With a German photographer in tow.

ARE YOU WORKING TO-GETHER?

NO, WE KNOW EACH OTHER FROM A PREVIOUS JOB.

I HAVEN'T WORKED IN TWO WEEKS.

I'M COMPLETELY BROKE.

Uo-oh! We all know what happens to my wallet when Neven is broke! It eases out of my trousers and starts spewing money!

J. SACCO S-02

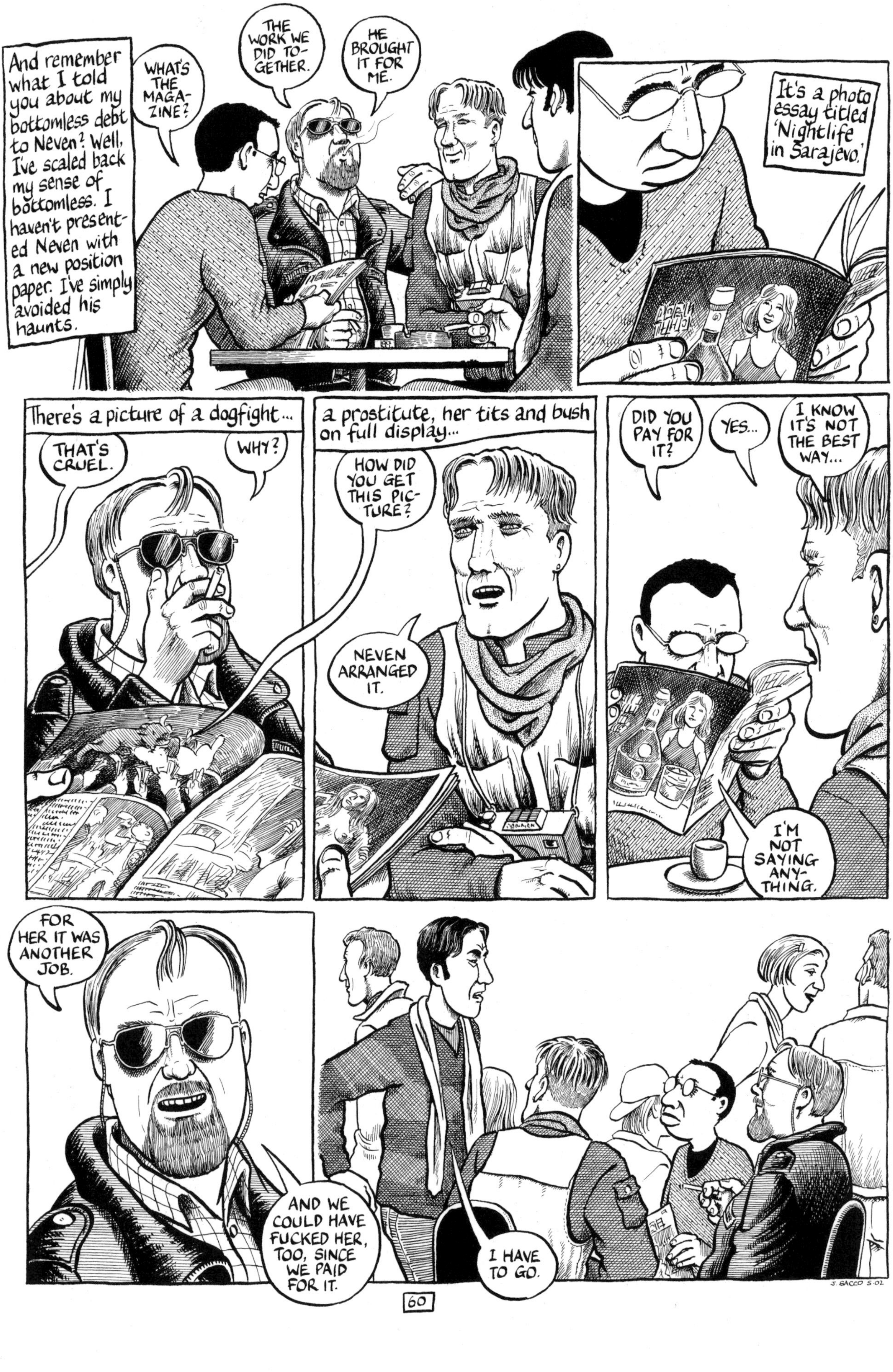
And remember what I told you about my bottomless debt to Neven? Well, I've scaled back my sense of bottomless. I haven't presented Neven with a new position paper. I've simply avoided his haunts.
WHAT'S THE MAGAZINE?
THE WORK WE DID TOGETHER.
HE BROUGHT IT FOR ME.
It's a photo essay titled 'Nightlife in Sarajevo.'
There's a picture of a dogfight...
THAT'S CRUEL.
WHY?
a prostitute, her tits and bush on full display...
HOW DID YOU GET THIS PICTURE?
NEVEN ARRANGED IT.
DID YOU PAY FOR IT?
YES...
I KNOW IT'S NOT THE BEST WAY...
I'M NOT SAYING ANYTHING.
FOR HER IT WAS ANOTHER JOB.
AND WE COULD HAVE FUCKED HER, TOO, SINCE WE PAID FOR IT.
I HAVE TO GO.
J. SACCO 5.02

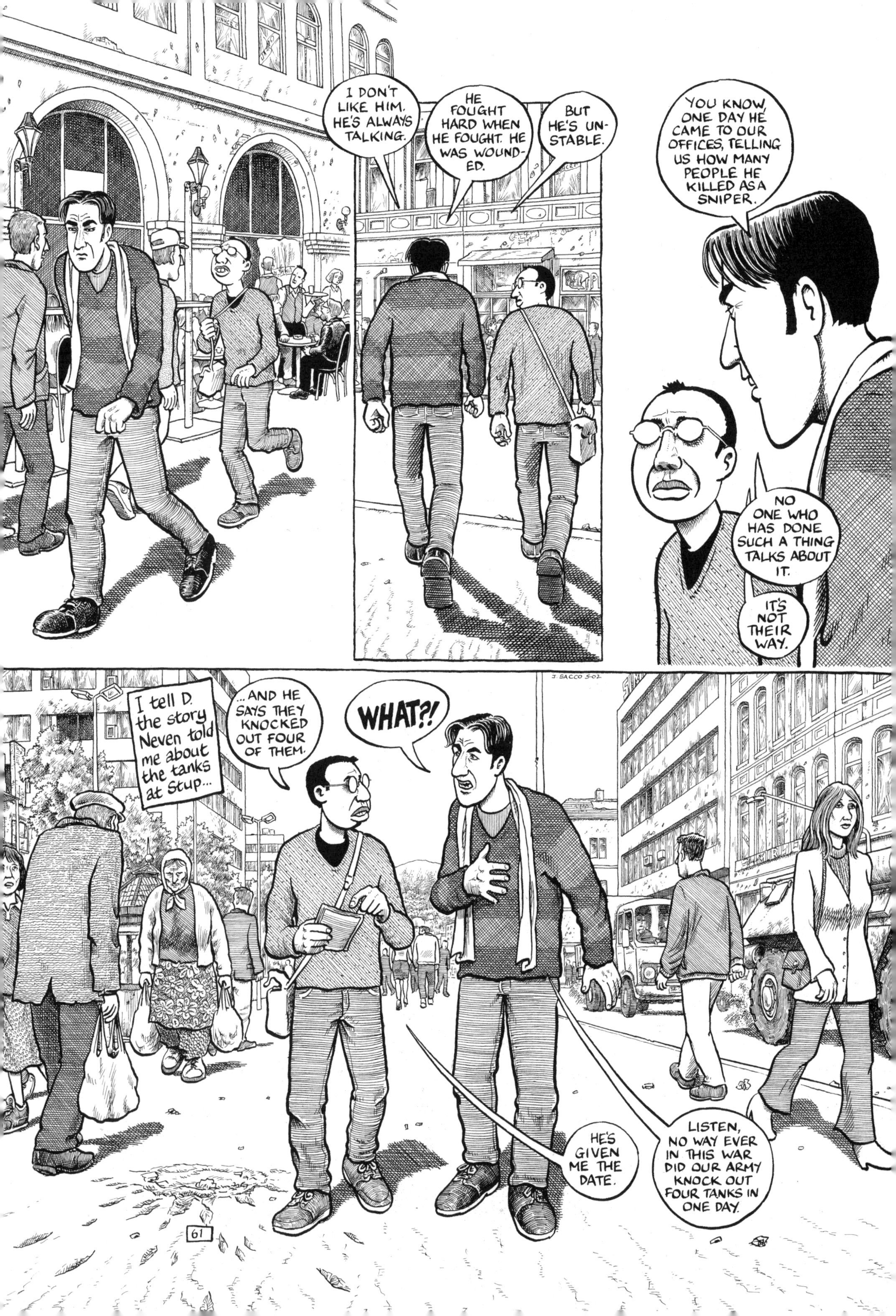
I DON'T LIKE HIM. HE'S ALWAYS TALKING.
HE FOUGHT HARD WHEN HE FOUGHT. HE WAS WOUNDED.
BUT HE'S UNSTABLE.
YOU KNOW, ONE DAY HE CAME TO OUR OFFICES, TELLING US HOW MANY PEOPLE HE KILLED AS A SNIPER.
NO ONE WHO HAS DONE SUCH A THING TALKS ABOUT IT.
IT'S NOT THEIR WAY.
J. SACCO 5-02
I tell D. the story Neven told me about the tanks at Stup...
...AND HE SAYS THEY KNOCKED OUT FOUR OF THEM.
WHAT?!
HE'S GIVEN ME THE DATE.
LISTEN, NO WAY EVER IN THIS WAR DID OUR ARMY KNOCK OUT FOUR TANKS IN ONE DAY.

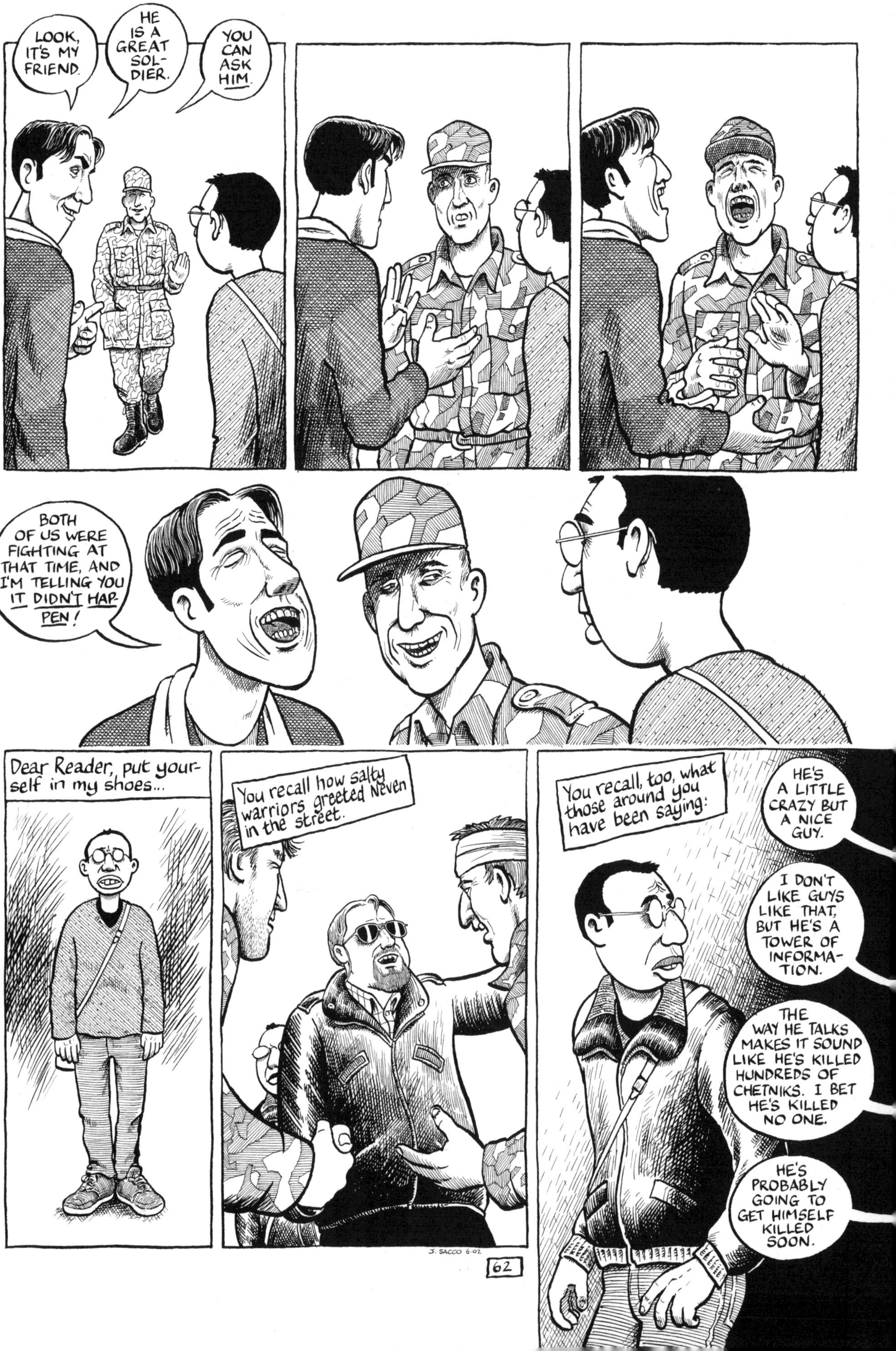
LOOK, IT'S MY FRIEND.
HE IS A GREAT SOL-DIER.
YOU CAN ASK HIM.
BOTH OF US WERE FIGHTING AT THAT TIME, AND I'M TELLING YOU IT DIDN'T HAP-PEN!
Dear Reader, put your-self in my shoes...
You recall how salty warriors greeted Neven in the street.
You recall, too, what those around you have been saying:
HE'S A LITTLE CRAZY BUT A NICE GUY.
I DON'T LIKE GUYS LIKE THAT, BUT HE'S A TOWER OF INFORMA-TION.
THE WAY HE TALKS MAKES IT SOUND LIKE HE'S KILLED HUNDREDS OF CHETNIKS. I BET HE'S KILLED NO ONE.
HE'S PROBABLY GOING TO GET HIMSELF KILLED SOON.
J. SACCO 6-02

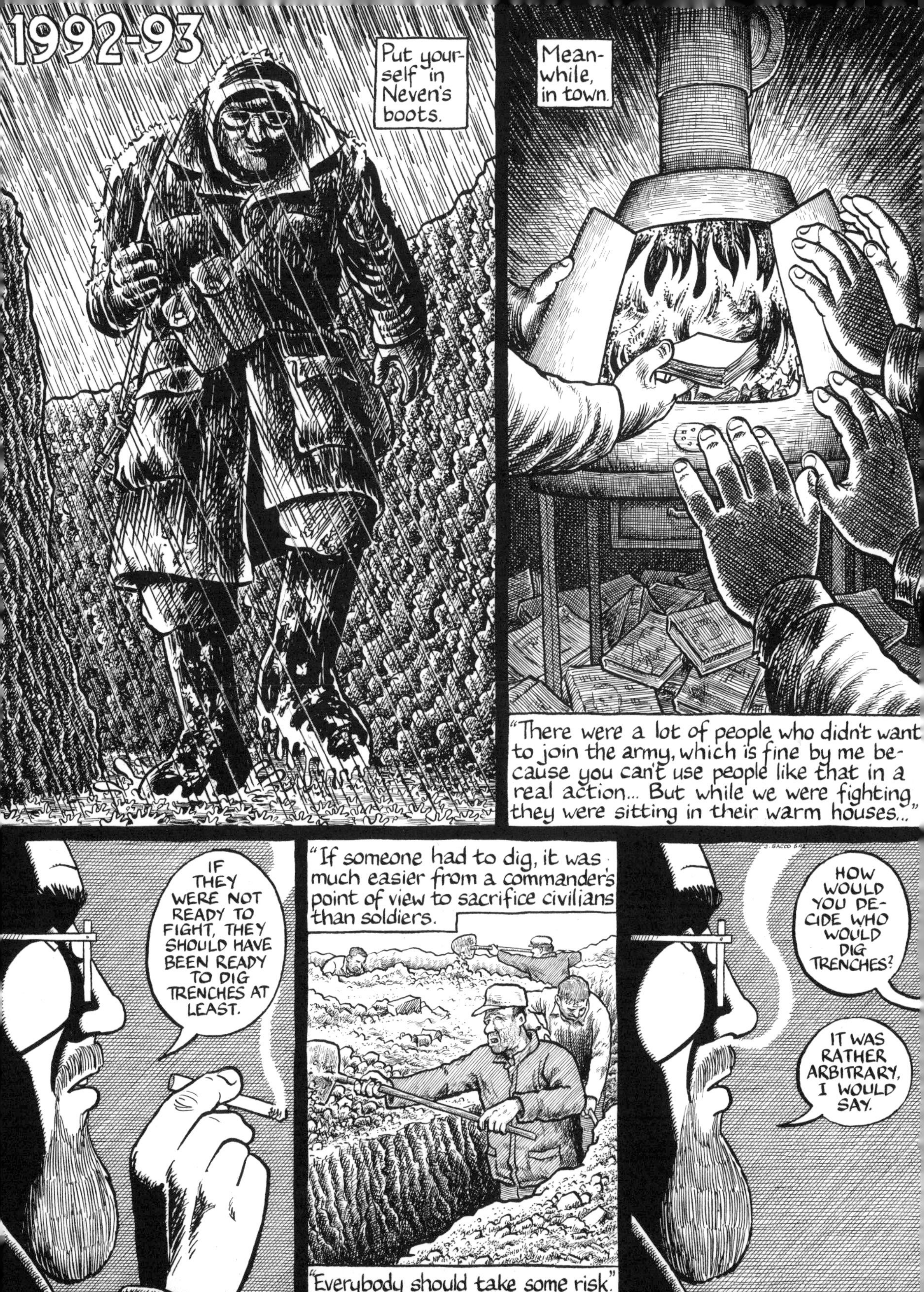
1992-93
Put yourself in Neven's boots.
Meanwhile, in town.
"There were a lot of people who didn't want to join the army, which is fine by me because you can't use people like that in a real action... But while we were fighting they were sitting in their warm houses..."
IF THEY WERE NOT READY TO FIGHT, THEY SHOULD HAVE BEEN READY TO DIG TRENCHES AT LEAST.
"If someone had to dig, it was much easier from a commander's point of view to sacrifice civilians than soldiers.
"Everybody should take some risk."
HOW WOULD YOU DECIDE WHO WOULD DIG TRENCHES?
IT WAS RATHER ARBITRARY, I WOULD SAY.

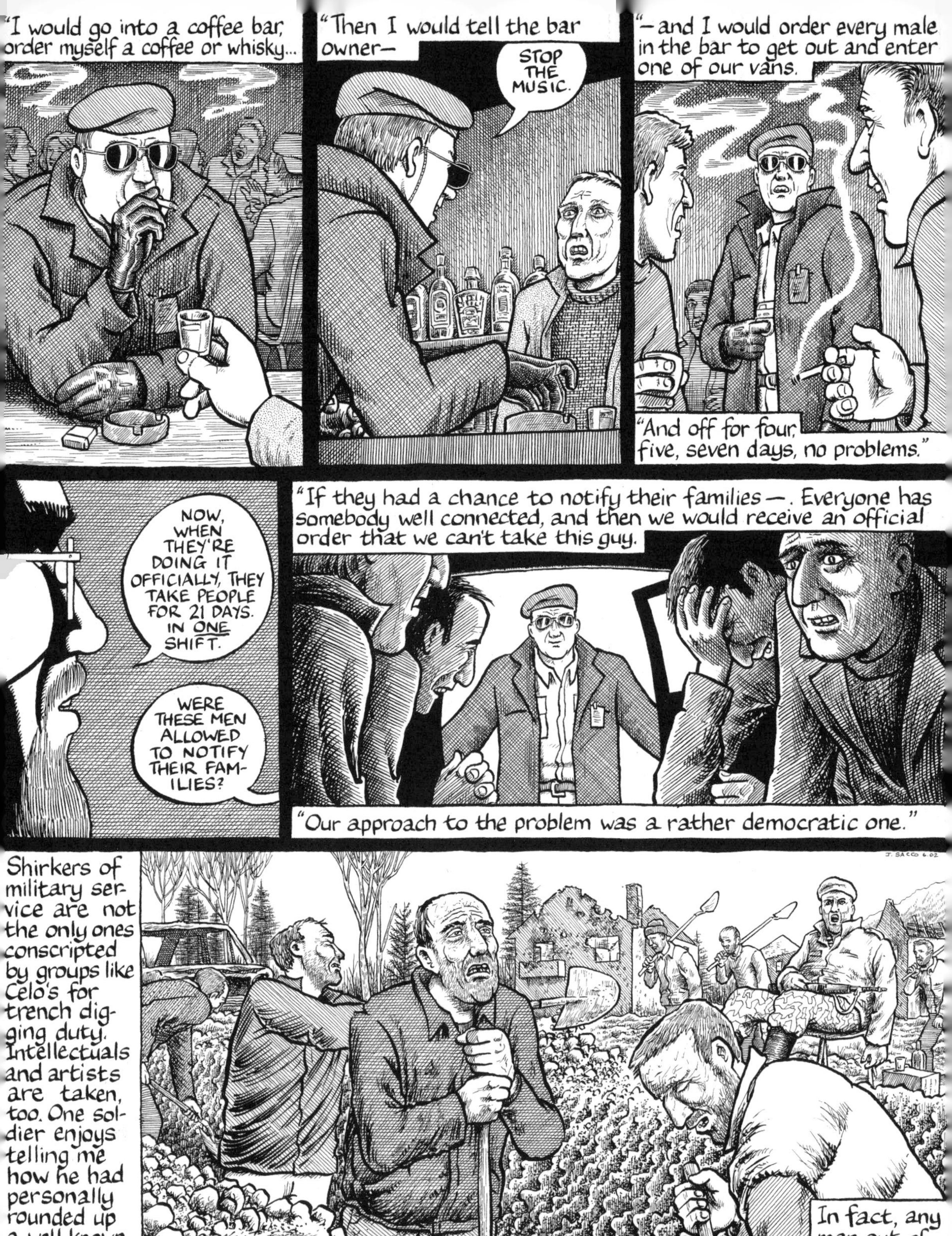
"I would go into a coffee bar, order myself a coffee or whisky...
"Then I would tell the bar owner—
STOP THE MUSIC.
"—and I would order every male in the bar to get out and enter one of our vans.
"And off for four, five, seven days, no problems."
NOW, WHEN THEY'RE DOING IT OFFICIALLY, THEY TAKE PEOPLE FOR 21 DAYS. IN ONE SHIFT.
WERE THESE MEN ALLOWED TO NOTIFY THEIR FAMILIES?
"If they had a chance to notify their families—. Everyone has somebody well connected, and then we would receive an official order that we can't take this guy.
"Our approach to the problem was a rather democratic one."
J. SACCO 6.02
Shirkers of military service are not the only ones conscripted by groups like Celo's for trench digging duty. Intellectuals and artists are taken, too. One soldier enjoys telling me how he had personally rounded up a well known theater director for Caco's 'Dig For Victory' campaign.
In fact, any man out of uniform might find himself plucked for this service.

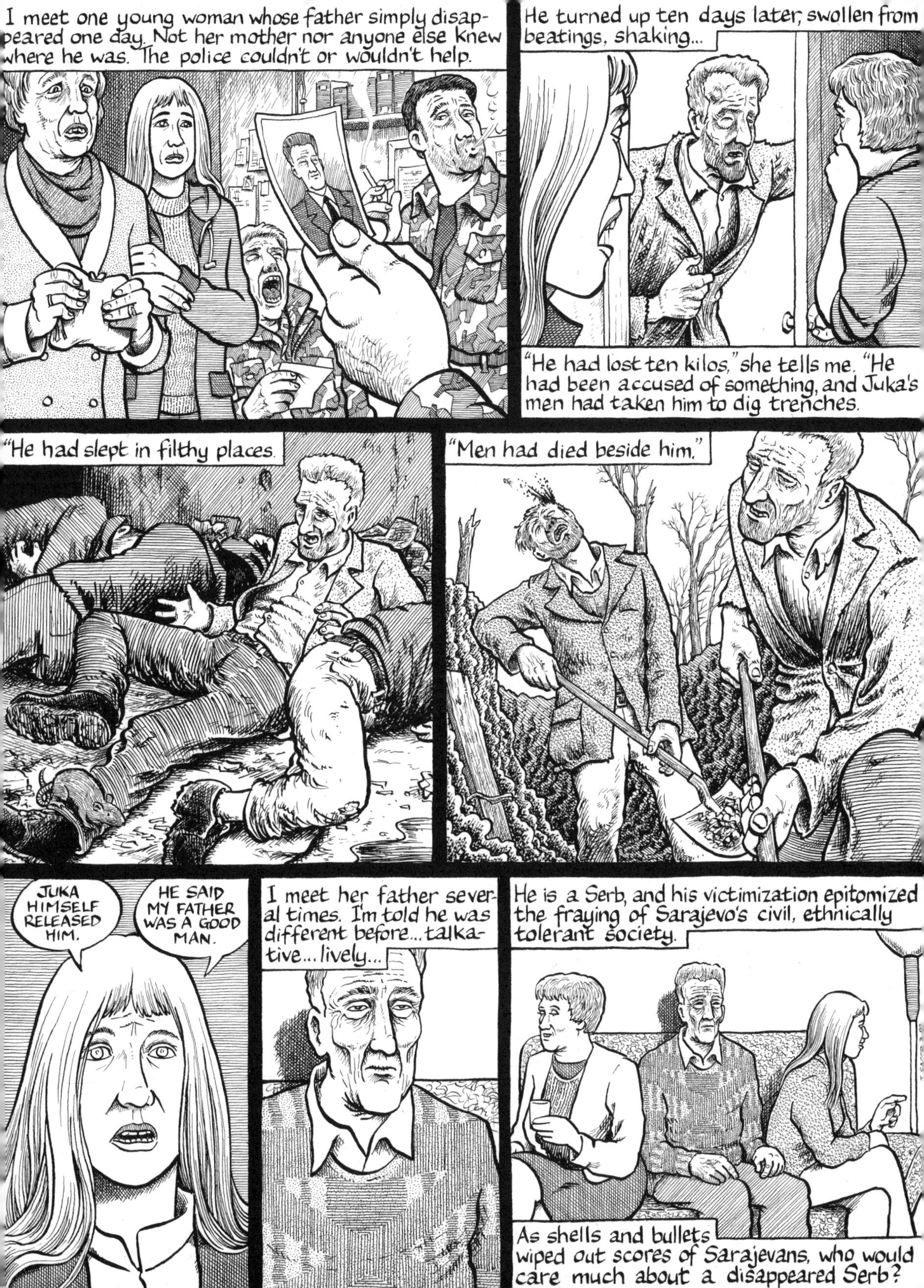
I meet one young woman whose father simply disappeared one day. Not her mother nor anyone else knew where he was. The police couldn't or wouldn't help.
He turned up ten days later, swollen from beatings, shaking...
"He had lost ten kilos," she tells me. "He had been accused of something, and Juka's men had taken him to dig trenches.
"He had slept in filthy places.
"Men had died beside him."
JUKA HIMSELF RELEASED HIM.
HE SAID MY FATHER WAS A GOOD MAN.
I meet her father several times. I'm told he was different before... talkative... lively...
He is a Serb, and his victimization epitomized the fraying of Sarajevo's civil, ethnically tolerant society.
As shells and bullets wiped out scores of Sarajevans, who would care much about a disappeared Serb?

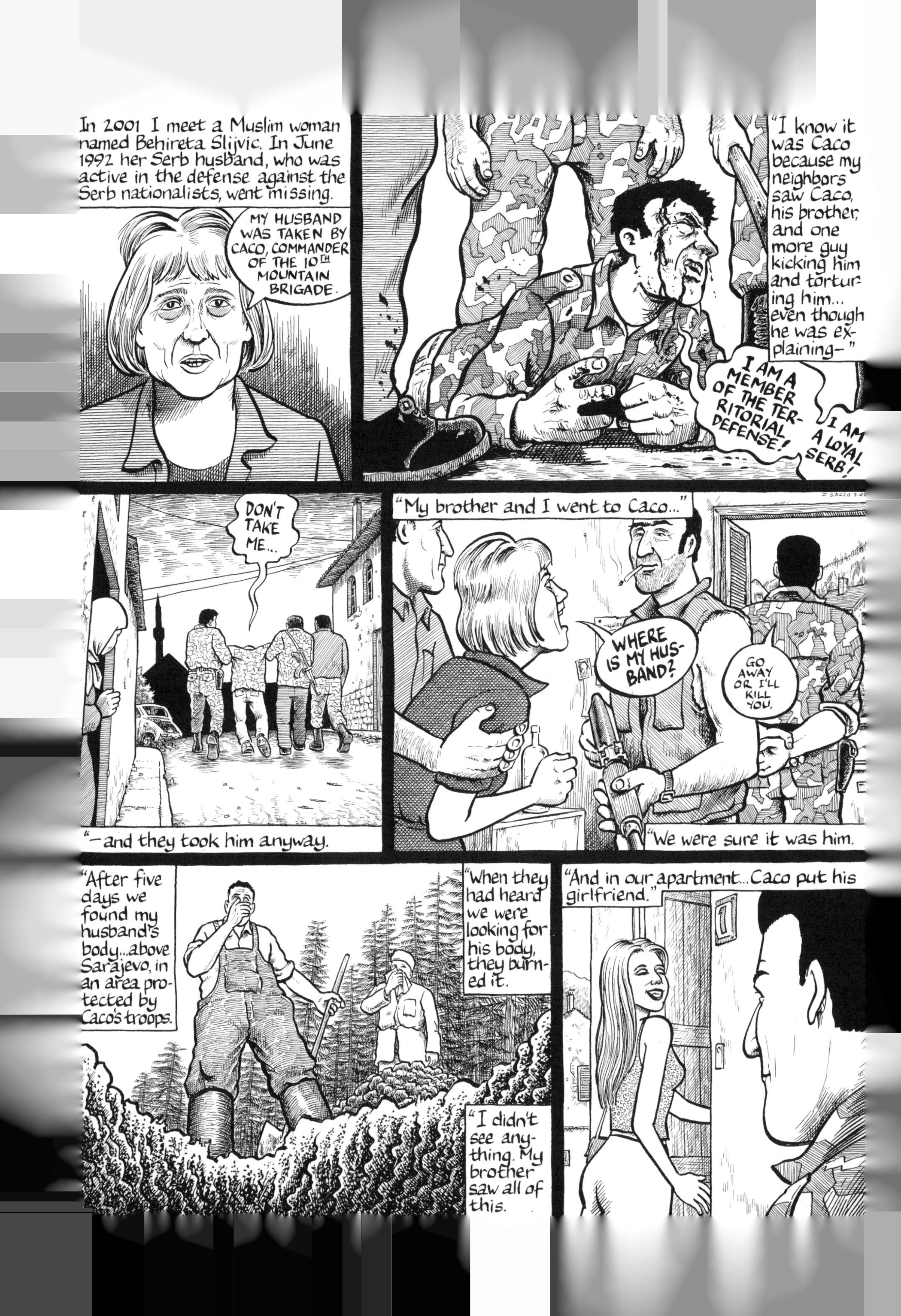
In 2001 I meet a Muslim woman named Behireta Slijvic. In June 1992 her Serb husband, who was active in the defense against the Serb nationalists, went missing.
MY HUSBAND WAS TAKEN BY CACO, COMMANDER OF THE 10TH MOUNTAIN BRIGADE.
"I know it was Caco because my neighbors saw Caco, his brother, and one more guy kicking him and torturing him... even though he was explaining–"
I AM A MEMBER OF THE TERRITORIAL DEFENSE!
I AM A LOYAL SERB!
DON'T TAKE ME...
"–and they took him anyway.
"My brother and I went to Caco..."
WHERE IS MY HUSBAND?
GO AWAY OR I'LL KILL YOU.
"We were sure it was him.
"After five days we found my husband's body...above Sarajevo, in an area protected by Caco's troops.
"When they had heard we were looking for his body, they burned it.
"I didn't see anything. My brother saw all of this.
"And in our apartment...Caco put his girlfriend."

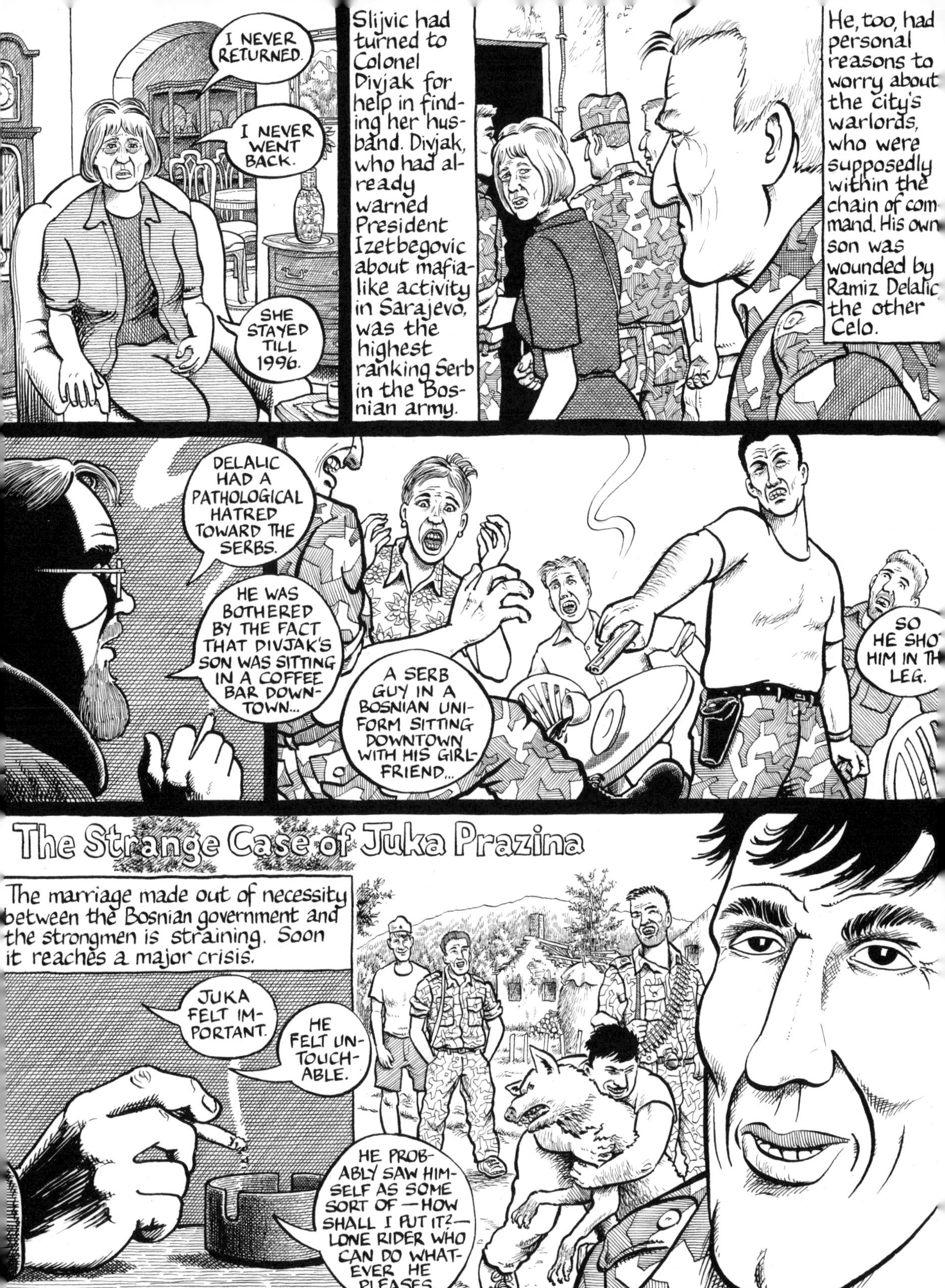
I NEVER RETURNED.
I NEVER WENT BACK.
SHE STAYED TILL 1996.
Slijvic had turned to Colonel Divjak for help in finding her husband. Divjak, who had already warned President Izetbegovic about mafia-like activity in Sarajevo, was the highest ranking Serb in the Bosnian army.
He, too, had personal reasons to worry about the city's warlords, who were supposedly within the chain of command. His own son was wounded by Ramiz Delalic, the other Celo.
DELALIC HAD A PATHOLOGICAL HATRED TOWARD THE SERBS.
HE WAS BOTHERED BY THE FACT THAT DIVJAK'S SON WAS SITTING IN A COFFEE BAR DOWNTOWN...
A SERB GUY IN A BOSNIAN UNIFORM SITTING DOWNTOWN WITH HIS GIRLFRIEND...
SO HE SHOT HIM IN THE LEG.
The Strange Case of Juka Prazina
The marriage made out of necessity between the Bosnian government and the strongmen is straining. Soon it reaches a major crisis.
JUKA FELT IMPORTANT.
HE FELT UNTOUCHABLE.
HE PROBABLY SAW HIMSELF AS SOME SORT OF — HOW SHALL I PUT IT? — LONE RIDER WHO CAN DO WHATEVER HE PLEASES.

Juka's personal heroics and T.V. appearances have transformed the one-time petty crook into an icon. Juka is highly regarded, even by educated Sarajevans, because "the fact that someone —anyone— would have the guts to stand up and fight was really appreciated," according to Vildana Selimbegovic, a journalist for 'Dani.'

The government cannot ignore Juka and his 3,000 well armed men... It names him commander of a reserve special police force.

The government also allows Juka to sit in on cabinet meetings... He clashes with General Sefer Halilovic, Bosnia's senior army officer.

WITH HALILOVIC, JUKA WAS LIKE, 'WHO THE FUCK ARE YOU TO GIVE ME ORDERS? I AM POLICE, YOU ARE ARMY.'

BUT THERE IS A LAW THAT, IN CASE OF WAR, THE ARMY IS SUPERIOR TO THE POLICE.

JUKA REFUSED TO ACCEPT THAT FACT.

When his police superiors cannot handle him, Juka is shifted to the army, which tries to appease him with the command of Special Units. But he publicly derides the high command and starts calling himself a general.

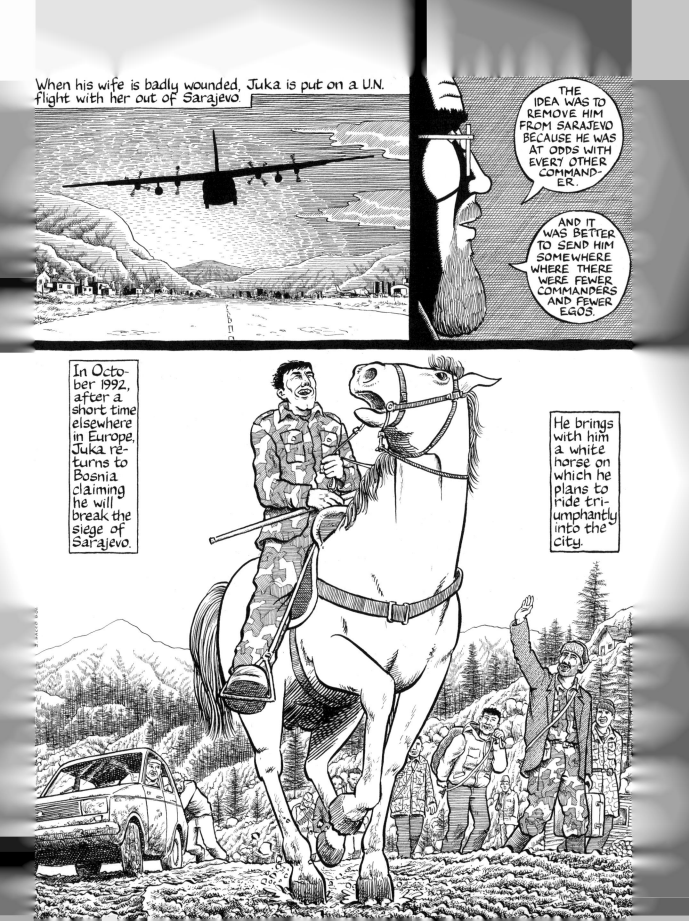

When his wife is badly wounded, Juka is put on a U.N. flight with her out of Sarajevo.

THE IDEA WAS TO REMOVE HIM FROM SARAJEVO BECAUSE HE WAS AT ODDS WITH EVERY OTHER COMMANDER.

AND IT WAS BETTER TO SEND HIM SOMEWHERE WHERE THERE WERE FEWER COMMANDERS AND FEWER EGOS.

In October 1992, after a short time elsewhere in Europe, Juka returns to Bosnia claiming he will break the siege of Sarajevo.

He brings with him a white horse on which he plans to ride triumphantly into the city.

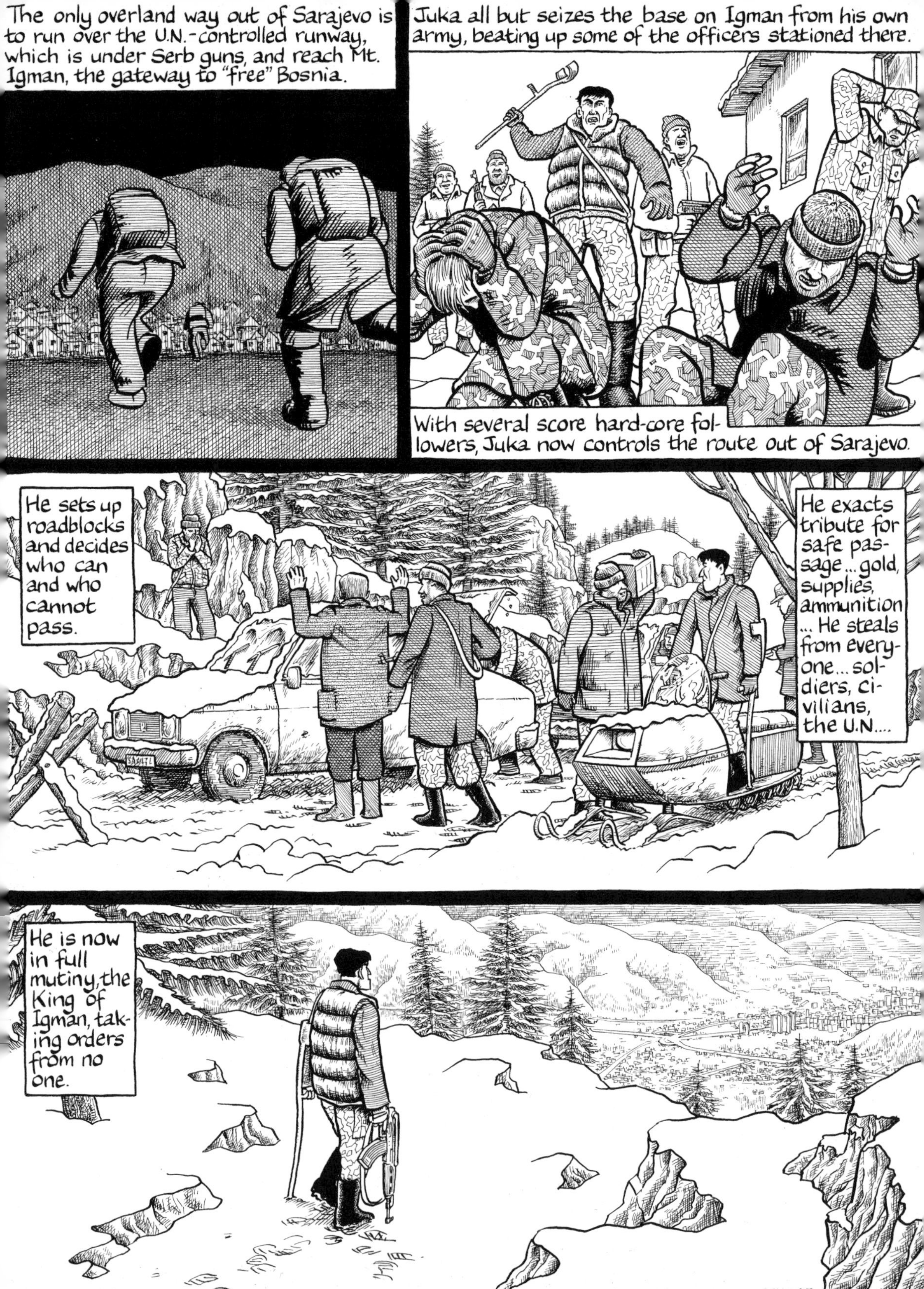
The only overland way out of Sarajevo is to run over the U.N.-controlled runway, which is under Serb guns, and reach Mt. Igman, the gateway to "free" Bosnia.
Juka all but seizes the base on Igman from his own army, beating up some of the officers stationed there.
With several score hard-core followers, Juka now controls the route out of Sarajevo.
He sets up roadblocks and decides who can and who cannot pass.
He exacts tribute for safe passage... gold, supplies, ammunition ... He steals from everyone... soldiers, civilians, the U.N....
He is now in full mutiny, the King of Igman, taking orders from no one.

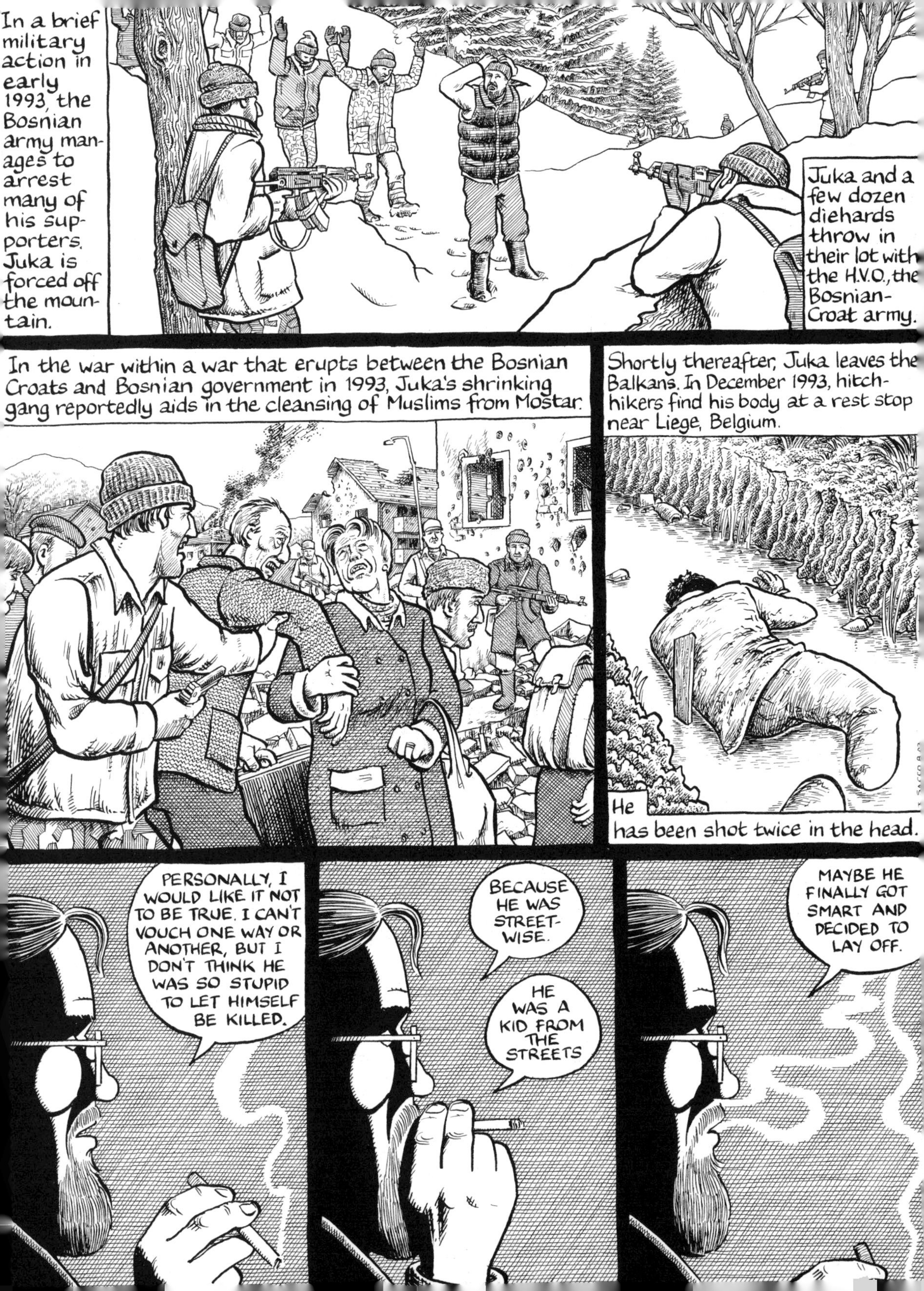
In a brief military action in early 1993, the Bosnian army manages to arrest many of his supporters. Juka is forced off the mountain.
Juka and a few dozen diehards throw in their lot with the H.V.O., the Bosnian-Croat army.
In the war within a war that erupts between the Bosnian Croats and Bosnian government in 1993, Juka's shrinking gang reportedly aids in the cleansing of Muslims from Mostar.
Shortly thereafter, Juka leaves the Balkans. In December 1993, hitch-hikers find his body at a rest stop near Liege, Belgium.
He has been shot twice in the head.
PERSONALLY, I WOULD LIKE IT NOT TO BE TRUE. I CAN'T VOUCH ONE WAY OR ANOTHER, BUT I DON'T THINK HE WAS SO STUPID TO LET HIMSELF BE KILLED.
BECAUSE HE WAS STREET-WISE.
HE WAS A KID FROM THE STREETS
MAYBE HE FINALLY GOT SMART AND DECIDED TO LAY OFF.

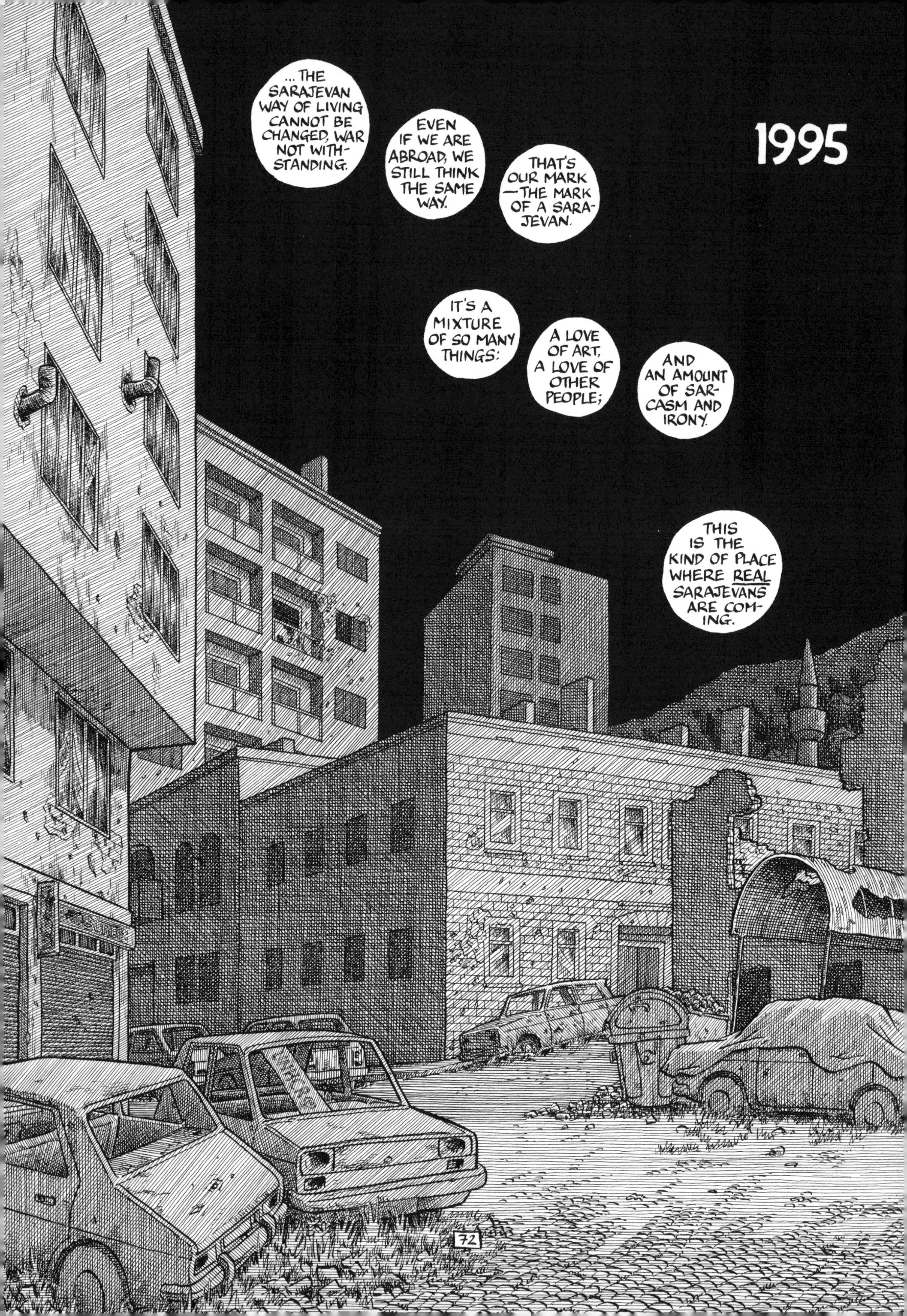
1995
...THE SARAJEVAN WAY OF LIVING CANNOT BE CHANGED, WAR NOT WITH-STANDING.
EVEN IF WE ARE ABROAD, WE STILL THINK THE SAME WAY.
THAT'S OUR MARK —THE MARK OF A SARA-JEVAN.
IT'S A MIXTURE OF SO MANY THINGS:
A LOVE OF ART, A LOVE OF OTHER PEOPLE;
AND AN AMOUNT OF SAR-CASM AND IRONY.
THIS IS THE KIND OF PLACE WHERE REAL SARAJEVANS ARE COM-ING.

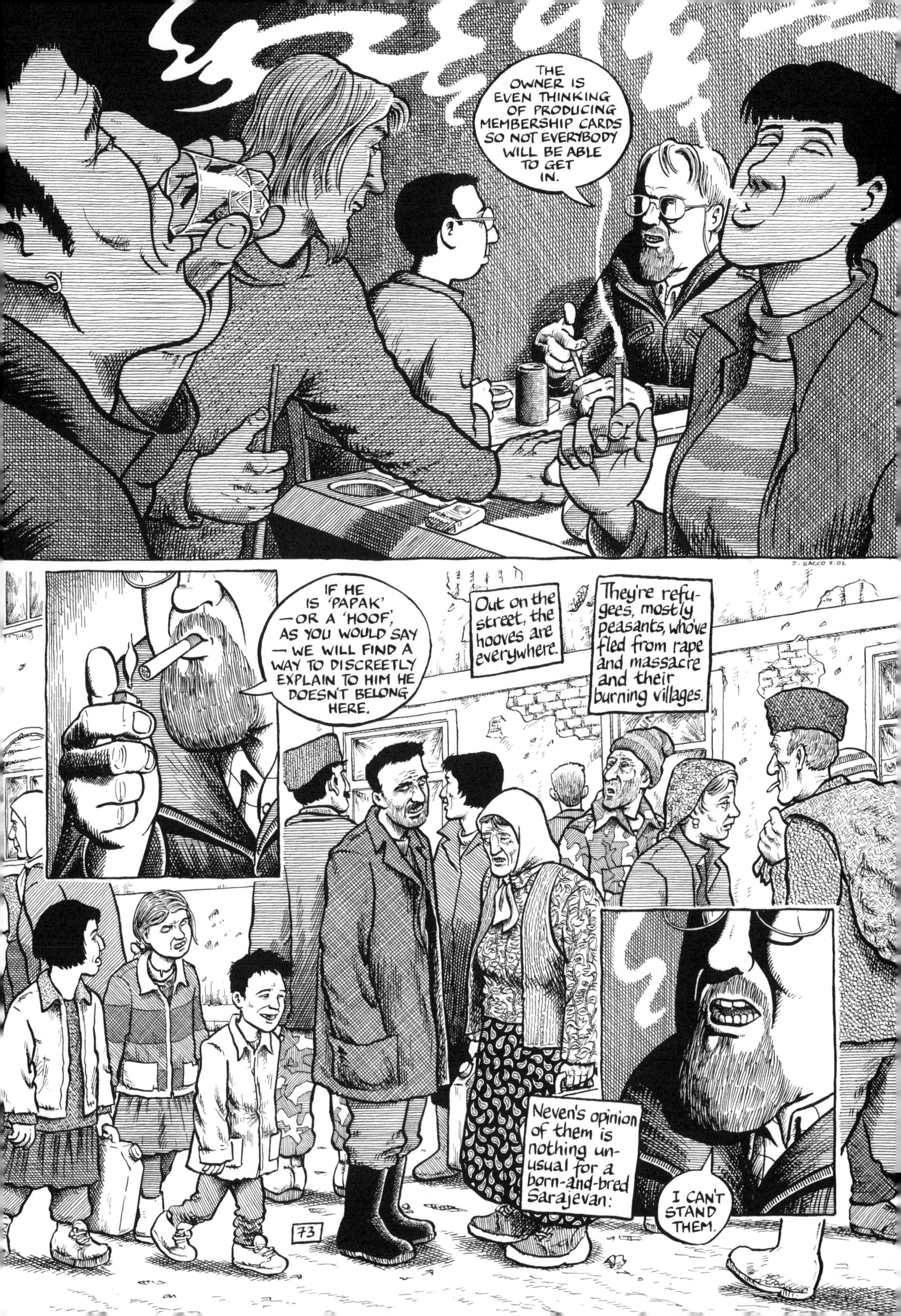

THE OWNER IS EVEN THINKING OF PRODUCING MEMBERSHIP CARDS SO NOT EVERYBODY WILL BE ABLE TO GET IN.
J. SACCO 7.02
IF HE IS 'PAPAK' —OR A 'HOOF', AS YOU WOULD SAY — WE WILL FIND A WAY TO DISCREETLY EXPLAIN TO HIM HE DOESN'T BELONG HERE.
Out on the street, the hooves are everywhere.
They're refugees, mostly peasants, who've fled from rape and massacre and their burning villages.
Neven's opinion of them is nothing unusual for a born-and-bred Sarajevan:
I CAN'T STAND THEM.

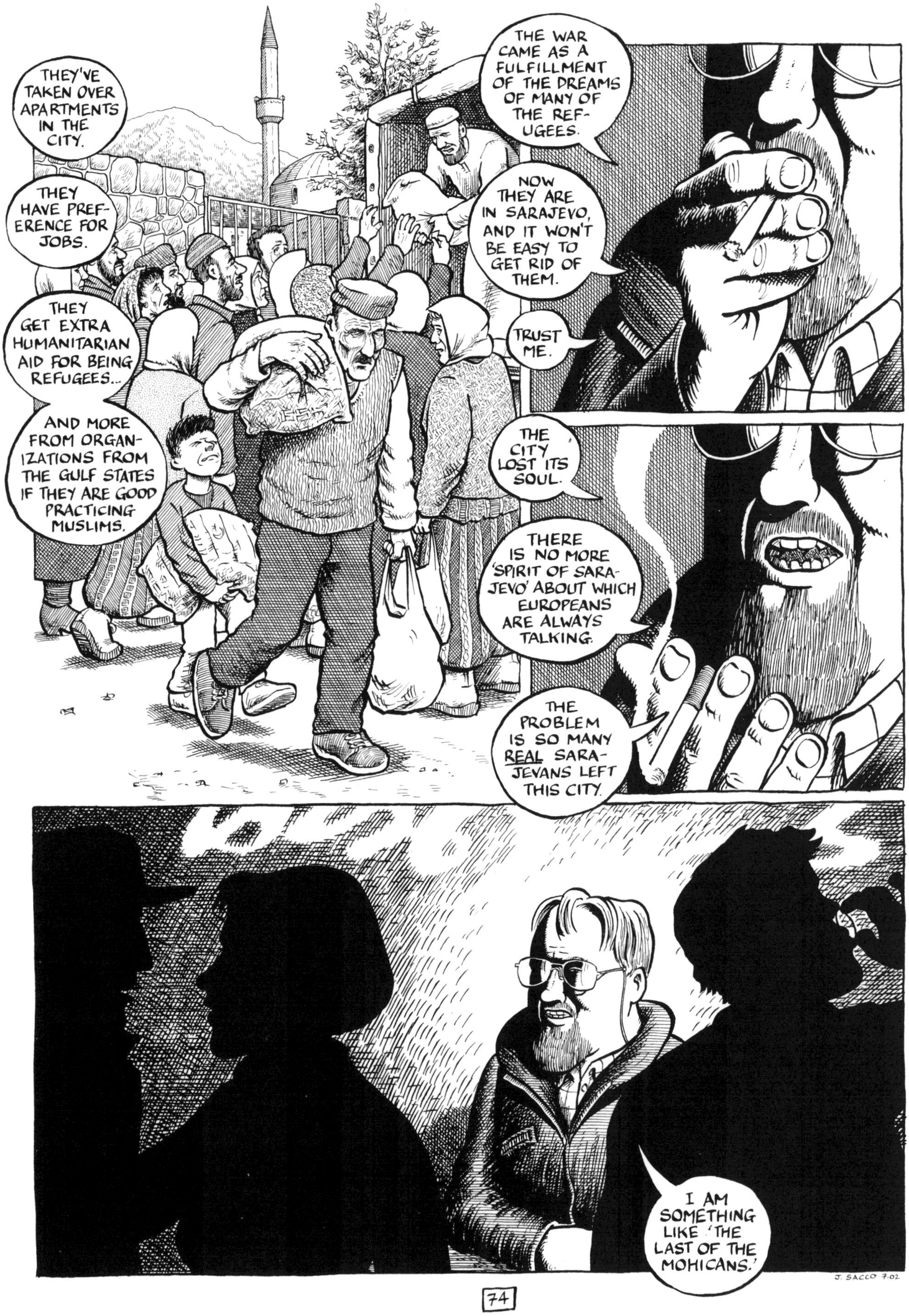

THEY'VE TAKEN OVER APARTMENTS IN THE CITY.
THEY HAVE PREFERENCE FOR JOBS.
THEY GET EXTRA HUMANITARIAN AID FOR BEING REFUGEES...
AND MORE FROM ORGANIZATIONS FROM THE GULF STATES IF THEY ARE GOOD PRACTICING MUSLIMS.
THE WAR CAME AS A FULFILLMENT OF THE DREAMS OF MANY OF THE REFUGEES.
NOW THEY ARE IN SARAJEVO, AND IT WON'T BE EASY TO GET RID OF THEM.
TRUST ME.
THE CITY LOST ITS SOUL.
THERE IS NO MORE 'SPIRIT OF SARAJEVO' ABOUT WHICH EUROPEANS ARE ALWAYS TALKING.
THE PROBLEM IS SO MANY REAL SARAJEVANS LEFT THIS CITY.
I AM SOMETHING LIKE 'THE LAST OF THE MOHICANS.'
J. SACCO 7.02

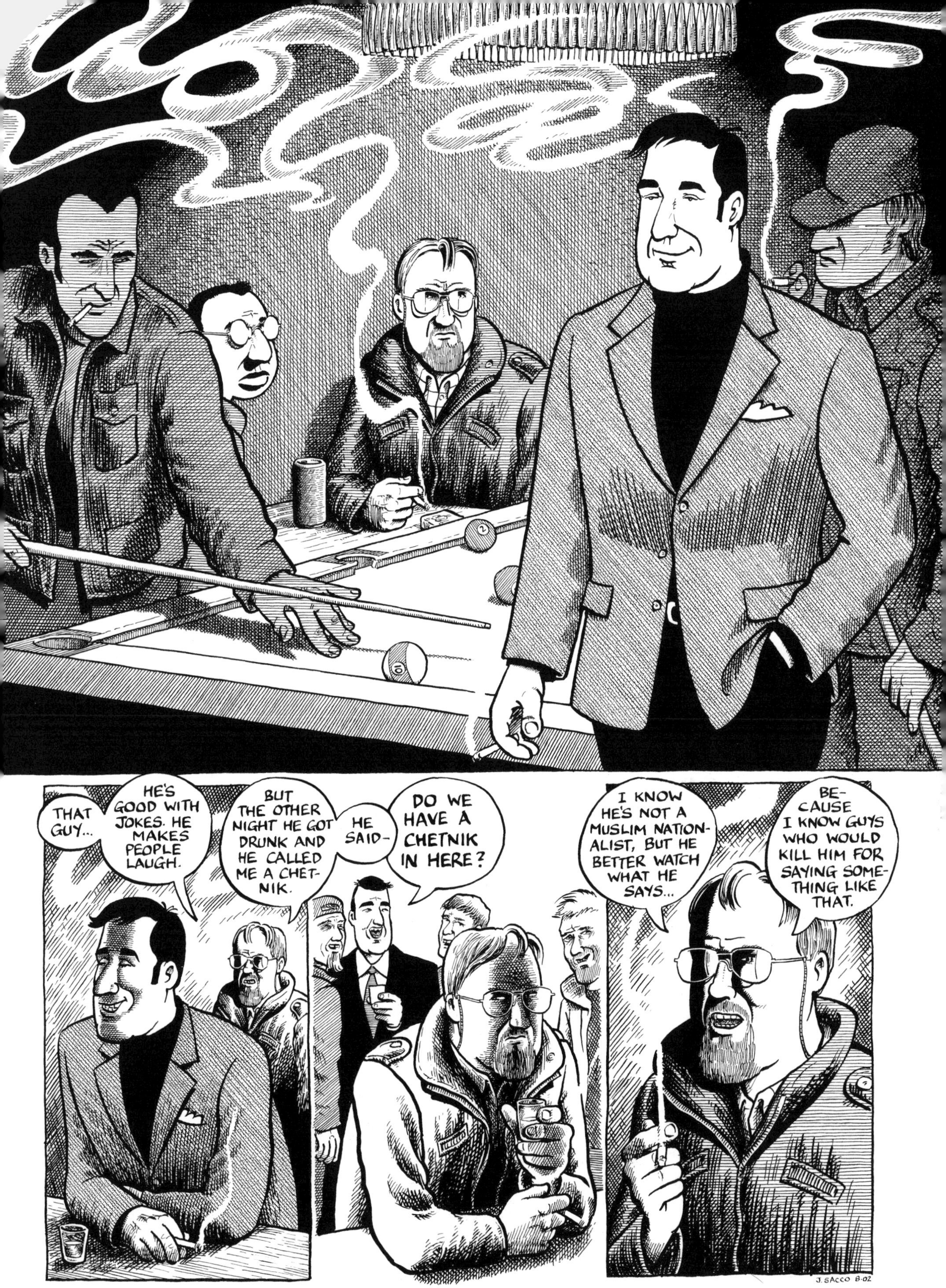

THAT GUY...
HE'S GOOD WITH JOKES. HE MAKES PEOPLE LAUGH.
BUT THE OTHER NIGHT HE GOT DRUNK AND HE CALLED ME A CHETNIK.
HE SAID—
DO WE HAVE A CHETNIK IN HERE?
I KNOW HE'S NOT A MUSLIM NATIONALIST, BUT HE BETTER WATCH WHAT HE SAYS...
BECAUSE I KNOW GUYS WHO WOULD KILL HIM FOR SAYING SOMETHING LIKE THAT.
J. SACCO 8-02

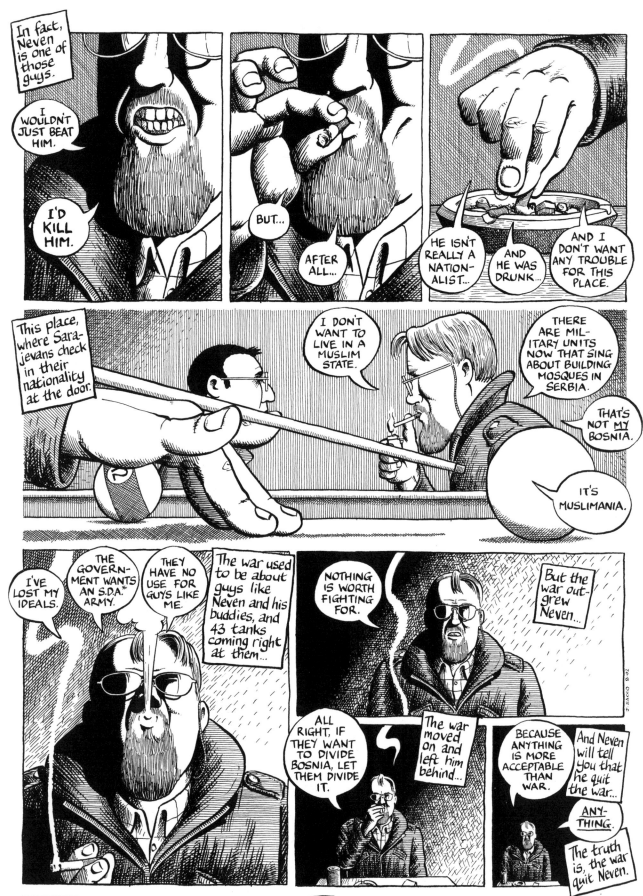

In fact, Neven is one of those guys.

I WOULDN'T JUST BEAT HIM.

I'D KILL HIM.

BUT...

AFTER ALL...

HE ISN'T REALLY A NATIONALIST...

AND HE WAS DRUNK...

AND I DON'T WANT ANY TROUBLE FOR THIS PLACE.

This place, where Sarajevans check in their nationality at the door.

I DON'T WANT TO LIVE IN A MUSLIM STATE.

THERE ARE MILITARY UNITS NOW THAT SING ABOUT BUILDING MOSQUES IN SERBIA.

THAT'S NOT MY BOSNIA.

IT'S MUSLIMANIA.

I'VE LOST MY IDEALS.

THE GOVERNMENT WANTS AN S.D.A.* ARMY.

THEY HAVE NO USE FOR GUYS LIKE ME.

The war used to be about guys like Neven and his buddies, and 43 tanks coming right at them...

ALL RIGHT, IF THEY WANT TO DIVIDE BOSNIA, LET THEM DIVIDE IT.

NOTHING IS WORTH FIGHTING FOR.

But the war outgrew Neven...

The war moved on and left him behind...

BECAUSE ANYTHING IS MORE ACCEPTABLE THAN WAR.

And Neven will tell you that he quit the war...

ANYTHING.

The truth is, the war quit Neven.

* S.D.A. — THE MUSLIM NATIONALIST PARTY

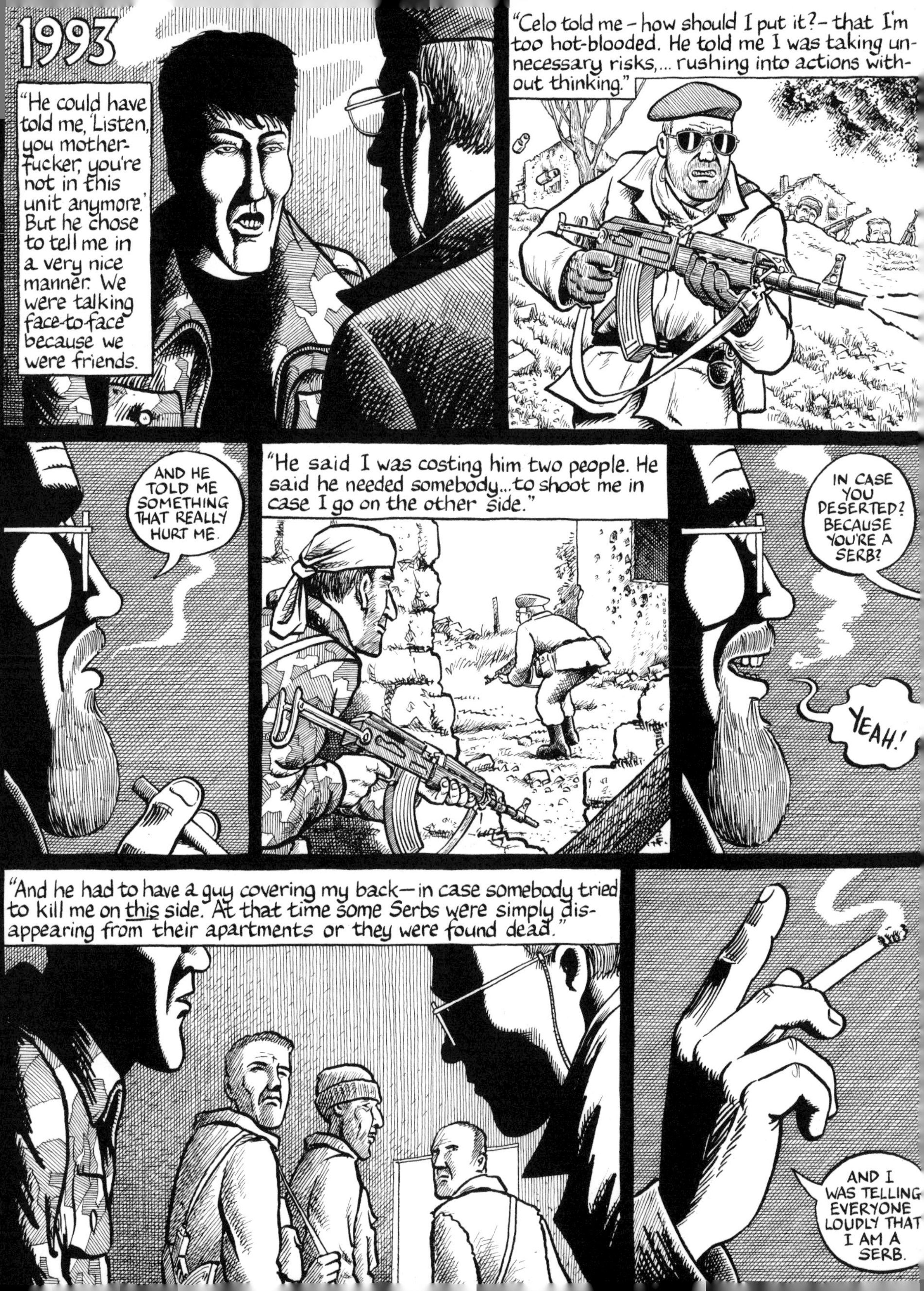
1993
"He could have told me, 'Listen, you mother-fucker, you're not in this unit anymore.' But he chose to tell me in a very nice manner. We were talking face-to-face because we were friends.
"Celo told me – how should I put it?– that I'm too hot-blooded. He told me I was taking unnecessary risks,... rushing into actions without thinking."
AND HE TOLD ME SOMETHING THAT REALLY HURT ME.
"He said I was costing him two people. He said he needed somebody...to shoot me in case I go on the other side."
IN CASE YOU DESERTED? BECAUSE YOU'RE A SERB?
YEAH!
"And he had to have a guy covering my back—in case somebody tried to kill me on this side. At that time some Serbs were simply disappearing from their apartments or they were found dead."
AND I WAS TELLING EVERYONE LOUDLY THAT I AM A SERB.

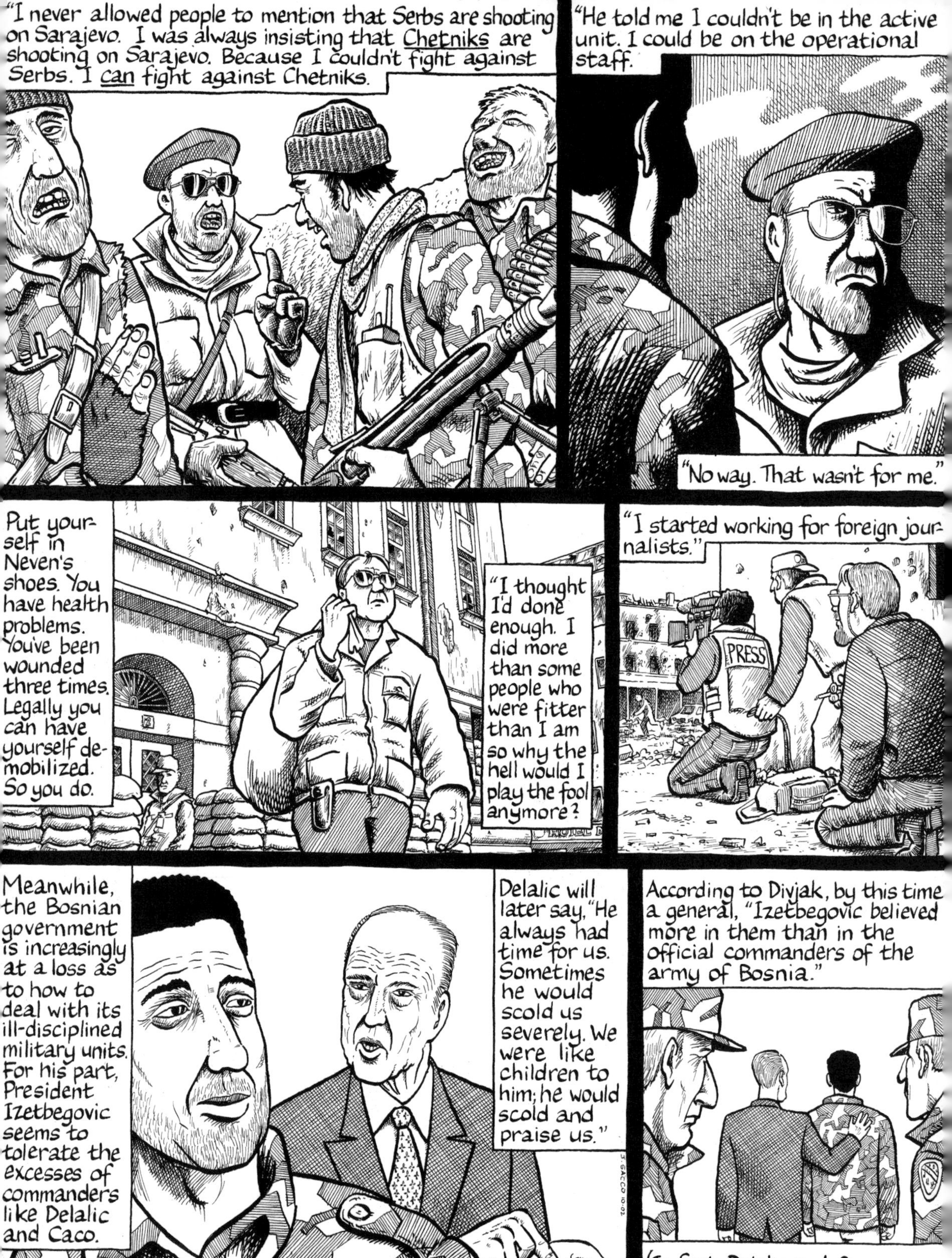

"I never allowed people to mention that Serbs are shooting on Sarajevo. I was always insisting that Chetniks are shooting on Sarajevo. Because I couldn't fight against Serbs. I can fight against Chetniks.
"He told me I couldn't be in the active unit. I could be on the operational staff.
"No way. That wasn't for me."
Put yourself in Neven's shoes. You have health problems. You've been wounded three times. Legally you can have yourself demobilized. So you do.
"I thought I'd done enough. I did more than some people who were fitter than I am so why the hell would I play the fool anymore?
"I started working for foreign journalists."
PRESS
Meanwhile, the Bosnian government is increasingly at a loss as to how to deal with its ill-disciplined military units. For his part, President Izetbegovic seems to tolerate the excesses of commanders like Delalic and Caco.
Delalic will later say, "He always had time for us. Sometimes he would scold us severely. We were like children to him; he would scold and praise us."
According to Divjak, by this time a general, "Izetbegovic believed more in them than in the official commanders of the army of Bosnia."
(In fact, Delalic and Caco were official commanders, technically answerable to the government.)

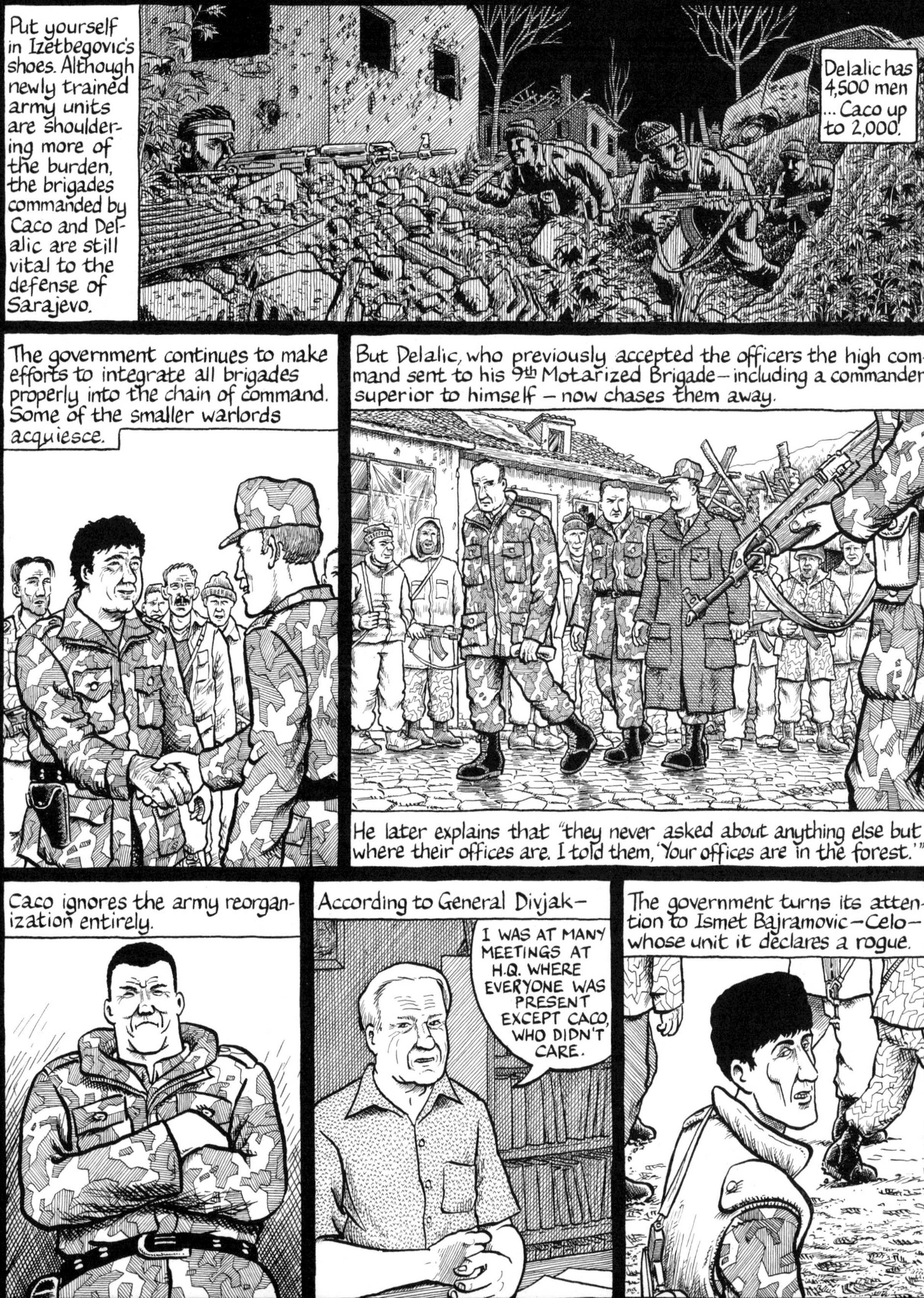
Put yourself in Izetbegovic's shoes. Although newly trained army units are shouldering more of the burden, the brigades commanded by Caco and Delalic are still vital to the defense of Sarajevo.
Delalic has 4,500 men ... Caco up to 2,000.
The government continues to make efforts to integrate all brigades properly into the chain of command. Some of the smaller warlords acquiesce.
But Delalic, who previously accepted the officers the high command sent to his 9th Motarized Brigade – including a commander superior to himself – now chases them away.
He later explains that "they never asked about anything else but where their offices are. I told them, 'Your offices are in the forest.'"
Caco ignores the army reorganization entirely.
According to General Divjak –
I WAS AT MANY MEETINGS AT H.Q. WHERE EVERYONE WAS PRESENT EXCEPT CACO, WHO DIDN'T CARE.
The government turns its attention to Ismet Bajramovic – Celo – whose unit it declares a rogue.

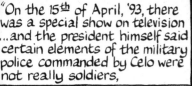

"On the 15th of April, '93, there was a special show on television ...and the president himself said certain elements of the military police commanded by Celo were not really soldiers,

"but were actually criminals,

"blah blah blah,

"killers,

"rapists,

"whatever you think...

"We were accused of breaking and entering,

"stealing,

"stopping commerce in the city...

"We were stunned by it. How else can you feel when you've lost so many friends and someone is saying you were not a soldier but a fucking criminal?

"And that's when I lost faith in this country."

Celo's unit is disbanded, its men dispersed into other units. Celo, who the war has made rich, opens up a nightclub.

Meanwhile, damning evidence is mounting against the other warlords. In May, General Divjak sends a letter to President Izetbegovic with detailed charges— including accusations of murder of citizens, particularly Serbs.

I DESCRIBED WHAT I KNEW ABOUT THEIR CRIMINAL ACTIVITIES,

ABOUT THE PEOPLE WHO HAD DISAPPEARED,

ABOUT WHO HAD TAKEN THEM.

But Izetbegovic won't upset his accommodation with the strongest of the strongmen until they threaten his authority or undermine the state.

J. SACCO 9·02

That moment seems to come in July when the government arrests Caco's chief of staff, who is sometimes blamed for certain excesses attributed to Caco. In response, Caco throws up barricades and takes hostages. Delalic lines up behind him. The stage is set for a confrontation between the government and two of its most powerful brigade commanders.

Only President Izetbegovic's personal intervention defuses the crisis, but Caco's and Delalic's zones now are essentially off limits to outside army officers.

According to 'Dani' journalist Vildana Selimbegovic—

THE HIGHER ECHELON WAS AFRAID TO GO THERE BECAUSE THEY RAN THE RISK OF BEING HUMILIATED BY CACO OR HIS TROOPS.

THEY DIDN'T REALLY HAVE THE GUTS TO GO THERE.

Caco in particular puts himself further and further above the law.

HE SNAPPED WHEN HE LOST HIS FINGERS.

"He was shooting a nitroglycerin gun. The gun malfunctioned, and the explosion took off three of his fingers.

"You can imagine what that means to a guitar player."

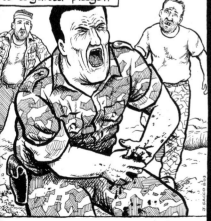

"Music was his whole life.

"He changed. That's beyond question...That must have affected his command abilities."

HE WAS TAKING PEOPLE FROM THE STREETS AND MAKING THEM DIG TRENCHES

BUT YOU WERE DOING THAT.

"But we were never putting guys in direct jeopardy. Some people were killed digging trenches for him. Whether it was by accident or design, I don't know."

And, increasingly, Sarajevans are whispering about horrible things said to be happening in Caco's area in a place called Kazani.

Government relations with Delalic haven't floundered entirely. In September, at the request of the high command, he sends some of his forces out of Sarajevo to aid troops fighting the Croats. (His soldiers are later implicated in a massacre of civilians in Grabovica.)

But the July barricades make clear that the one-time heroes of Sarajevo are all but beyond redemption. They have undermined the government's authority at home and embarrassed it abroad.

Since the beginning of the war, the government has managed to build up military units loyal to itself, and plans are underfoot to settle the question of the warlords once and for all.

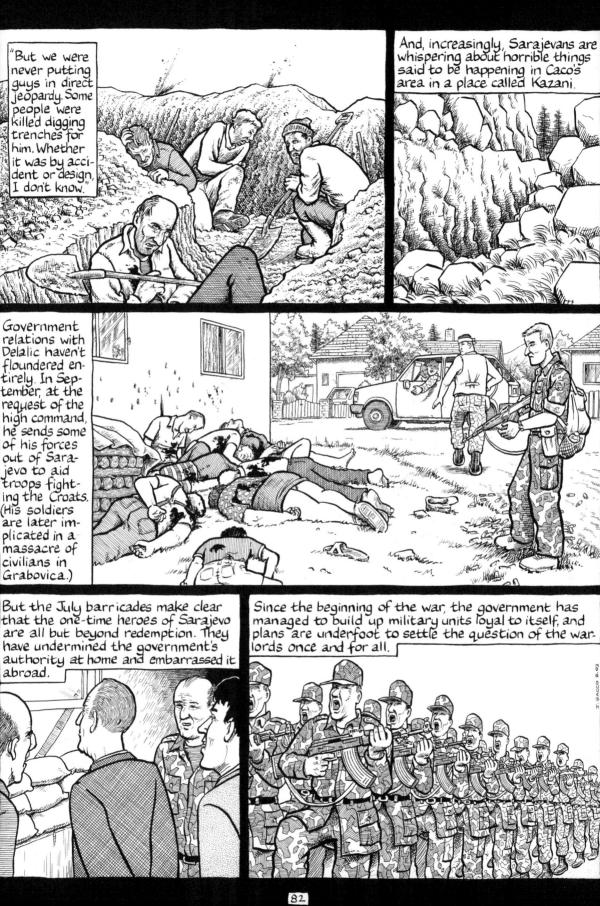

THE GOVERNMENT'S FIRST ACTION WAS TO GET RID OF CELO.

IF YOU REMOVE HIM, EVERYBODY ELSE WILL HEEL TO THE HIGHER COMMAND.

SO THEY TRIED TO KILL HIM.

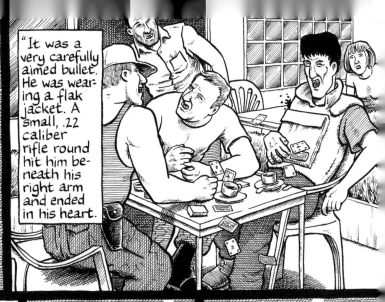

"It was a very carefully aimed bullet. He was wearing a flak jacket. A small, .22 caliber rifle round hit him beneath his right arm and ended in his heart.

"He lost four and a half liters of blood, and still he was strong enough to say,"

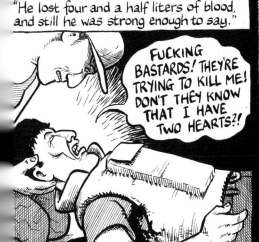

FUCKING BASTARDS! THEY'RE TRYING TO KILL ME! DON'T THEY KNOW THAT I HAVE TWO HEARTS?!

THEY SAID THAT THE BULLET CAME FROM ENEMY POSITIONS, WHICH WERE 1,200 METERS FROM THAT PLACE.

IF SOMEONE CAN EXPLAIN TO ME HOW A .22 CALIBER BULLET CAN TRAVEL 1,200 METERS, I WILL KISS HIS ASS IN WASHINGTON SQUARE AT WHATEVER TIME HE CHOOSES.

In fact, in 2001 Munir Alibabic, who in 1993 was Bosnia's intelligence services chief in Sarajevo, as well as a top police official, tells me he learned the attempted assassination—

—WAS DONE BY SEVA UNITS.

The Seva was a notorious paramilitary group established by the Interior Ministry.

A SMALL AMOUNT OF MONEY—WELL, NOT SMALL, BUT SMALL FOR CELO—CHANGED HANDS WITH A FRENCH COLONEL WHO WAS IN CHARGE OF AIRLIFTS TO AVIANO.

And so Celo is Medivac'd to Italy.

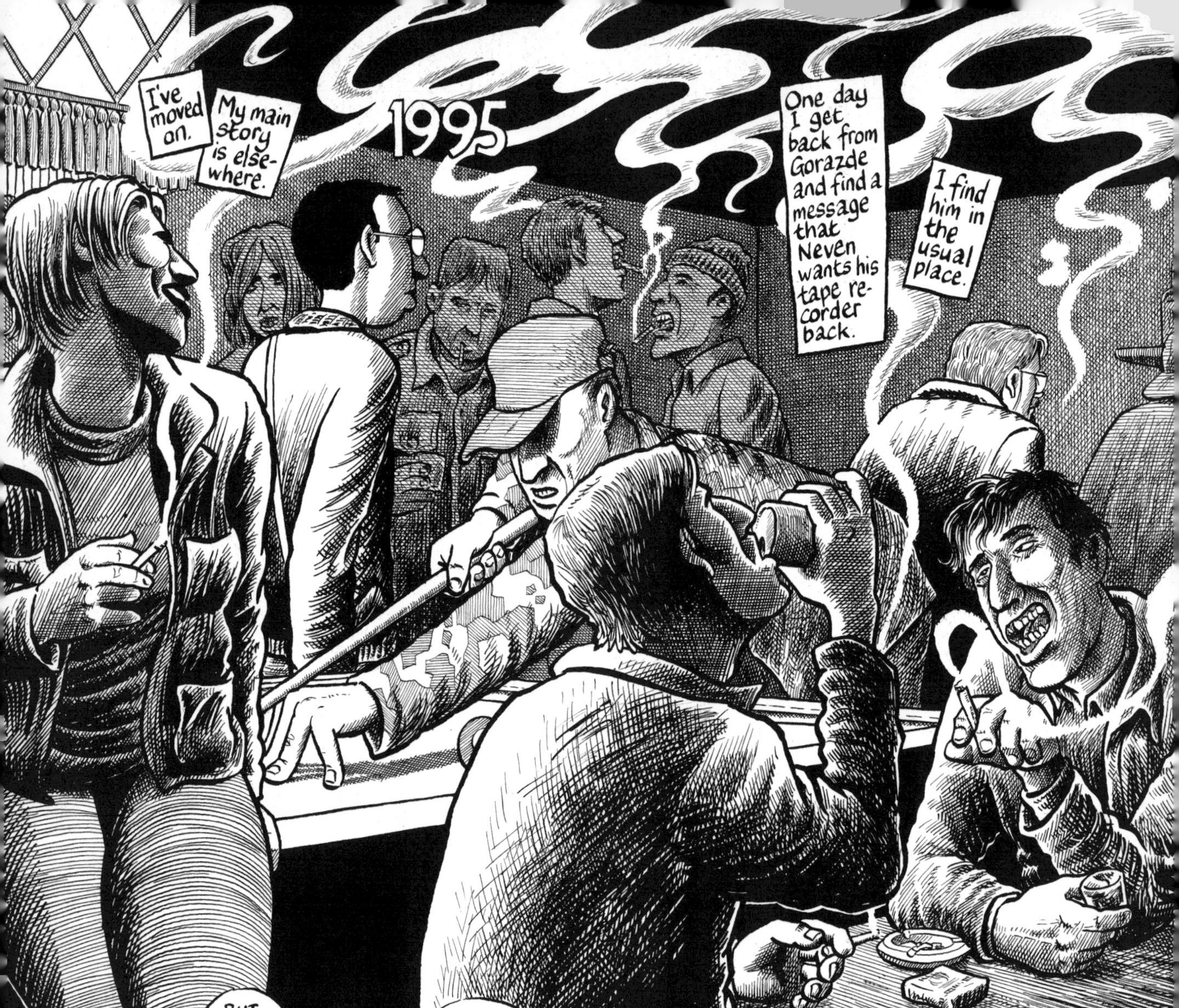

1995
I've moved on.
My main story is elsewhere.
One day I get back from Gorazde and find a message that Neven wants his tape recorder back.
I find him in the usual place.

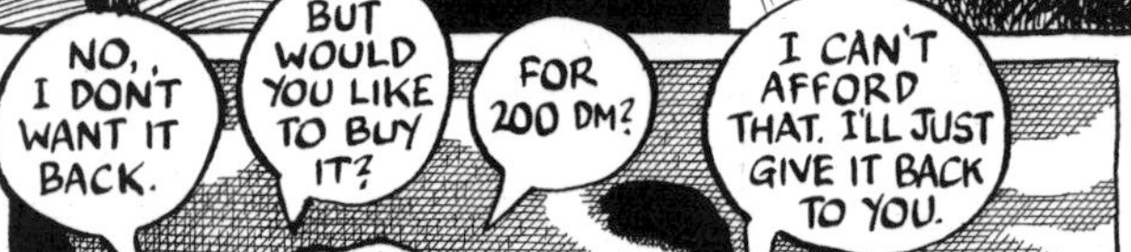

NO, I DON'T WANT IT BACK.
BUT WOULD YOU LIKE TO BUY IT?
FOR 200 DM?
I CAN'T AFFORD THAT. I'LL JUST GIVE IT BACK TO YOU.
NO, YOU CAN KEEP IT FOR NOW.

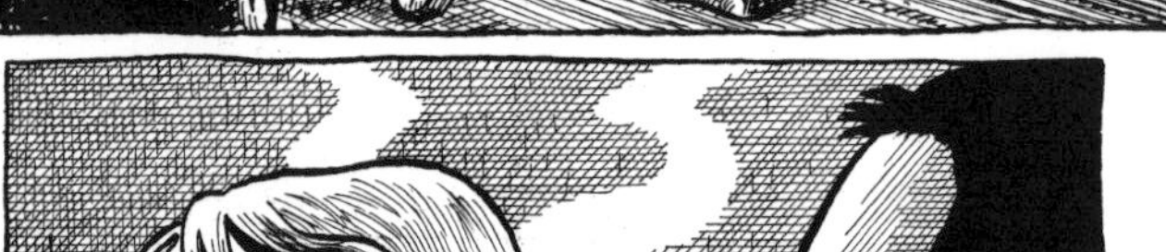

SO WHAT'S NEW?
I AM NO LONGER BANNED FROM THE HOTEL BOSNA.
I'VE BEEN WORKING FOR A JAPANESE JOURNALIST.
AFTER TWO DAYS' WORK I WAS ABLE TO PAY OFF SOME OF MY MAJOR DEBTS.
J. SACCO 11-02

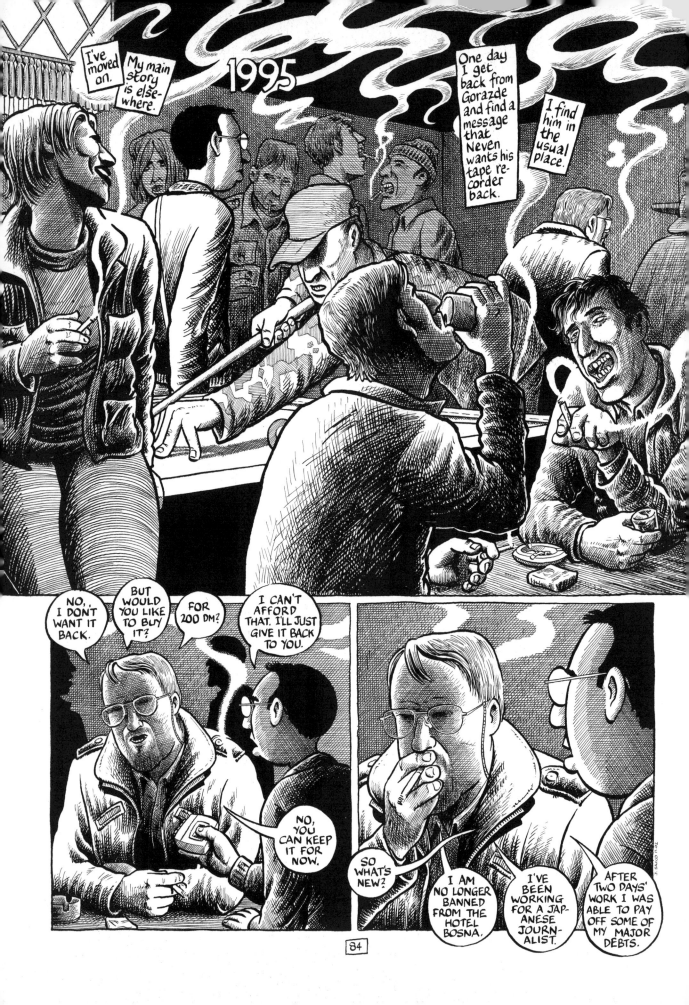

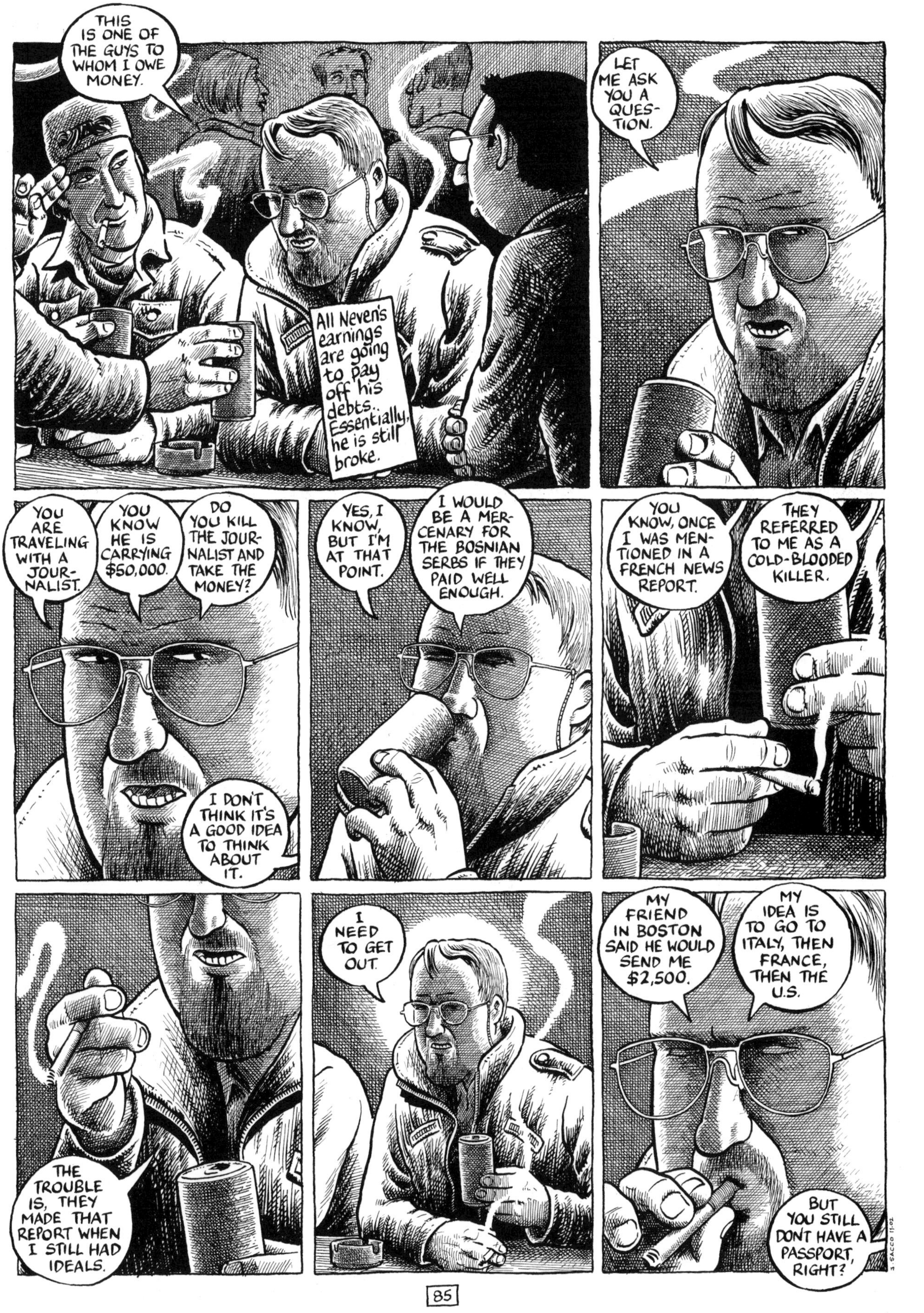

THIS IS ONE OF THE GUYS TO WHOM I OWE MONEY.
All Neven's earnings are going to pay off his debts. Essentially, he is still broke.
LET ME ASK YOU A QUESTION.
YOU ARE TRAVELING WITH A JOURNALIST.
YOU KNOW HE IS CARRYING $50,000.
DO YOU KILL THE JOURNALIST AND TAKE THE MONEY?
I DON'T THINK IT'S A GOOD IDEA TO THINK ABOUT IT.
YES, I KNOW, BUT I'M AT THAT POINT.
I WOULD BE A MERCENARY FOR THE BOSNIAN SERBS IF THEY PAID WELL ENOUGH.
YOU KNOW, ONCE I WAS MENTIONED IN A FRENCH NEWS REPORT.
THEY REFERRED TO ME AS A COLD-BLOODED KILLER.
THE TROUBLE IS, THEY MADE THAT REPORT WHEN I STILL HAD IDEALS.
I NEED TO GET OUT.
MY FRIEND IN BOSTON SAID HE WOULD SEND ME $2,500.
MY IDEA IS TO GO TO ITALY, THEN FRANCE, THEN THE U.S.
BUT YOU STILL DON'T HAVE A PASSPORT, RIGHT?
J. SACCO 11.02

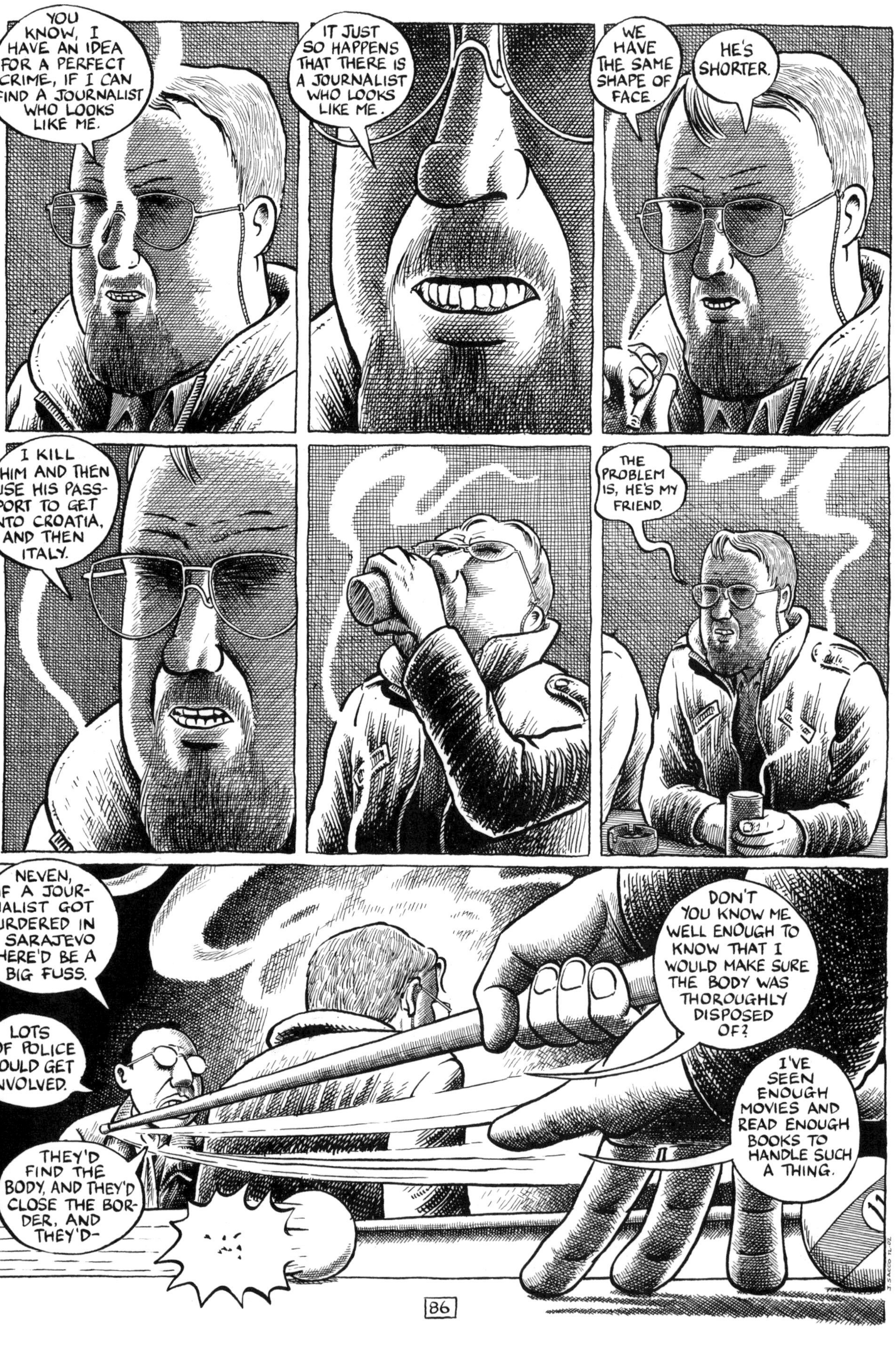
YOU KNOW, I HAVE AN IDEA FOR A PERFECT CRIME, IF I CAN FIND A JOURNALIST WHO LOOKS LIKE ME.
IT JUST SO HAPPENS THAT THERE IS A JOURNALIST WHO LOOKS LIKE ME.
WE HAVE THE SAME SHAPE OF FACE.
HE'S SHORTER.
I KILL HIM AND THEN USE HIS PASSPORT TO GET INTO CROATIA, AND THEN ITALY.
THE PROBLEM IS, HE'S MY FRIEND.
NEVEN, IF A JOURNALIST GOT MURDERED IN SARAJEVO THERE'D BE A BIG FUSS.
LOTS OF POLICE WOULD GET INVOLVED.
THEY'D FIND THE BODY, AND THEY'D CLOSE THE BORDER, AND THEY'D-
DON'T YOU KNOW ME WELL ENOUGH TO KNOW THAT I WOULD MAKE SURE THE BODY WAS THOROUGHLY DISPOSED OF?
I'VE SEEN ENOUGH MOVIES AND READ ENOUGH BOOKS TO HANDLE SUCH A THING.

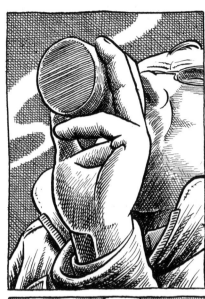

I NEED TO CALL MY FRIEND IN BOSTON AND HAVE HIM CALL ME BACK.

I NEED 20 MARKS TO MAKE THE CALL.

I'm not going to budge.

MAYBE I NEED ONLY 10 MARKS.

Well...

after all...

I am using his tape recorder.

ACTUALLY I DO NEED 20 MARKS.

I give him 20, but it's time to cut my losses.

Though I suppose I should pay for the drinks, too.

FOUR MARKS.

— says Neven, the pro.

87

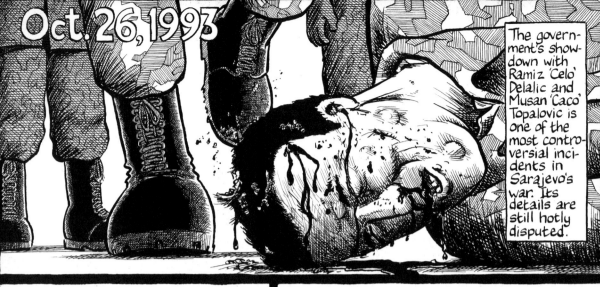

Oct. 26, 1993

The government's showdown with Ramiz 'Celo' Delalic and Musan 'Caco' Topalovic is one of the most controversial incidents in Sarajevo's war. Its details are still hotly disputed.

According to Alibabic, the intelligence boss and police chief at the time, "A plan was put together to get rid of the criminal individuals..."

I PARTICIPATED IN THE PLAN, WHICH INVOLVED A COMBINATION OF MILITARY FORCES AND POLICE OFFICERS.

THE PLAN WAS TO BESIEGE THEM, TO MAKE THE NOOSE TIGHTER, AND THEN TO ARREST THEM.

When he sees his headquarters has been surrounded by soldiers and police, Delalic takes hostages.

After a brief firefight and a call to President Izetbegovic, however, he gives himself up.

But in the operation against Caco's brigade, things go wrong. According to Alibabic, nine policemen are sent in to arrest Caco before the original plan can unfold.

THEY WERE CAPTURED AND LATER MUTILATED, THOSE NINE PEOPLE.

J. SACCO 12-02

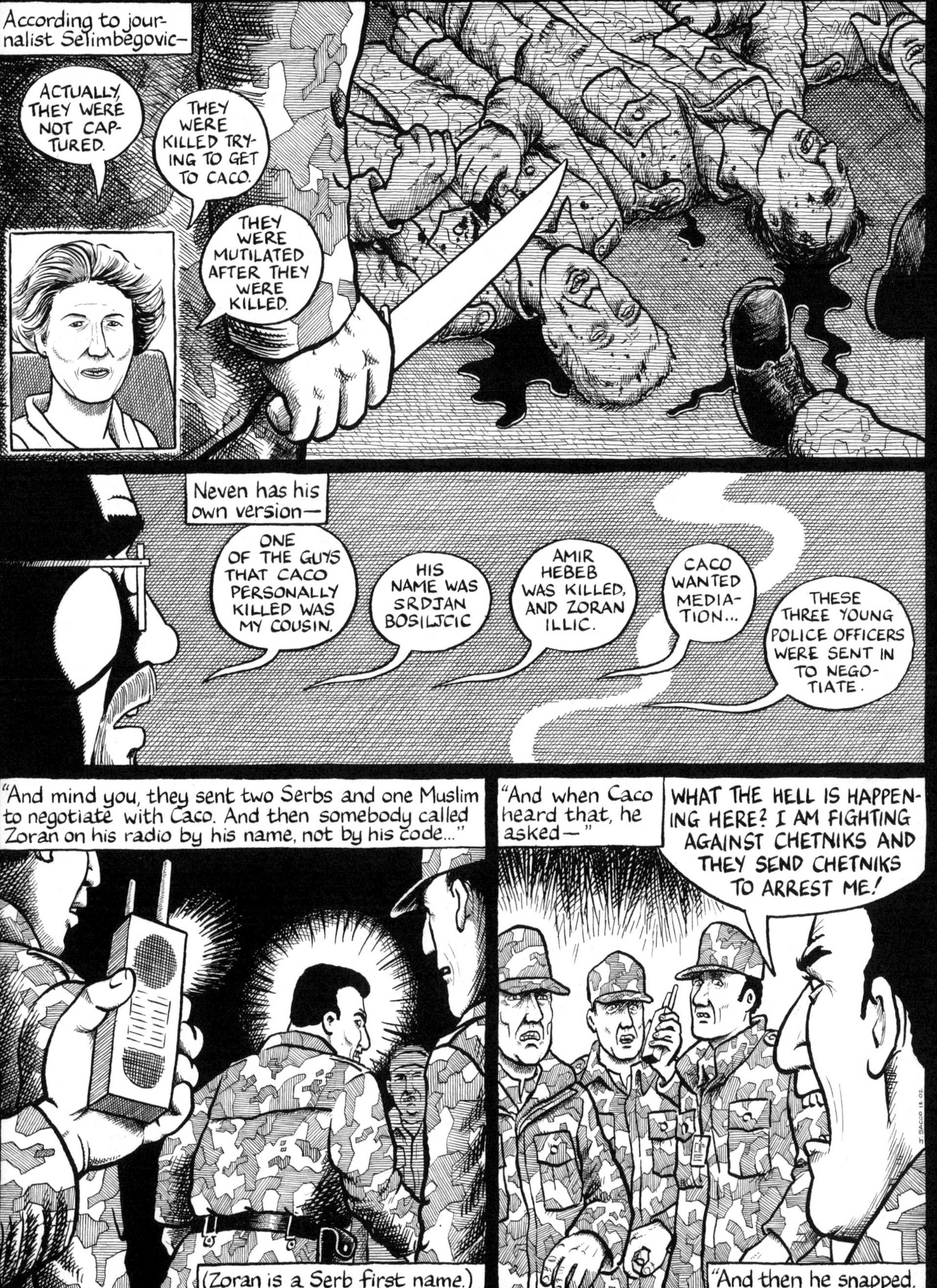
According to journalist Selimbegovic—
ACTUALLY, THEY WERE NOT CAPTURED.
THEY WERE KILLED TRYING TO GET TO CACO.
THEY WERE MUTILATED AFTER THEY WERE KILLED.
Neven has his own version—
ONE OF THE GUYS THAT CACO PERSONALLY KILLED WAS MY COUSIN.
HIS NAME WAS SRDJAN BOSILJCIC
AMIR HEBEB WAS KILLED, AND ZORAN ILLIC.
CACO WANTED MEDIATION...
THESE THREE YOUNG POLICE OFFICERS WERE SENT IN TO NEGOTIATE.
"And mind you, they sent two Serbs and one Muslim to negotiate with Caco. And then somebody called Zoran on his radio by his name, not by his code..."
(Zoran is a Serb first name.)
"And when Caco heard that, he asked—"
WHAT THE HELL IS HAPPENING HERE? I AM FIGHTING AGAINST CHETNIKS AND THEY SEND CHETNIKS TO ARREST ME!
"And then he snapped.

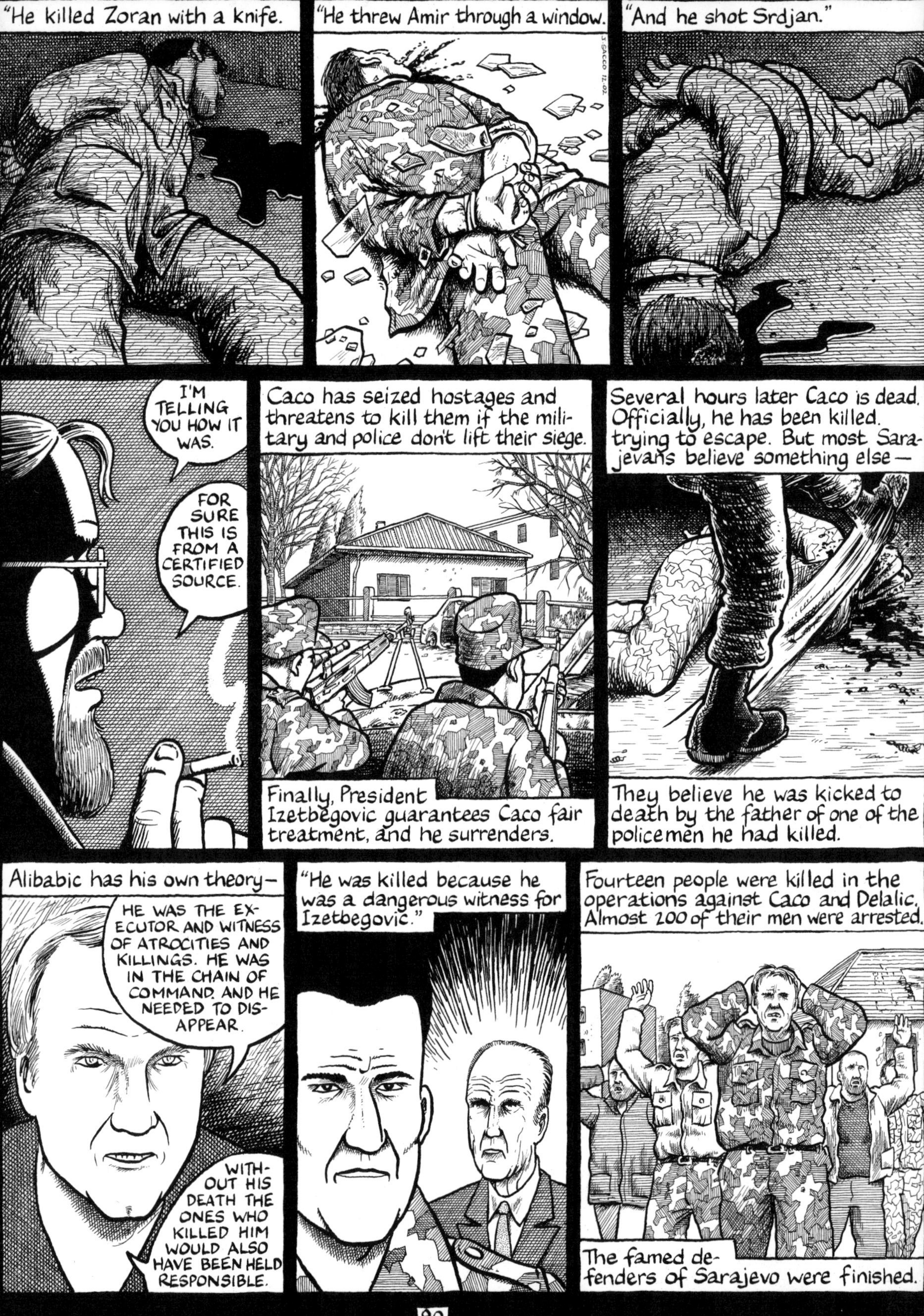
"He killed Zoran with a knife.
"He threw Amir through a window.
"And he shot Srdjan."
J. SACCO 12.02
I'M TELLING YOU HOW IT WAS.
FOR SURE THIS IS FROM A CERTIFIED SOURCE.
Caco has seized hostages and threatens to kill them if the military and police don't lift their siege.
Finally, President Izetbegovic guarantees Caco fair treatment, and he surrenders.
Several hours later Caco is dead. Officially, he has been killed trying to escape. But most Sarajevans believe something else—
They believe he was kicked to death by the father of one of the policemen he had killed.
Alibabic has his own theory—
HE WAS THE EXECUTOR AND WITNESS OF ATROCITIES AND KILLINGS. HE WAS IN THE CHAIN OF COMMAND AND HE NEEDED TO DISAPPEAR.
WITHOUT HIS DEATH THE ONES WHO KILLED HIM WOULD ALSO HAVE BEEN HELD RESPONSIBLE.
"He was killed because he was a dangerous witness for Izetbegovic."
Fourteen people were killed in the operations against Caco and Delalic. Almost 200 of their men were arrested.
The famed defenders of Sarajevo were finished.

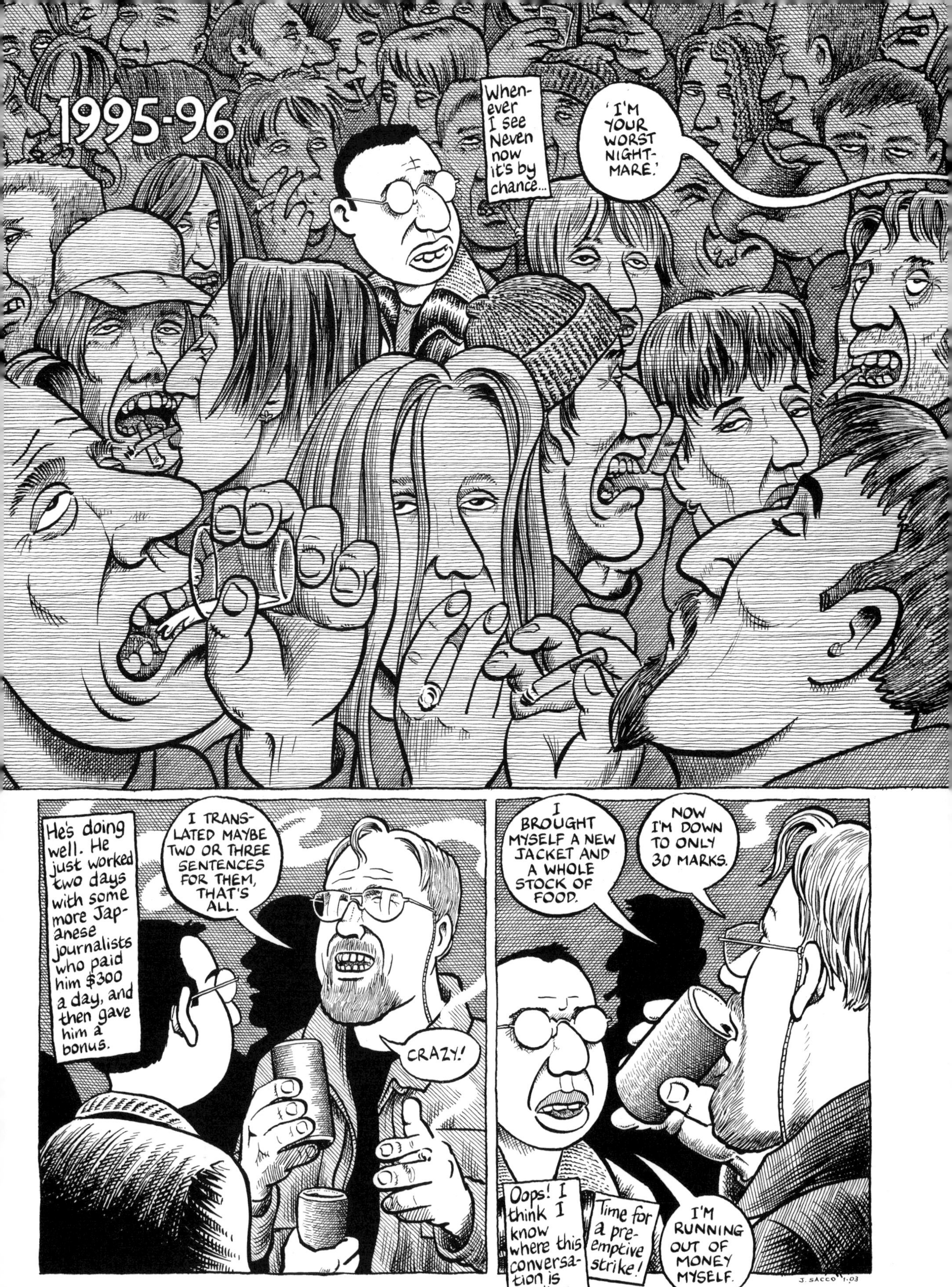
1995-96
Whenever I see Neven now it's by chance...
'I'M YOUR WORST NIGHTMARE.'
He's doing well. He just worked two days with some more Japanese journalists who paid him $300 a day, and then gave him a bonus.
I TRANSLATED MAYBE TWO OR THREE SENTENCES FOR THEM, THAT'S ALL.
CRAZY!
I BROUGHT MYSELF A NEW JACKET AND A WHOLE STOCK OF FOOD.
NOW I'M DOWN TO ONLY 30 MARKS.
Oops! I think I know where this conversation is heading...
Time for a preemptive strike!
I'M RUNNING OUT OF MONEY MYSELF.
J. SACCO 1.03

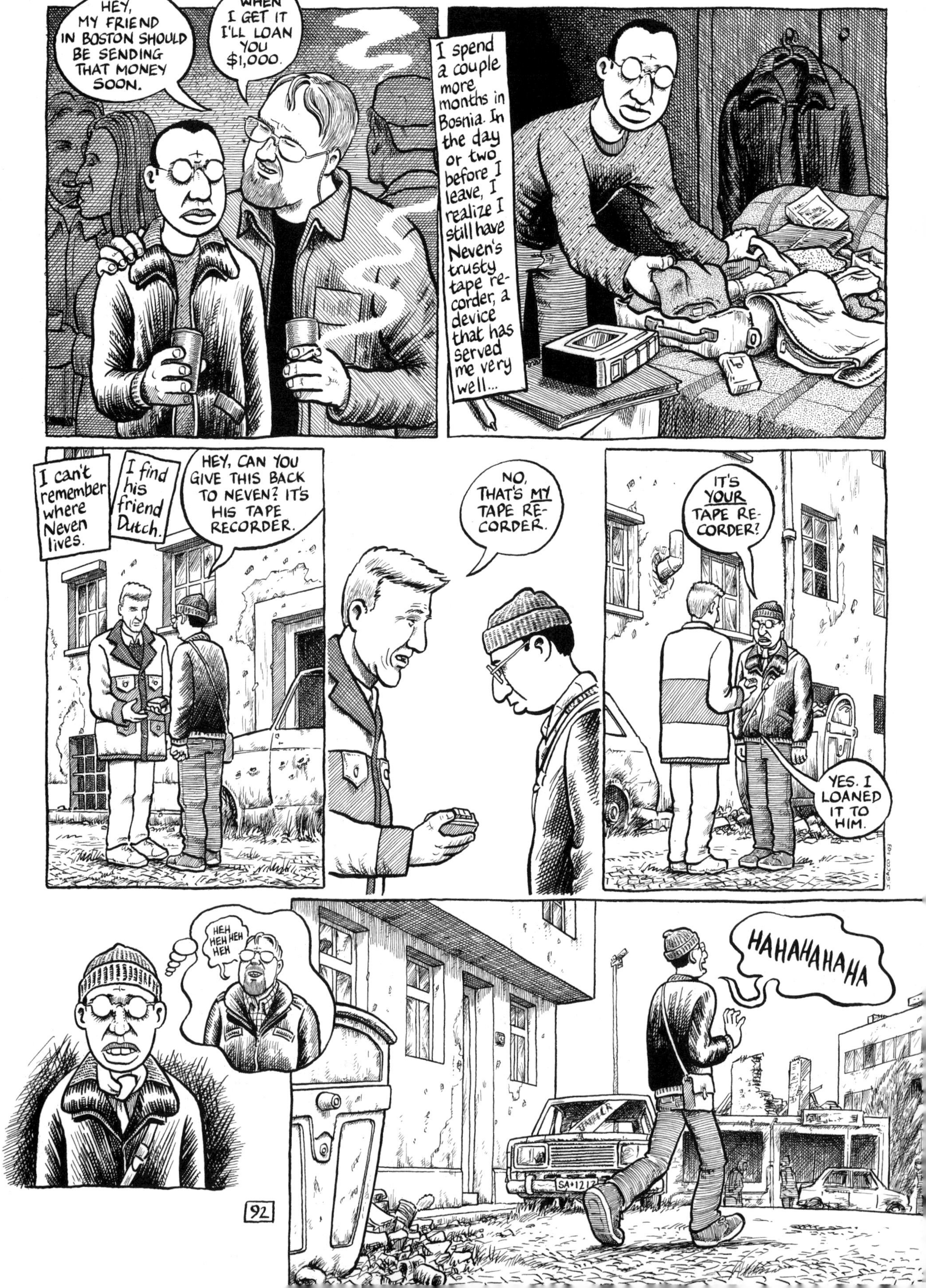
HEY, MY FRIEND IN BOSTON SHOULD BE SENDING THAT MONEY SOON.
WHEN I GET IT I'LL LOAN YOU $1,000.
I spend a couple more months in Bosnia. In the day or two before I leave, I realize I still have Neven's trusty tape re-corder, a device that has served me very well...
I can't remember where Neven lives.
I find his friend Dutch.
HEY, CAN YOU GIVE THIS BACK TO NEVEN? IT'S HIS TAPE RECORDER.
NO, THAT'S MY TAPE RE-CORDER.
IT'S YOUR TAPE RE-CORDER?
YES. I LOANED IT TO HIM.
HEH HEH HEH HEH
HAHAHAHAHA
SA•1212

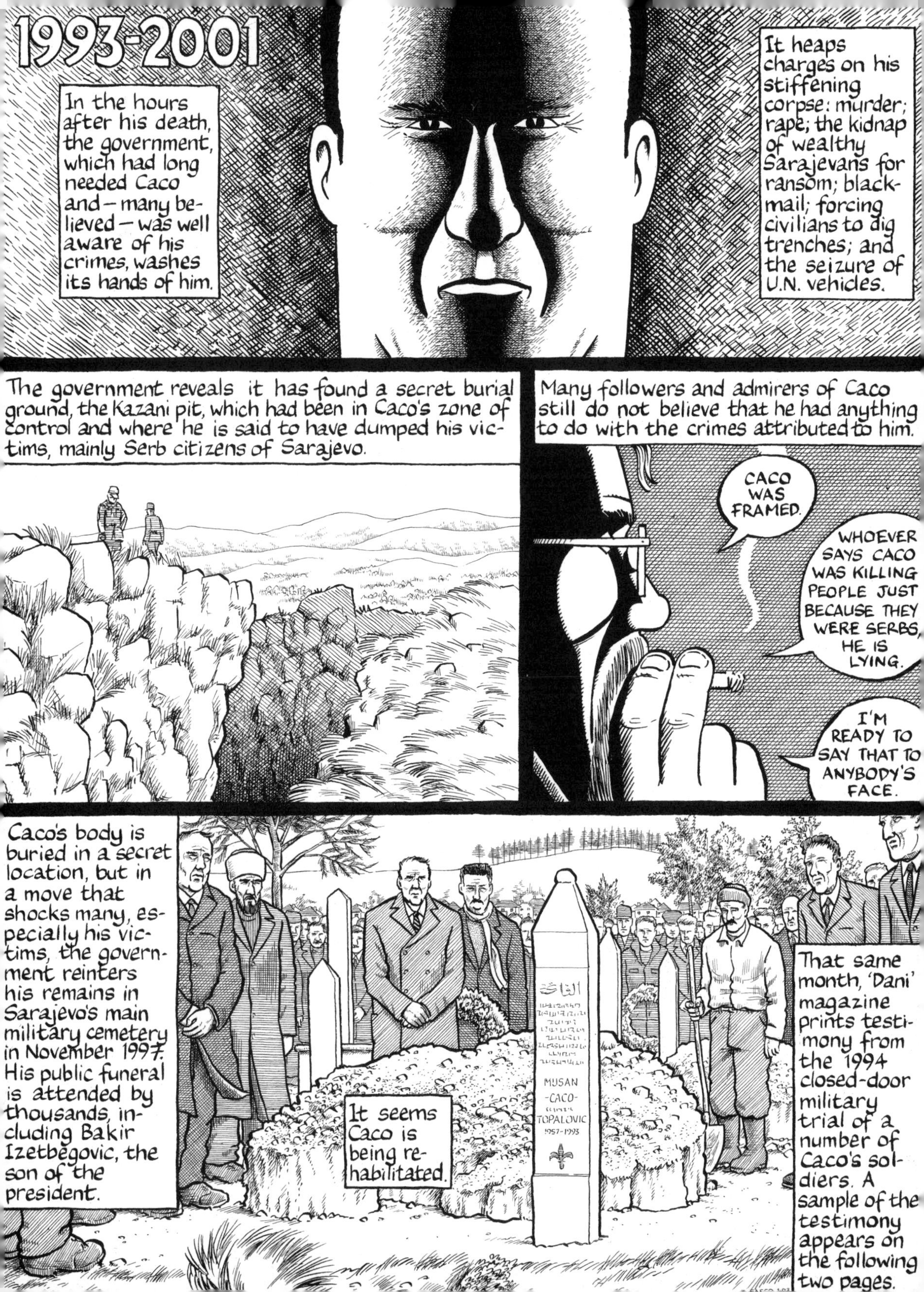
1993-2001
In the hours after his death, the government, which had long needed Caco and—many believed—was well aware of his crimes, washes its hands of him.
It heaps charges on his stiffening corpse: murder; rape; the kidnap of wealthy Sarajevans for ransom; blackmail; forcing civilians to dig trenches; and the seizure of U.N. vehicles.
The government reveals it has found a secret burial ground, the Kazani pit, which had been in Caco's zone of control and where he is said to have dumped his victims, mainly Serb citizens of Sarajevo.
Many followers and admirers of Caco still do not believe that he had anything to do with the crimes attributed to him.
CACO WAS FRAMED.
WHOEVER SAYS CACO WAS KILLING PEOPLE JUST BECAUSE THEY WERE SERBS, HE IS LYING.
I'M READY TO SAY THAT TO ANYBODY'S FACE.
Caco's body is buried in a secret location, but in a move that shocks many, especially his victims, the government reinters his remains in Sarajevo's main military cemetery in November 1997. His public funeral is attended by thousands, including Bakir Izetbegovic, the son of the president.
MUSAN -CACO- TOPALOVIC 1957-1993
It seems Caco is being rehabilitated.
That same month, 'Dani' magazine prints testimony from the 1994 closed-door military trial of a number of Caco's soldiers. A sample of the testimony appears on the following two pages.

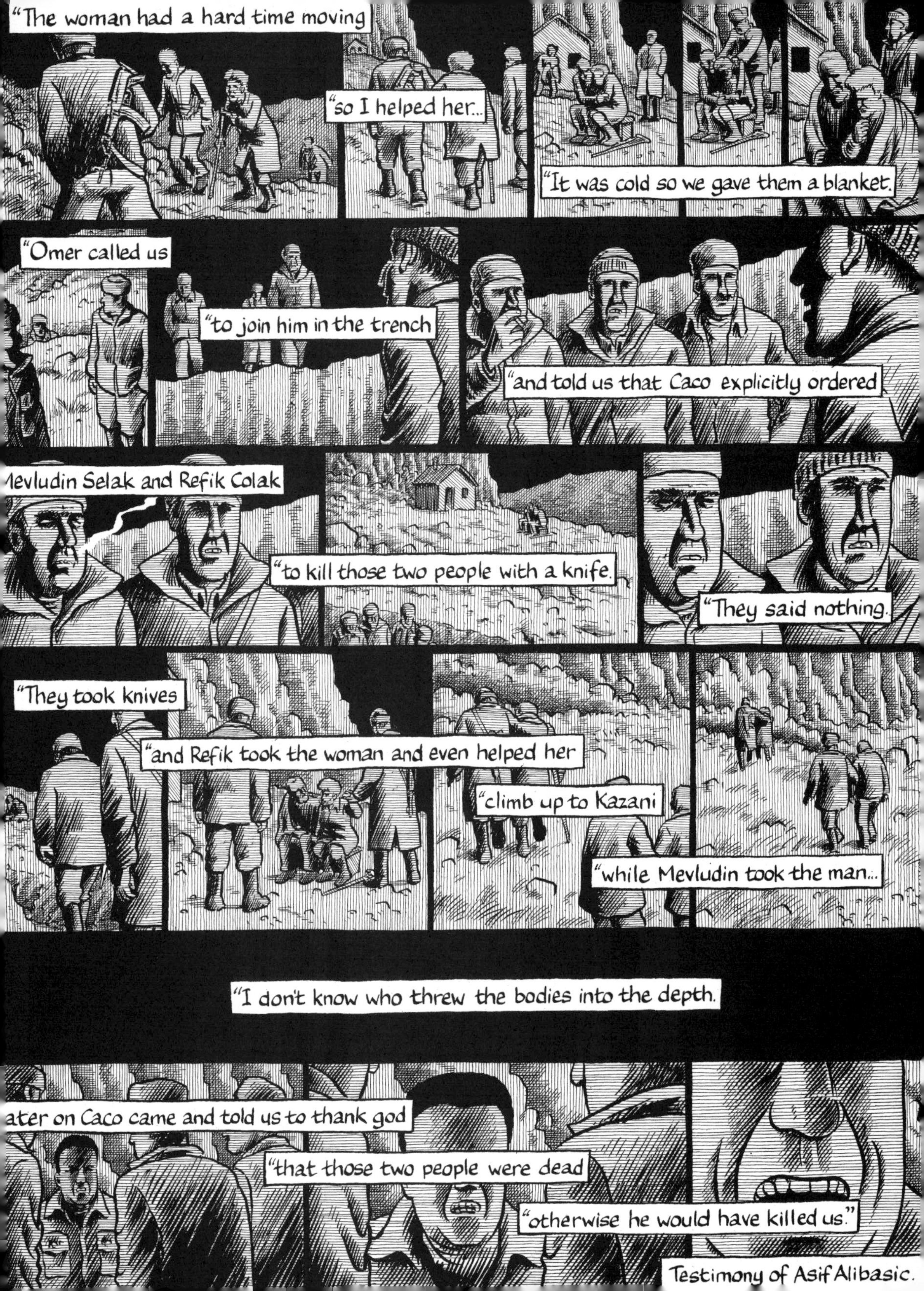
"The woman had a hard time moving
"so I helped her...
"It was cold so we gave them a blanket.
"Omer called us
"to join him in the trench
"and told us that Caco explicitly ordered
Mevludin Selak and Refik Colak
"to kill those two people with a knife.
"They said nothing.
"They took knives
"and Refik took the woman and even helped her
"climb up to Kazani
"while Mevludin took the man...
"I don't know who threw the bodies into the depth.
ater on Caco came and told us to thank god
"that those two people were dead
"otherwise he would have killed us."
Testimony of Asif Alibasic.

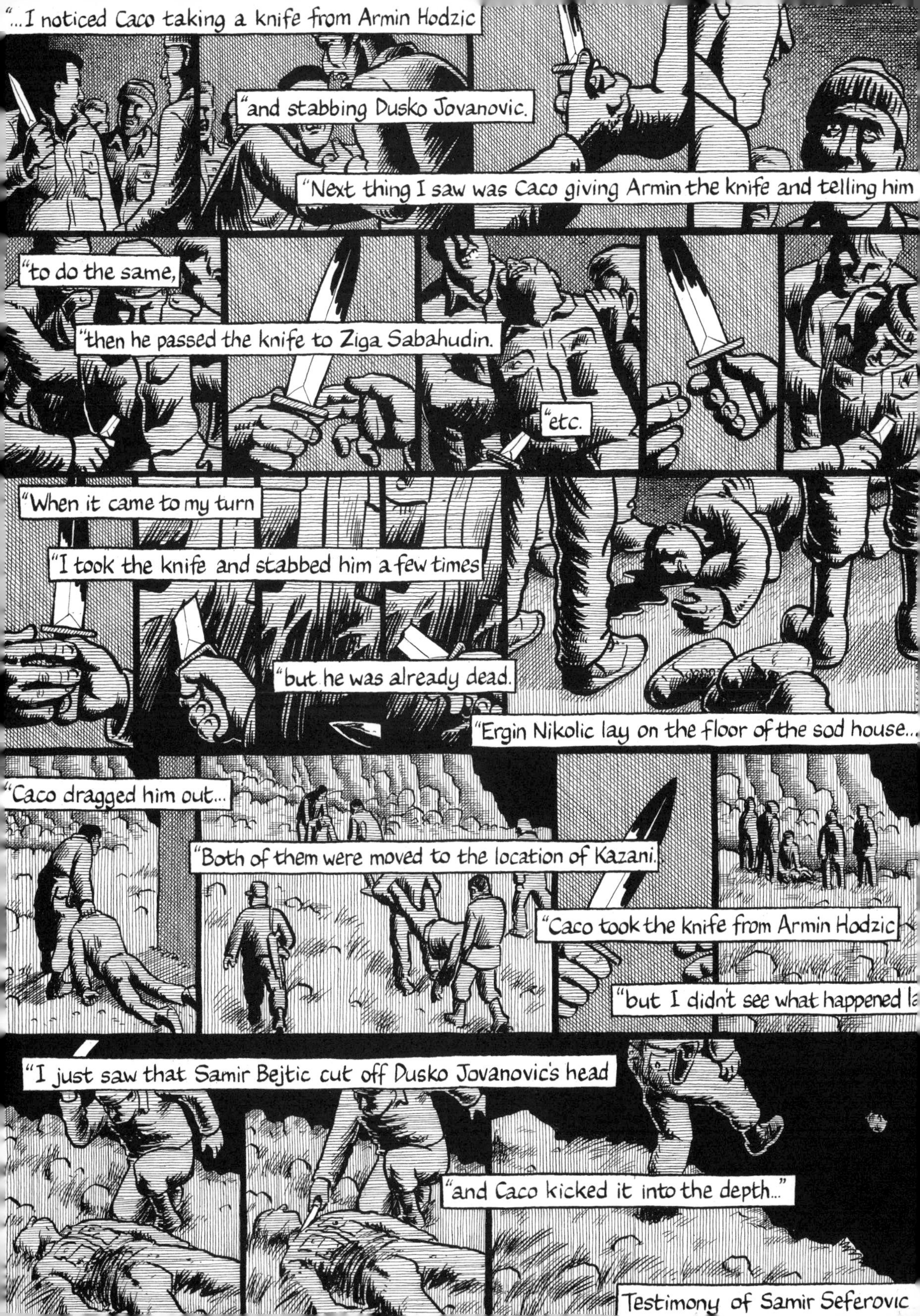
"...I noticed Caco taking a knife from Armin Hodzic
"and stabbing Dusko Jovanovic.
"Next thing I saw was Caco giving Armin the knife and telling him
"to do the same,
"then he passed the knife to Ziga Sabahudin.
"etc.
"When it came to my turn
"I took the knife and stabbed him a few times
"but he was already dead.
"Ergin Nikolic lay on the floor of the sod house...
"Caco dragged him out...
"Both of them were moved to the location of Kazani.
"Caco took the knife from Armin Hodzic
"but I didn't see what happened la
"I just saw that Samir Bejtic cut off Dusko Jovanovic's head
"and Caco kicked it into the depth..."
Testimony of Samir Seferovic

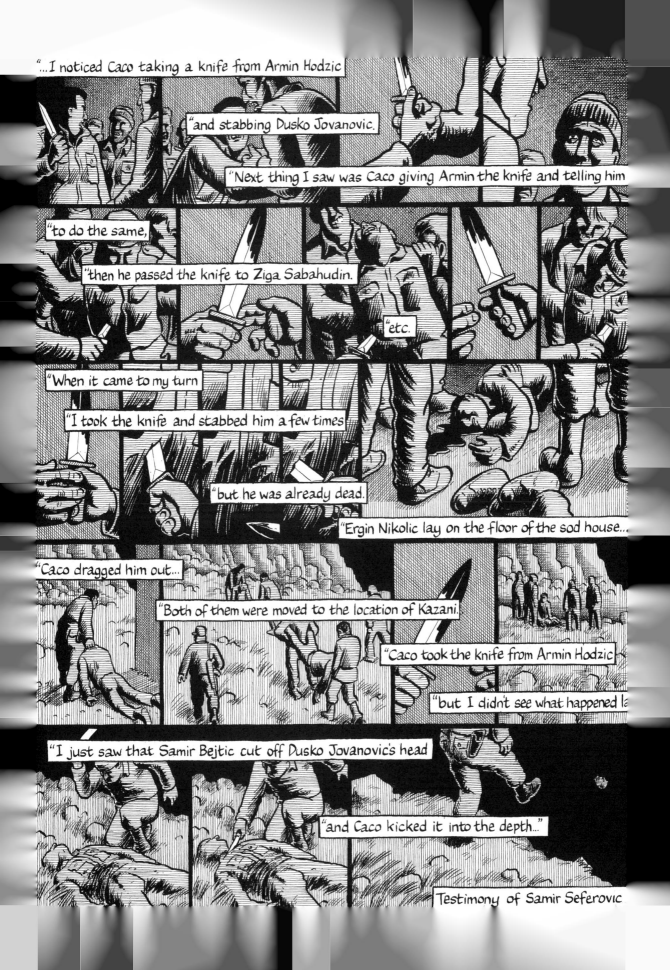

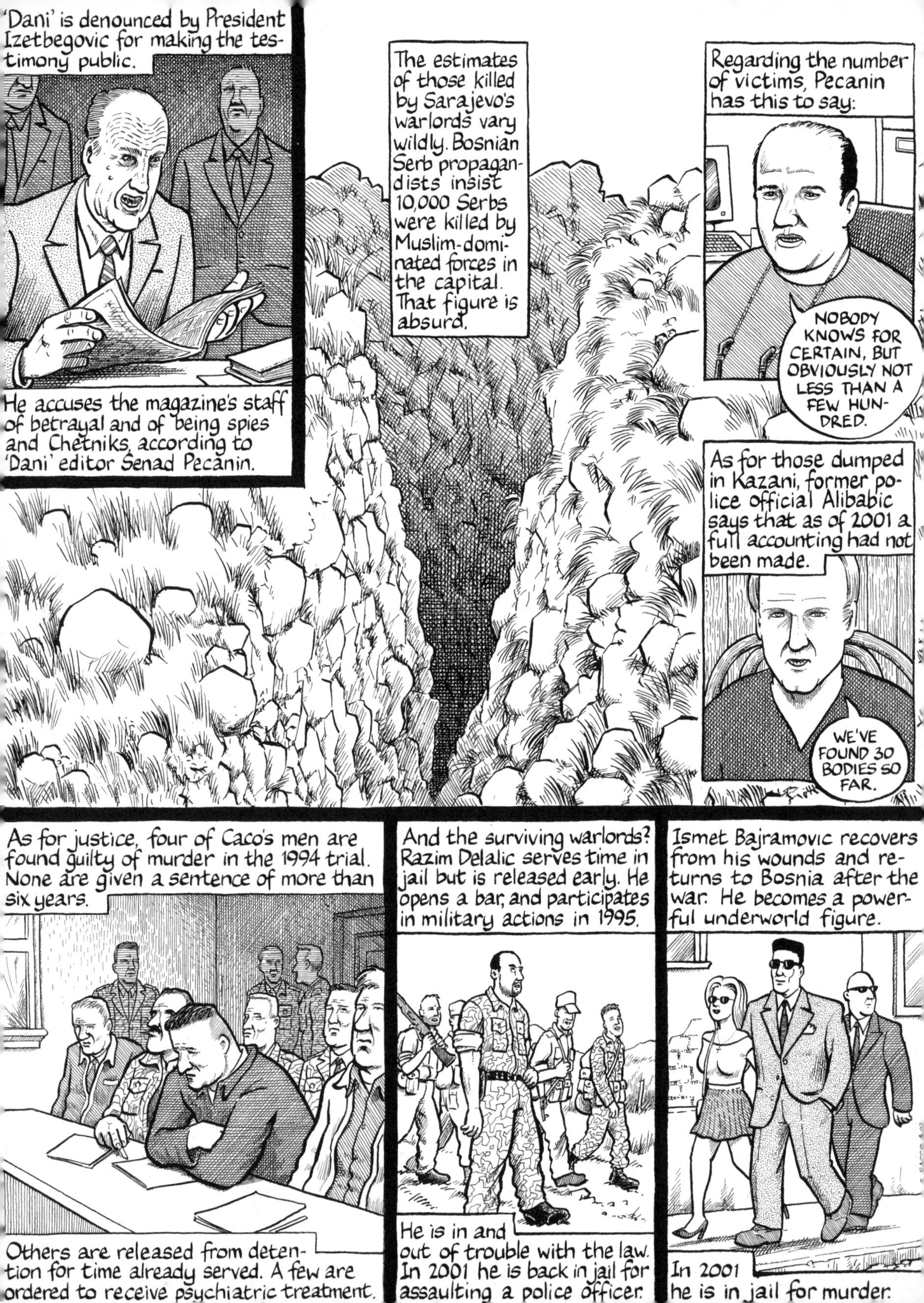
'Dani' is denounced by President Izetbegovic for making the testimony public.
He accuses the magazine's staff of betrayal and of being spies and Chetniks, according to 'Dani' editor Šenad Pecanin.
The estimates of those killed by Sarajevo's warlords vary wildly. Bosnian Serb propagandists insist 10,000 Serbs were killed by Muslim-dominated forces in the capital. That figure is absurd.
Regarding the number of victims, Pecanin has this to say:
NOBODY KNOWS FOR CERTAIN, BUT OBVIOUSLY NOT LESS THAN A FEW HUNDRED.
As for those dumped in Kazani, former police official Alibabic says that as of 2001 a full accounting had not been made.
WE'VE FOUND 30 BODIES SO FAR.
As for justice, four of Caco's men are found guilty of murder in the 1994 trial. None are given a sentence of more than six years.
Others are released from detention for time already served. A few are ordered to receive psychiatric treatment.
And the surviving warlords? Razim Delalic serves time in jail but is released early. He opens a bar, and participates in military actions in 1995.
He is in and out of trouble with the law. In 2001 he is back in jail for assaulting a police officer.
Ismet Bajramovic recovers from his wounds and returns to Bosnia after the war. He becomes a powerful underworld figure.
In 2001 he is in jail for murder.

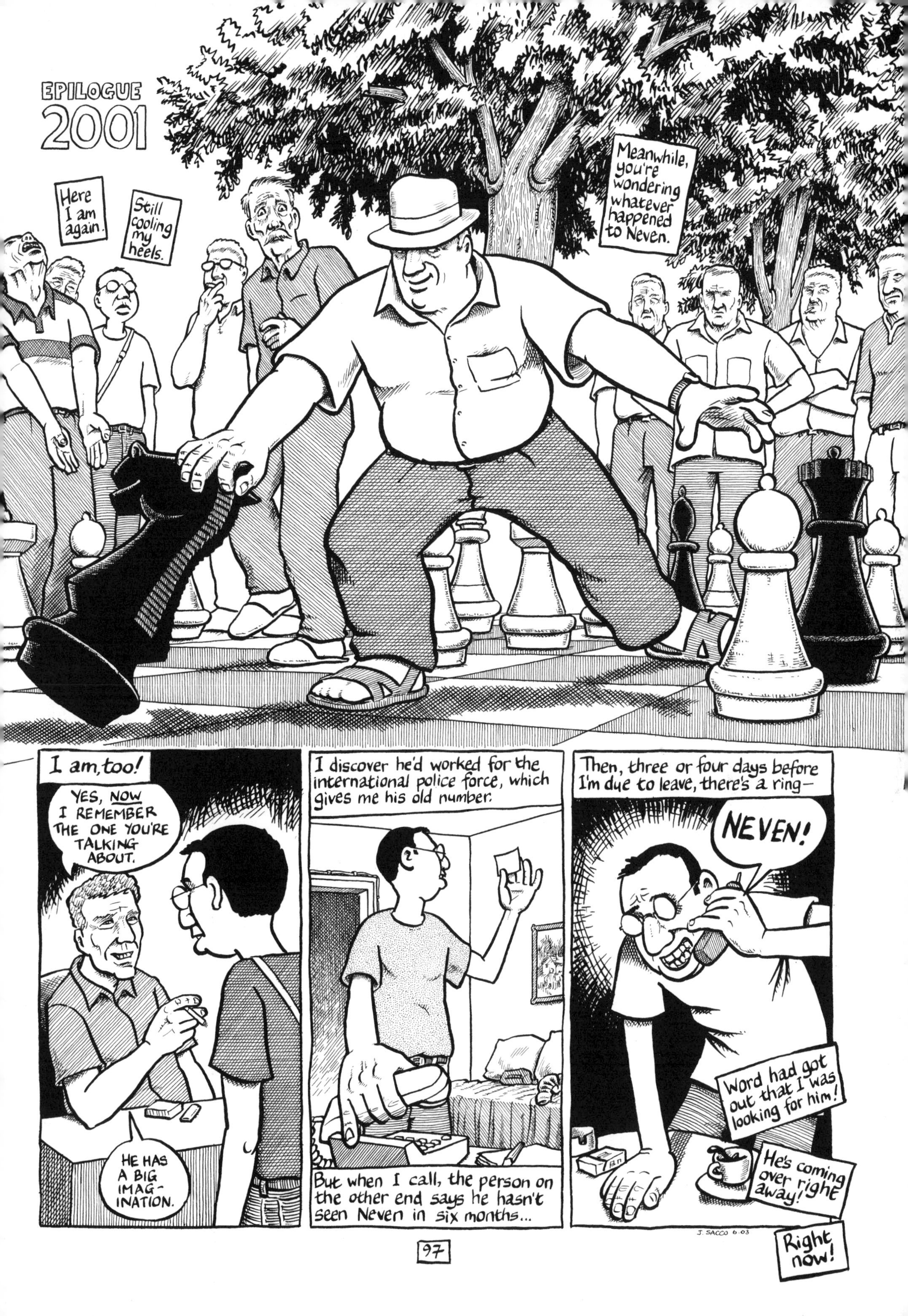

EPILOGUE
2001
Here I am again.
Still cooling my heels.
Meanwhile, you're wondering whatever happened to Neven.
I am, too!
YES, NOW I REMEMBER THE ONE YOU'RE TALKING ABOUT.
HE HAS A BIG IMAG-INATION.
I discover he'd worked for the international police force, which gives me his old number.
But when I call, the person on the other end says he hasn't seen Neven in six months...
Then, three or four days before I'm due to leave, there's a ring—
NEVEN!
Word had got out that I was looking for him!
He's coming over right away!
Right now!
J. SACCO 6.03

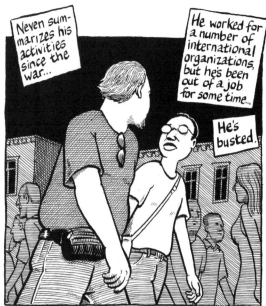

Neven summarizes his activities since the war...

He worked for a number of international organizations, but he's been out of a job for some time...

He's busted.

I explain what I'm doing in Sarajevo.

I tell him I need his help.

I need a fixer.

$100 PER DAY.

This is very good news for Neven.

He insists on paying for my beer.

Okay! Gotta go!

I have another engagement with old friends from Gorazde.

Neven has learned that my old friends are young ladies.

I'VE GOT NOTHING ELSE TO DO THIS EVENING.

J. SACCO 7.03

Soon we're embarking on a double date at a nearby ice cream parlor.

Lejla talks to me about her fondness for Nietzsche...

while Neven chats up Alma with some choice war stories.

WE ARE TALKING ABOUT SOME ACTIONS.

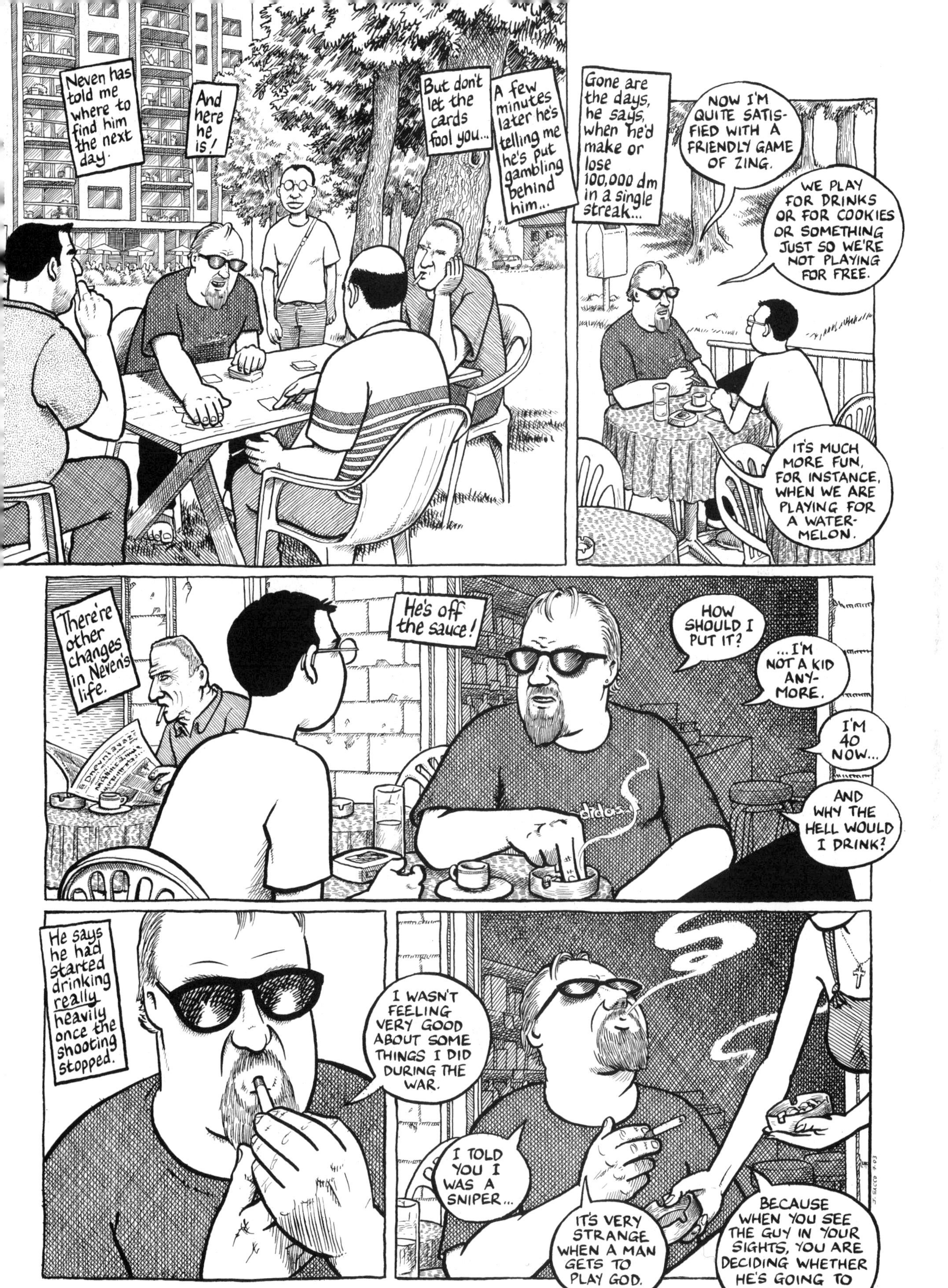

Neven has told me where to find him the next day.
And here he is!
But don't let the cards fool you...
A few minutes later he's telling me he's put gambling behind him...
Gone are the days, he says, when he'd make or lose 100,000 dm in a single streak...
NOW I'M QUITE SATISFIED WITH A FRIENDLY GAME OF ZING.
WE PLAY FOR DRINKS OR FOR COOKIES OR SOMETHING JUST SO WE'RE NOT PLAYING FOR FREE.
IT'S MUCH MORE FUN, FOR INSTANCE, WHEN WE ARE PLAYING FOR A WATER-MELON.
There're other changes in Neven's life.
He's off the sauce!
HOW SHOULD I PUT IT?
...I'M NOT A KID ANY-MORE.
I'M 40 NOW...
AND WHY THE HELL WOULD I DRINK?
He says he had started drinking really heavily once the shooting stopped.
I WASN'T FEELING VERY GOOD ABOUT SOME THINGS I DID DURING THE WAR.
I TOLD YOU I WAS A SNIPER...
IT'S VERY STRANGE WHEN A MAN GETS TO PLAY GOD.
BECAUSE WHEN YOU SEE THE GUY IN YOUR SIGHTS, YOU ARE DECIDING WHETHER HE'S GOING TO LIVE OR DIE.

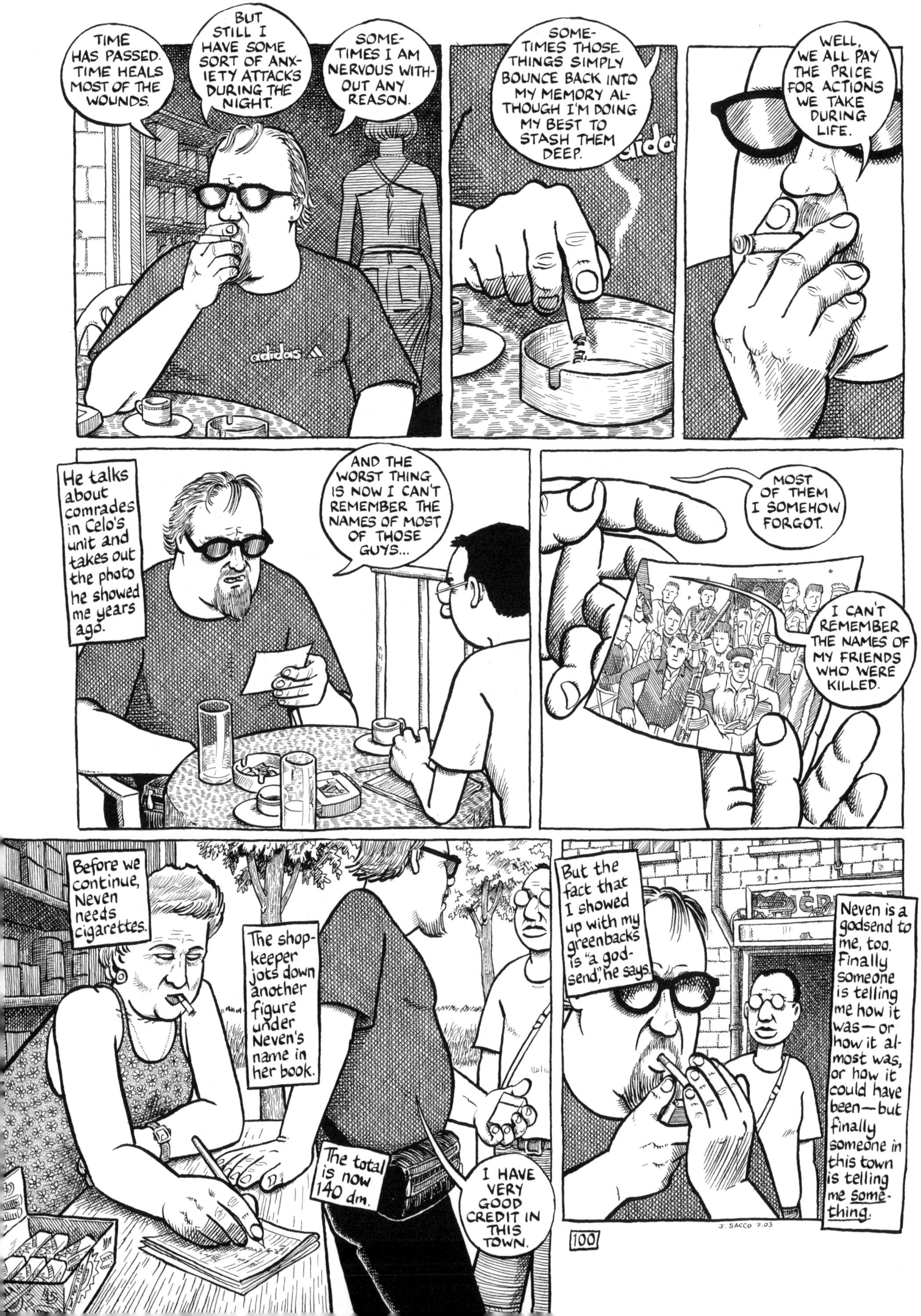

TIME HAS PASSED. TIME HEALS MOST OF THE WOUNDS.
BUT STILL I HAVE SOME SORT OF ANXIETY ATTACKS DURING THE NIGHT.
SOMETIMES I AM NERVOUS WITHOUT ANY REASON.
adidas
SOMETIMES THOSE THINGS SIMPLY BOUNCE BACK INTO MY MEMORY ALTHOUGH I'M DOING MY BEST TO STASH THEM DEEP.
WELL, WE ALL PAY THE PRICE FOR ACTIONS WE TAKE DURING LIFE.
He talks about comrades in Celo's unit and takes out the photo he showed me years ago.
AND THE WORST THING IS NOW I CAN'T REMEMBER THE NAMES OF MOST OF THOSE GUYS...
MOST OF THEM I SOMEHOW FORGOT.
I CAN'T REMEMBER THE NAMES OF MY FRIENDS WHO WERE KILLED.
Before we continue, Neven needs cigarettes.
The shopkeeper jots down another figure under Neven's name in her book.
The total is now 140 dm.
I HAVE VERY GOOD CREDIT IN THIS TOWN.
But the fact that I showed up with my greenbacks is "a godsend," he says.
Neven is a godsend to me, too. Finally someone is telling me how it was—or how it almost was, or how it could have been—but finally someone in this town is telling me something.
J. SACCO 7.03

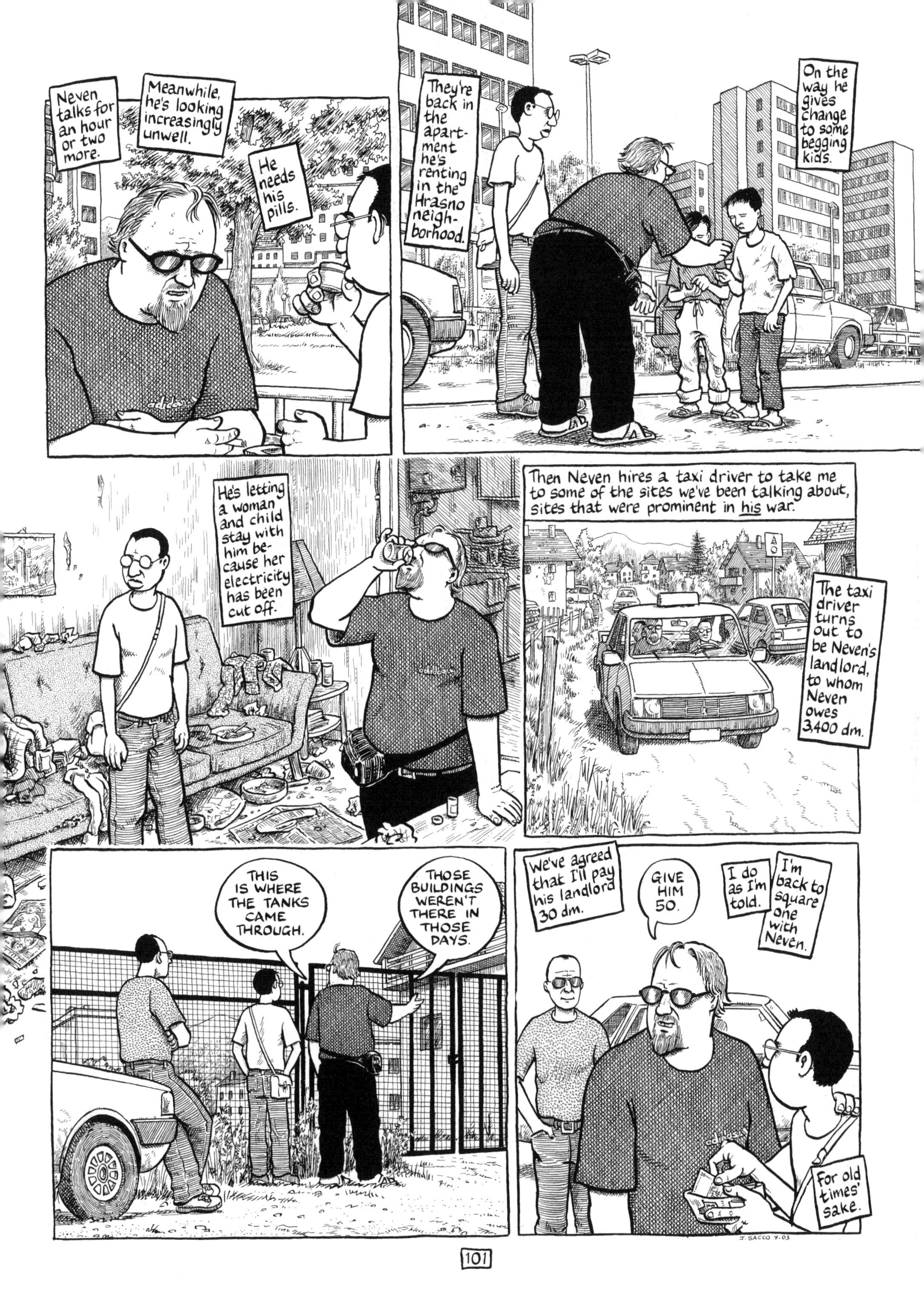

Neven talks for an hour or two more.
Meanwhile, he's looking increasingly unwell.
He needs his pills.
They're back in the apartment he's renting in the Hrasno neighborhood.
On the way he gives change to some begging kids.
He's letting a woman and child stay with him because her electricity has been cut off.
Then Neven hires a taxi driver to take me to some of the sites we've been talking about, sites that were prominent in his war.
The taxi driver turns out to be Neven's landlord, to whom Neven owes 3,400 dm.
THIS IS WHERE THE TANKS CAME THROUGH.
THOSE BUILDINGS WEREN'T THERE IN THOSE DAYS.
We've agreed that I'll pay his landlord 30 dm.
GIVE HIM 50.
I do as I'm told.
I'm back to square one with Neven.
For old times' sake.
J. SACCO 7.03

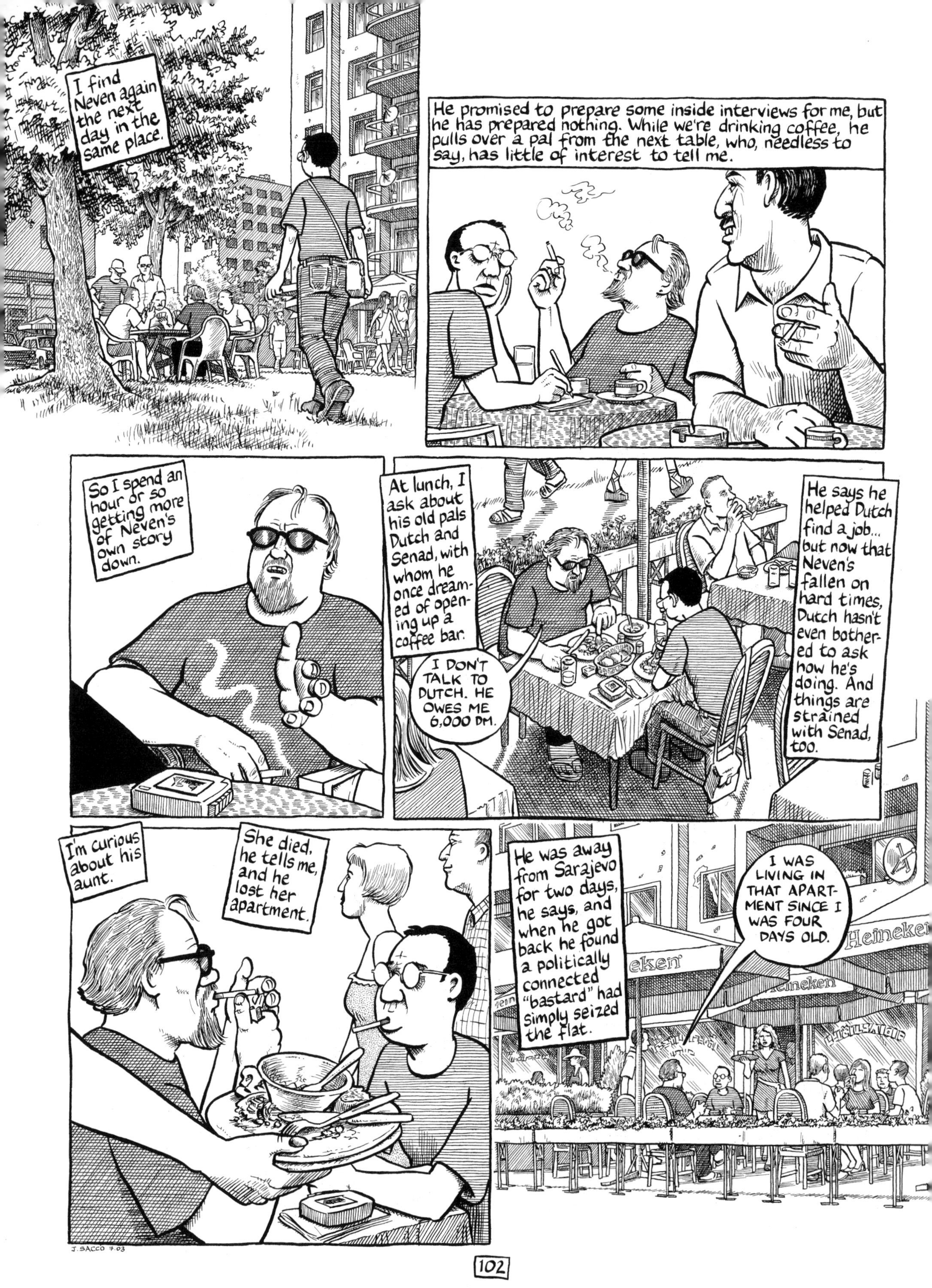
I find Neven again the next day in the same place.
He promised to prepare some inside interviews for me, but he has prepared nothing. While we're drinking coffee, he pulls over a pal from the next table, who, needless to say, has little of interest to tell me.
So I spend an hour or so getting more of Neven's own story down.
At lunch, I ask about his old pals Dutch and Senad, with whom he once dreamed of opening up a coffee bar.
I DON'T TALK TO DUTCH. HE OWES ME 6,000 DM.
He says he helped Dutch find a job... but now that Neven's fallen on hard times, Dutch hasn't even bothered to ask how he's doing. And things are strained with Senad, too.
I'm curious about his aunt.
She died, he tells me, and he lost her apartment.
He was away from Sarajevo for two days, he says, and when he got back he found a politically connected "bastard" had simply seized the flat.
I WAS LIVING IN THAT APARTMENT SINCE I WAS FOUR DAYS OLD.
Heineken
J. SACCO 7.03

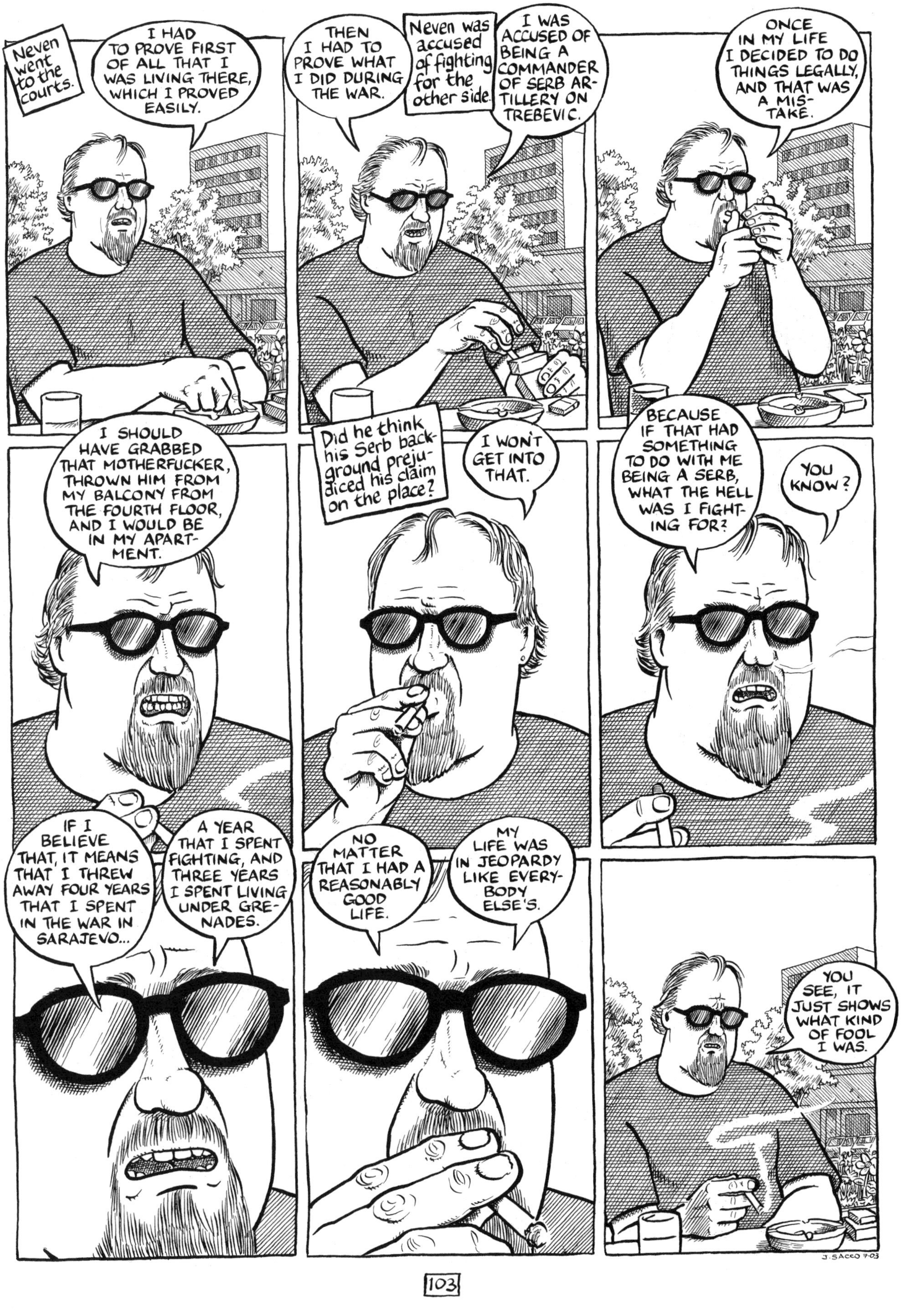

Neven went to the courts.
I HAD TO PROVE FIRST OF ALL THAT I WAS LIVING THERE, WHICH I PROVED EASILY.
THEN I HAD TO PROVE WHAT I DID DURING THE WAR.
Neven was accused of fighting for the other side.
I WAS ACCUSED OF BEING A COMMANDER OF SERB ARTILLERY ON TREBEVIC.
ONCE IN MY LIFE I DECIDED TO DO THINGS LEGALLY, AND THAT WAS A MISTAKE.
I SHOULD HAVE GRABBED THAT MOTHERFUCKER, THROWN HIM FROM MY BALCONY FROM THE FOURTH FLOOR, AND I WOULD BE IN MY APARTMENT.
Did he think his Serb background prejudiced his claim on the place?
I WON'T GET INTO THAT.
BECAUSE IF THAT HAD SOMETHING TO DO WITH ME BEING A SERB, WHAT THE HELL WAS I FIGHTING FOR?
YOU KNOW?
IF I BELIEVE THAT, IT MEANS THAT I THREW AWAY FOUR YEARS THAT I SPENT IN THE WAR IN SARAJEVO...
A YEAR THAT I SPENT FIGHTING, AND THREE YEARS I SPENT LIVING UNDER GRENADES.
NO MATTER THAT I HAD A REASONABLY GOOD LIFE.
MY LIFE WAS IN JEOPARDY LIKE EVERYBODY ELSE'S.
YOU SEE, IT JUST SHOWS WHAT KIND OF FOOL I WAS.
J. SACCO 7-03

I LOVE THIS CITY, BUT IT'S KILLING ME.

AS I TOLD YOU, ONE WAY OR ANOTHER, I AM GOING TO GET MY ASS OUT OF HERE.

AS SOON AS POSSIBLE.

He's not looking too well.

He needs to take his pill.

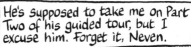

He's supposed to take me on Part Two of his guided tour, but I excuse him. Forget it, Neven.

Goodbye. Take care of yourself.

He walks back to where his pals are playing cards.

And I go see someone who knew Neven well, someone whose opinion I trust.

J. SACCO 8·03

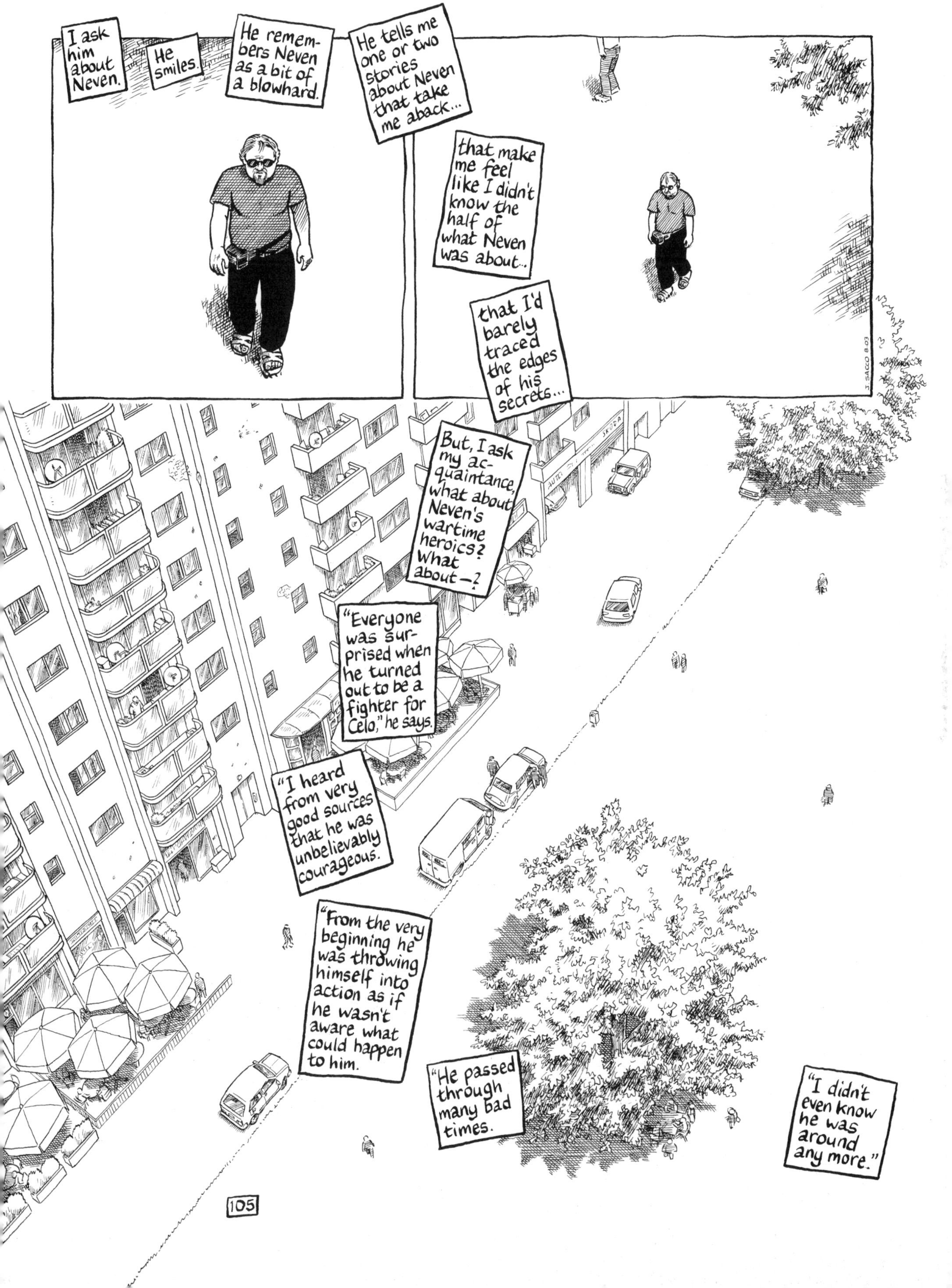

I ask him about Neven.
He smiles.
He remembers Neven as a bit of a blowhard.
He tells me one or two stories about Neven that take me aback...
that make me feel like I didn't know the half of what Neven was about...
that I'd barely traced the edges of his secrets...
J. SACCO 8.03
But, I ask my acquaintance, what about Neven's wartime heroics? What about—?
"Everyone was surprised when he turned out to be a fighter for Celo," he says.
"I heard from very good sources that he was unbelievably courageous.
"From the very beginning he was throwing himself into action as if he wasn't aware what could happen to him.
"He passed through many bad times.
"I didn't even know he was around any more."

LAST WORDS

A NOTE ON THE TWO CELOS

As indicated in the book, two of Sarajevo's warlords—**Ismet Bajramovic** and **Ramiz Delalic**—were nicknamed Celo. To avoid too much confusion, I usually refer to Ismet Bajramovic (who is central to Neven's story) as Celo, and I usually refer to Ramiz Delalic by his last name. During the war, however, most Sarajevans were apt to think of Delalic, who had a larger unit and was around longer, when someone mentioned the name Celo.

ACKNOWLEDGEMENTS

First off, great thanks to the **John Simon Guggenheim Memorial Foundation** for providing a grant which got me back to Bosnia for additional research and bought me the time needed to produce this book.

In Sarajevo, special thanks to my old pal **Edin Culov** for helping out with translations at interviews and to **Lejla Efendic** for translating Bosnian-language articles into English. Thanks also to the staff at **Dani** magazine, particularly **Senad Pecanin** and **Vildana Selimbegovic**, who were always helpful to me during the war and upon my return visit. **Dani** was my primary source for the histories of the various warlords and most of the quotes attributed to them. Thanks to those few among Sarajevo's former police and army officials who took the time to answer my questions, namely **Munir Alibabic** and **Josan Divjak**. Thanks also to **Ferida Durakovic, Ivana Sekularac, Srdjan Vuletic**, and **Alma Mirvic**. In New York City, thanks to my other old pal **Soba** for all that last-minute help tracking down photos and information.

Thanks also to **Chris Oliveros**, Drawn & Quarterly publisher, for being patient while I stretched out the deadline for this book. He is a very easy man to work for.

Finally, the most thanks to **Neven**. Good luck to you always.

ABOUT THE AUTHOR

JOE WAS BORN IN MALTA IN 1960. He moved around the world to Australia, before settling in Los Angeles in 1972. As a child he vividly remembers buying war comics and **Mad** magazine 1950s reprints. He studied at the University of Oregon and graduated with a degree in journalism in 1981. That same year he received his first rejection slip from **RAW** that noted his strip had "almost been published."

Joe continued to travel extensively in the 1980s, living in Europe and Malta. He worked as a cartoonist and editor for various presses, including **The Comics Journal**.

Joe traveled to the Middle East for the first time in 1991 and came away from Israel and the Occupied Territories with the material that would make up his groundbreaking comic book series **Palestine** (1995, Fantagraphics). Sacco was the recipient of the prestigious American Book Award in 1996 for **Palestine**.

In 1995, just prior to the end of the Bosnian War, Sacco traveled to Sarajevo and its surrounding areas. There he began his book **Safe Area Gorazde** (2000, Fantagraphics), a fierce condemnation of the political impotence and badly planned UN operations during the Bosnian conflict. He continues to travel to and write about the situation in Bosnia. He has an infrequent series called **Stories from Bosnia** with D&Q.

Joe's work has been exhibited at art galleries and universities around the world, and he has lectured on political conflict, journalism, and the art of comics.

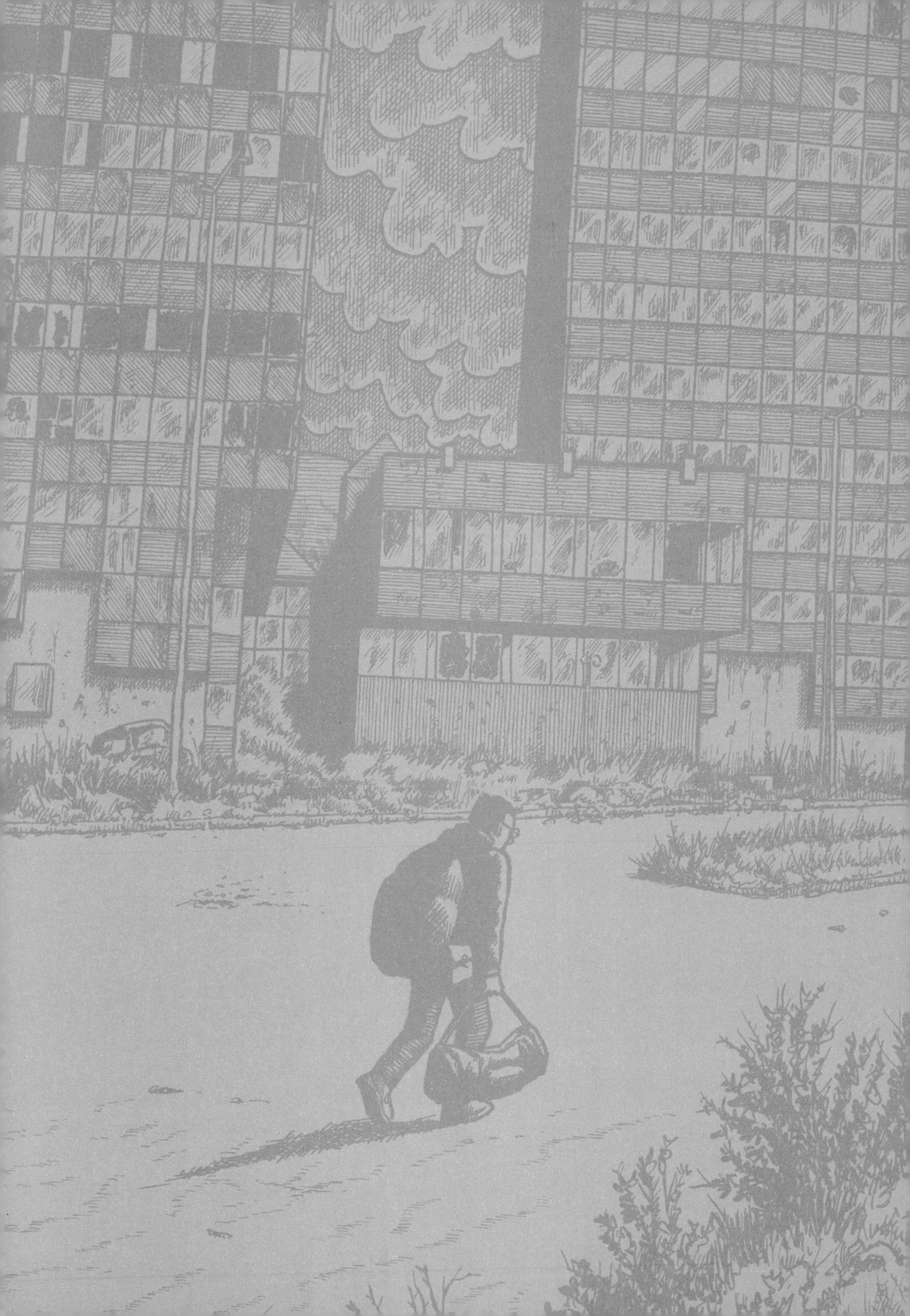